ALASKA'S
DEADLY
DOZEN

MOST NOTORIOUS MURDER CASES

TOM BRENNAN

Epicenter Press Inc.
Alaska Book Adventures™

Epicenter Press Inc.
Alaska Book Adventures™

Epicenter Press is a regional press publishing nonfiction
books about the arts, history, environment, and diverse
cultures and lifestyles of Alaska and the Pacific Northwest.
For more information, visit www.EpicenterPress.com

Alaska's Deadly Dozen

Cover design: Scott Book
Interior design: Melissa Vail Coffman

ISBN: 978-1-60381-339-6 (Trade Paperback)

ISBN: 978-1-60381-340-2 (Ebook)

Produced in the United States of America

10 9 8 7 6 5 4 3 2 1

To the men and women who enforce the law in the towns, cities and wild country of the Last Frontier.

Contents

Acknowledgments

THE IDEA FOR THIS BOOK originated with Lael Morgan, acquisitions editor at Epicenter Press and my long-time mentor. And special thanks are due to my wife Marnie, who reads and does a first-pass edit on everything I write. Information and inspiration has also come from my friend Colonel Tom Anderson, retired director of Alaska State Troopers, the late Trooper Major Walt Gilmour, my friend and editor Paul Jenkins, Homicide Detective Monique Doll of the Anchorage Police Department, blogger Simone LeClere, UPI editor Jeff Berliner, columnist Amy Armstrong, columnist Lameredith, retired Alaska State Trooper Sergeant Jim McCann, columnist Michael Kern, Anchorage Daily News columnist James Halpin, KUAC editor Dan Bross, Fairbanks Daily News-Miner columnist Dorothy Chomicz, KTUU-TV reporter Derek Minemyer, KTVA reporter Daniella Rivera, CBS News reporter Erin Donaghue, Must Read Alaska columnist Suzanne Downing, Heavy.com editor Tom Cleary, Bangor Daily News reporter Seth Koenig, Fairbanks Daily News-Miner reporter Robin Wood, Anchorage Daily News reporter Madeline McGee, Medium.com writer Robin Barefield, Lewiston Sun Journal reporter Christopher Williams, retired Alaska State Trooper investigator Dean Bivins, retired Alaska State Trooper Lorry Schuerch, author Kim Rich, UPI reporter Andrew MacLeod, author/journalist Tom Kizzia, Anchorage Daily News reporter Megan Holland, plus friend and author Leland Hale.

CHAPTER 1

Murder in a Hunting Camp - 1969

NORMAN "BUTCH" JOHNSON was a California boy whose carpenter father took a job in the far-off city of Anchorage, Alaska, a job that often involved working on projects in remote Arctic communities. Butch was 20 years old and could have gone on his own, but he decided to stick with his parents and moved north with them despite the ominously unfamiliar location. He was accustomed to moving because his father, Al Johnson, constantly moved around California to take carpentry assignments. Alaska was then booming because of major oil discoveries on the state's North Slope, with high-paying jobs opening for skilled people like carpenters. It was a promising position for Al but Alaska was another world for Butch and the adjustment was difficult.

The frequent moves and changing of schools disrupted his education, which was difficult enough because he tested low in intelligence. Butch rarely got into trouble and tried to please his parents but his handicaps sometimes made him a troubled youth. He had little interest in school and dropped out at age 16. He then took a number of low-skill jobs and felt he had little to lose when he followed his parents into the Far North. Butch couldn't find a job that suited him in Anchorage, so he decided to continue his education and enrolled at Anchorage Community College to work toward a high school equivalency certificate.

Butch's lack of a job and his weak school performance weighed on him and his morale was sagging, so his dad decided to cheer him up with a hunting trip in the Alaska wilderness. His father felt an adventure in the wild country might be just the thing to bolster the boy's attitude and increase his self-confidence. Butch had hunted rabbits and doves in California so he was accustomed to tracking and shooting wild creatures. Al felt a big-game trip in the wild country would fit in with his son's interests and give him the emotional boost the boy seemed to need.

For Christmas of 1969 Butch's parents gave him a lever-action Winchester 30-30 rifle, an appropriate weapon for a wilderness hunting adventure. Al was then working on a housing project in Kiana, an Inupiat Eskimo village of about 300 people in the Northwest Arctic portion of Alaska, just north of the Arctic Circle. Al was a supervisor on the project, which involved recruiting unpaid Eskimo workers to create sweat equity ownership of houses by helping to build them.

Al asked Freddie Jackson, a 43-year-old Inupiat and one of the few paid employees on the project, to take his son along on a caribou hunting trip when the boy came up from Anchorage in late January. Freddie agreed and invited two of his friends to join them, Clarence Arnold, 39, from the Arctic city of Kotzebue, and Oscar Henry Sr., 64, a resident of the small village of Kiana near the area Freddie preferred to hunt. The men liked the idea because they could hunt caribou and lay in a supply of meat for their freezers while doing a favor for Freddie's boss. The three men left Kiana on snow machines and motored up the Kobuk River to set up a tent camp, then returned to Kiana to await Butch's arrival.

When the boy arrived and the time came to head for their tent camp, the weather was horrible, 50 below zero with no wind and ice fog in low-lying areas, among the toughest conditions the Arctic can throw at you. Ordinarily, Alaskans prefer to remain indoors near the fire when such conditions prevail, putting off travel until the weather improves. Traveling in extreme cold would be difficult and keeping machinery running was a challenge, but Freddie Jackson and his friends were accustomed to tough weather and knew how to dress for and deal with it. Since Butch Johnson was on a relatively tight schedule, they elected to get him outfitted and bundled up, and headed for camp despite the harsh conditions. The boy expected to hunt and he would be taken hunting.

The Arctic was by then emerging from the depths of winter and the December days were behind them, days when the sun rose just above the horizon for about three hours, providing little light and no heat, but a usable day. By late January the sun rose before noon and was above the horizon until late afternoon. Spring was still far off, but the hunters were tired of staying indoors and anxious to get out into the countryside and doing something useful.

On Friday, January 23, Clarence and Oscar fired up their snow machines and headed north on the frozen surface of the Kobuk River 65 miles to their tent camp, with gear-laden sleds trailing behind their snow travelers. At camp they set up an additional white tent, settled in, built a fire in their wood-stove and set a kettle on to heat water. They cooked a meal, worked on their equipment and waited for Freddie and Butch to arrive.

IN KIANA, FREDDIE AND HIS NEIGHBORS had outfitted Butch with Arctic gear, including a warm parka and the Eskimo boots called mukluks. The boots were made for him by an Eskimo family that befriended Al Johnson and was helping prepare for his son's great adventure. The mukluks were the perfect footgear to keep one's feet warm in cold weather. Freddie had access to only one snow machine, his own—spare machines were not to be had—so Butch was required to ride in the sled behind Freddie's Arctic Cat. Unlike the snow machine, the sled had no windshield and no suspension, so Butch had to hang on tight to avoid being bounced out while the sled careened behind Freddie's machine. Adding to his discomfort, Butch was almost constantly sprayed by snow thrown up by the spinning tracks of the Arctic Cat. There was little danger in the trip but considerable discomfort and Butch's mood began to sour. It was an unpromising start to a trip about which the boy had considerable misgivings. They left Kiana at 1 p.m. and arrived at their camp by late afternoon, with Butch exhausted and in a foul mood because of his arduous journey.

The four men grabbed their rifles and hunted briefly, but saw no caribou. They returned to camp, had dinner and climbed into their sleeping bags. Next morning they took off on the three snow machines with Butch riding doggedly behind in Freddie's sled. A few miles from camp they spotted a small herd of caribou and looped around to get ahead of the animals and find a suitable shooting position. The Eskimos leaned heavily on their accelerators and Butch's sled careened and bounced over the snow berms, an even rougher ride than on the flat ice of the Kobuk River. Early in the chase Butch leaned over to pull his rifle from its scabbard, lost his balance and was flipped out of the sled when it hit a bump.

Freddie didn't want to miss his chance at the caribou so he kept going, figuring he could come back for the boy once he had a caribou down. Meanwhile, Butch was forced to hike along behind the speeding snow vehicles, struggling to catch up. Butch stumbled exhausted into a field where his three compatriots were field-dressing the animals they had brought down.

Butch was bone-weary and furious at being left behind and ignored. He wasn't sure the others intended to return for him and felt abandoned. He thought they might not care if he froze to death on the trail behind them. Butch helped dress out the fallen caribou but worked with little enthusiasm and growing fury at his companions. He had never worked on a newly killed large animal and found the work confusing and messy. It was disturbing but seemed the only way to get back to camp in a hurry. Butch watched in disgust as one of the Eskimos slit open the belly of a female caribou and pulled an unborn baby from the animal's inert body. He felt sick to his stomach. The three Inupiat wondered at the boy's inexperience and lack of hunter skills, but worked silently to avoid provoking him.

———

WHEN THEY PREPARED TO HEAD BACK to camp, Clarence Arnold's machine wouldn't start because of the cold. He loaded up what meat he could carry and hiked the mile-long trail behind the others. When he reached the tents Arnold told the others he had seen snow machine lights on the river ice. A short time later, Clarence Wood, a 32-year-old neighbor from Kiana, motored into camp to say hello, warm up and have a cup of coffee. His friends invited him to stay for a bowl of caribou soup. Butch Johnson was nowhere to be seen even though his three companions were hard at work processing their kill, working on their snow machines, hauling ice for water and chopping wood for the stove.

Clarence Wood first saw Butch sitting on a food box inside the main tent. One of the men needed access to the box and asked Butch to move. The boy rose and walked sullenly to his bunk. He hadn't uttered a word since Clarence arrived. Oscar Henry knew little English so the four Inupiats spoke Eskimo, telling Butch they would not be talking about him. They then began joking in a typical men's conversation, laughing at each other's comments. Butch simmered on his bunk, growing ever more irritated by his companions' unintelligible conversation. At one point they told Clarence Wood about their young friend's misadventure in falling out of the sled and having to hike to the shooting grounds. It was obvious then that the Eskimos were in fact talking about him and his grim mood deepened. After dinner Clarence Wood climbed back onto his snow machine and headed up the river, leaving the other four men to the quiet of their wilderness camp.

Wood later commented that he thought it unusual that Butch didn't help with the work at all, leaving it for his companions to do his share. "No one said anything about it," he said, "but I had the feeling that they would have felt a little better if the boy would at least make an attempt to help."

THE NEXT AFTERNOON pilot Harold Lie and Dr. Ray Lang flew over the trail in search of wolves, which they hoped to shoot from the air. They were in Lie's Super Cub, a light aircraft with two in-line seats that could fly low and slow over the snow machine trail near the Kobuk Sand Dunes. Lie spotted what looked like a wolf in the trail. He shouted, "Get ready", and pushed open the upper half of the aircraft's right door. Dr. Lang raised his shotgun and pushed the muzzle out into the frigid slipstream, peering ahead for the wolf. The creature below suddenly stood up, raised its arms, waved at the Super Cub and then dropped to the ground.

"Wait," Lee shouted. "It's a man."

Below them Butch Johnson waved furiously, worrying that he was about to be shot, perhaps not because they thought he was a wolf. Lie circled and landed, easing his plane's skis onto the snow. Butch ran to the Super Cub and its two occupants looked out to a shocking sight. The wolf that turned out to be a man was covered with blood. He told them that he had been running all night and day because a man had invaded their hunting camp, argued with his Eskimo companions and murdered them all. He had escaped with his life but worried that the killer might be behind him.

The two men loaded Butch into the seat behind the pilot and Dr. Lang wedged himself into the cargo area, his knees jammed on either side of their terrified passenger's shoulders.

Harold Lie was puzzled by Butch Johnson's story. Something didn't ring true; the blood-covered clothing was curious, among other things. Butch fell asleep just after the skis left the ground. Since the boy made him nervous, Lie reached into his survival gear bag, pulled out a hatchet and placed it near his control column.

Lie then flipped on his radio and called the Public Health Service operator in Kiana. He said they had just rescued a man on the trail who said he had witnessed the murder of his three hunting companions. The operator then radioed the Alaska State Trooper office in Kotzebue, a rural city 40 miles southwest of Kiana. The Super Cub then landed in Kiana where Butch was taken to see the public health nurse, checked over and put to bed. Harold Lie recruited another friend to accompany him and flew to the hunting camp, dropping low to see what they could. From the air they spotted one body lying in the snow outside a tent. There was no sign of life. Dusk was fast approaching so they turned and flew back to Kiana.

———

In Kotzebue, Trooper Bob Boatright chartered an aircraft and asked Police Chief William Stevens to join him for the flight to the hunting camp. They were unable to land there so the aircraft flew on to Kiana and found a community in shock over reports of the triple homicide. The only survivor was a young white man whose story seemed suspicious and involved an unknown Eskimo who invaded their camp and killed everyone but him.

The rumors quickly spread through Kiana's small community and anger seemed to be growing and directed at all whites. The school superintendent requested permission to move white teachers out of the village. When word of the unrest in Kiana reached trooper officials, they called on Trooper Lorenz "Lorry" Schuerch who was then on traffic duty in Fairbanks. Schuerch was the troopers' first part-Eskimo officer and had been born in Kiana. The agency had long had Alaska Native officers, actively recruited them to deal with law enforcement problems in remote Alaska villages. Their success was proving that officers having local knowledge and rapport with Native village residents could be valuable assets able to deal with problems in remote communities more effectively than non-Native officers from more urban environments, especially in delicate situations.

Lorry Schuerch had been a State Trooper for two years and lived in Kiana for most of his early life. His father owned a trading post and his brother was mayor. Victim Freddie Jackson had been one of his closest friends. Trooper Schuerch jumped on the first plane to Kotzebue then caught a smaller plane for the flight to Kiana. There he found Boatwright interviewing local witnesses about Butch Johnson's behavior and organized a search party to follow Butch's trail back to the tent camp. He asked the searchers to pick up anything interesting along the trail and any evidence at the camp, then gather up the victims' personal gear, take down the tents and prepare the camp to be vacated.

When Trooper Boatright interviewed Butch, the boy told him he had gotten a good look at the murderer and would be able to identify him if he saw him again. He told Boatman the killer "was about five foot nine, kind of fat, wearing a dark blue Comfy hip-length parka with a light-colored wolf ruff. He had brown, down-filled Army-type trousers with zippers in the legs, dark store-bought snow boots with rubber soles and cloth tops, and wearing a black ear band with the word 'Alaska' written across it.

"He was driving a yellow snow machine pulling a cargo-type sled that was filled. There was a canvas across the load, and I don't know what was in it. I was in my sleeping bag in the back of the tent, and he and the other Eskimos were talking in the front of the tent. I guess they started arguing, as they were raising their voices."

"This guy that was visiting got up and left the tent, and we turned out the lamps. He started his machine and then it died . . . Shortly after it stopped, there was a bunch of shots and one of the men with me hollered 'No, no' and I guess he took one of the first shots, as he fell partway across me. I slipped out of my sleeping bag and out the back of the tent and ran a short distance and hid behind a tree. The guy kept firing and firing, both small and large caliber, and then all was quiet.

"I saw the fellow walk up to the tent, do something inside, and then come out again. He looked around for a while, then got on the machine and left, heading toward Kiana. I stayed put until the sound of his machine became faint, and then I went to the back of the tent . . . Everyone was dead."

Butch told Boatright that he tried unsuccessfully to start one of the snow machines then took off down the trail without a weapon. "I didn't want to stick around because I was afraid the guy might come after me."

Butch Johnson's description of the killer sounded a lot like Clarence Wood, but the boy said he had met Clarence when he came through camp and he was definitely not the murderer. Boatright advised Butch that he himself was in fact a suspect and recommended that he and his father leave Kiana as quickly as possible. Both departed Kiana for Kotzebue within an hour and then flew on to Anchorage. There they were met by another trooper and given information on when and where to appear for additional interviews.

THE KIANA COMMUNITY was then in an uproar and Trooper Lorry Schuerch's first job was to try to get people calmed down. His presence was a big help. Because he was one of them, the villagers felt their side would be presented fairly and justice would be done. Schuerch made multiple visits before stopping at the home of Paul Henry, son of murder victim Oscar Henry. Paul was reportedly drinking and had threatened to shoot every white man in Kiana. His threats were a major worry for his fellow village residents, both Eskimo and white. Schuerch found Paul sitting at his kitchen table, a bottle in front of him. The trooper was Paul Henry's second cousin and had known him for years.

Lorry took a seat at the table and asked Paul: "Mind if I have a drink." His cousin poured him one and handed it across the table. Lorry sipped the drink and gave a low-key lecture, telling Paul to stay calm and warning him against making threats. He said such behavior could put him in jail, especially if he shot someone.

"I don't care," Paul moaned, pain in his voice and the lines of his face.

"I want your rifles," Lorry demanded.

"You don't have a warrant," Paul countered.

"I'm not talking as a trooper," Lorry replied. "I'm talking as your cousin. Give me your rifles!"

Paul reluctantly agreed and Lorry took his weapons to some of Paul's relatives in another part of town and asked them to hold them until Paul sobered up and stopped the threats. The family showdown eased tensions in the village greatly and the people turned their discussions from thoughts of revenge to the process of calming things down and dealing with their shock and grief.

BOATRIGHT FLEW TO THE BLOODY TENT CAMP the next day with Chief Stevens from Kotzebue, Kiana Mayor Vincent Schuerch, a helper and a pilot. The aircraft landed upriver from the camp, then circled while the two officers approached the tents on foot, treading quietly with guns drawn, ready to deal with a gunman if the killer was still there. They cleared the camp and found nothing but the three dead men and their gear. They determined the camp was abandoned and signaled the others that it was safe to land.

The body of Freddie Jackson lay in front of one tent, his hands grasping the ends of a pine bough, the middle portion of the bow clenched in his teeth. He had obviously been shot in the tent, crawled outside and bit down on the bough to deal with his pain, then was finished off by one or more bullets. The body lay in a pool of frozen blood that extended down through the snow to the tundra, suggesting that his heart had been pumping long after he fell there.

The frozen bodies of Clarence Arnold and Oscar Henry lay inside the tent. Clarence had been shot multiple times. Oscar had been wounded with his pants at half-mast. He had been getting dressed when the gunman found him and the killer smashed his head with a gun butt after Oscar fell. The officers found a spent .243 slug in the coffee pot which had drained through the hole it left. They found the bloody bolt of a .243 rifle under a sleeping bag near Oscar's head, obviously from the rifle used to bash Oscar's skull.

Boatright walked around the tent camp and could find no snow machine tracks other than those left by the three victims and by Clarence Wood during his brief visit. Boatright drew a map of the murder scene, logged the evidence and authorized his party to load the bodies onto their aircraft for the flight to Kiana, and then on to Anchorage for autopsy.

When they returned to the village, Mayor Schuerch rounded up a 13-man search party to run up the river on snow machines and backtrack the trail from the spot where the flying hunters had first spotted Butch Johnson. They would search for evidence and look for any unknown snow machine tracks. The party searched all day until dark, then returned the next day. They found no sign of unknown travelers but about a mile and a quarter from the hunting camp, one of the searchers spotted footprints running off the trail to a spot where the snow had been disturbed. Digging down they found Freddie Jackson's .243 Winchester, blood crusted on its butt and its bolt missing. At the tent camp the searchers gathered up the personal gear of the victims, their guns, clothing and sleeping bags, and hauled it to back to Kiana.

———

CLARENCE WOOD HEARD on the radio about the shooting at his friends' camp and headed for Kiana, knowing that the troopers would want to talk to him. There he was interviewed by Boatright and offered the names of witnesses who had seen him the night of the murders, after he left the hunting camp, and would be able to testify to his whereabouts and behavior. Boatright and Trooper Schuerch questioned the witnesses and decided Clarence Wood was an unlikely suspect.

Trooper Investigator Dean Bivins interviewed Butch Johnson at his home the morning after the boy and his father returned. The story Butch told Bivins was very different from the one he had given when interviewed by Trooper Boatright in Kiana. This time he said that when he and the other hunters returned to the tents from hunting, they found a sleeping bag had disappeared and their belongings were strewn around the tent. He described Clarence Woods visit, his dinner with the three friends and his departure. Then an unknown man arrived on a snowmobile and had a cup of coffee with his three companions before beginning to argue with them. The visitor started to leave and Butch said he heard the man's snow machine start as they were preparing for bed. Then the snow machine was turned off and moments later bullets began tearing through the tent's walls. Butch said he slipped out the back and heard his friends shouting behind him. He said he hid behind some trees and watched as the visitor left the tent, fired up his snow machine and headed off toward Kiana. Butch said he went inside and found everyone dead so he gathered up his clothes and tried to start one of the snow machines. He couldn't get it going so he took off running up the trail.

Two days later Butch was interviewed again at Trooper Headquarters. When confronted by the mounting evidence, he admitted he was angry, left the tent to go to the bathroom, went to the gun storage area, took his 30-30 from its case and began firing through the tent wall, hitting all three of his companions. Freddie Jackson ran to the front of the tent and Butch shot him as he exited. He said he shot his fellow hunters in a panic and headed off on the trail unaware that at least two of them were still alive, though bleeding badly. When he heard Freddie Jackson trying to start a snow machine he ran back and shot him again, finishing him off. He then went into the tent, grabbed Freddie Jackson's .243 and took several shots at the others. When the gun ran out of bullets, he beat Oscar Henry to death with its butt. Butch failed to notice that the bolt of the .243 had fallen out while he was beating Oscar with the rifle. Freddie Jackson had been shot four times, Oscar Henry had three bullet wounds and Clarence had six wounds from at least four different bullets.

———

BUTCH JOHNSON WAS TRIED in an Anchorage courtroom in January, 1971. His lawyer argued that at the time of the killings the boy was suffering from a mental disease and was not responsible for his actions. Psychiatrist Dr. J. Ray Langdon testified that he had examined Butch and his records and felt that at the time of the murders the boy "had what we would call a 'psychotic lapse; he was divorced from reality.'" Langdon said that in the frigid and unfamiliar circumstances the boy considered the snow-covered field where the Eskimos shot the caribou a massacre ground. "Norman was in an unfamiliar situation in the extremely cold Arctic wilderness . . . Norman was experiencing what was primarily a panic."

Dr. Barbara Ure, another psychiatrist testifying on Butch's behalf, said: "He was already insecure as to who he was. Having lost contact with his culture and his geography, he was displaced. He had absolutely no preparation for this caribou hunt." She said he identified with the dead caribou mother and its unborn baby, felt threatened by his Eskimo companions, who were speaking a language he didn't understand and didn't appear to like him. In his mind he was shooting them in self-defense."

The trial judge denied Butch's plea of temporary insanity and found him guilty of three counts of second-degree murder. He sentenced the 21-year-old to life in prison but ordered that he be given psychiatric treatment while there. The judge's ruling left it to the parole board to decide if and when he would not be a threat to other people and set free.

Butch was sent to a California prison which offered better psychiatric care than was available in Alaska facilities and released on parole just four years later. He was discharged from parole in May 1986 on recommendation of his parole officer. An Alaska parole officer told reporters that such an early discharge from parole is so rare that parolees rarely even ask for it. It was apparently considered justified because Butch's behavior both in prison and on parole was exemplary and justified such treatment.

When word of Johnson's release got back to Kiana the villagers were shocked and outraged. They found it hard to believe and felt three murders justified long imprisonment. Many considered it an official statement that Eskimo lives are valued less than whites and those who murder them deserve minimal punishment.

CHAPTER 2

An Aspiring Hit Man - 1970

SOME SAW GARY ZIEGER as a hard-working young man with a nice personality. Others considered him a murderous punk, a despicable human being who avoided paying for his crimes until he got crosswise with his friends.

Zieger was just 17 when he first came to the attention of authorities. In late 1970 a young woman was shocked when her boyfriend told her he knew about a murder that took place in Anchorage six months earlier. The woman was aghast and told him that he had to go to the police. The boy was hesitant but changed his mind when she told him she wouldn't marry him unless he did the right thing. He called the Alaska State Troopers.

The witness told the troopers he was riding around in Zieger's truck when Gary stopped to pick up a young Alaska Native man and drove him to a secluded spot at the Anchorage dump. There Zieger borrowed his friend's pistol, held it to the Native's head and demanded oral sex. The young man complied but afterward Zieger shot and killed him and threw his body over an embankment. The body was found the next day but there was virtually no evidence and no information about the crime, so the murder was investigated but listed as unsolved.

When the witness called six months later, troopers dispatched an investigator to the young man's apartment to pick up the gun Zieger borrowed for the murder. But the officer did not have a search warrant and had to wait outside until one arrived. While he waited Zieger showed up, entered the apartment and quickly left. When the warrant arrived and the trooper was able to enter the apartment, the pistol was nowhere to be found.

Troopers returned to the site where the body was discovered, used a metal detector and found several empty cartridges from a 9 mm pistol. The expended shells had been there for about six months. They also studied the lands and grooves on the cartridges and determined they had been fired from a weapon sold by the Sears sporting goods department to a member of the witness' family.

Investigators were convinced the young man's story was true and that Zieger had murdered the young Native. But without the pistol, they had nothing but the boy's testimony to go on and that was not enough to make the case.

———

YOUNG WOMEN WERE OFTEN GOING MISSING in Anchorage during that time. Some were dancers and prostitutes who left town without notice, others were murdered by baker Robert Hansen (see following chapter *With Help From His Friends*) and still others are now attributed to Gary Zieger.

One murder believed to be Zieger's was that of Zingre "ZeZe" Mason, a pretty, 20-year-old ground hostess for Japan Airlines. The young woman's car was in the shop for repairs on August 22, 1972 and she decided, despite warnings from her friends, to hitchhike to the repair shop to pick it up. She stepped to the side of the road nearest her home and stuck out her thumb. When she failed to show up for work the next day, ZeZe's co-workers reported her missing. Her parents called the repair shop and were told her car was still there.

On August 28, children playing under a tree near a gravel pit at the intersection of Sand Lake Road and Dimond Boulevard stumbled over her near-naked body and ran screaming for help.

———

TROOPER SERGEANT WALTER GILMOUR was appalled by the growing death toll and determined to crack the murder cases, to break the cycle. He arranged to have all available investigators assigned to work with him on a task force for the purpose. Since there was no clear indication whether ZeZe Mason's murder took place in State Troopers' area of responsibility or that of the Anchorage Police Department, APD sent one of its detectives to work with the state trooper team.

Gilmour's task force worked 20 hours without a break, then cut back to 16-hour shifts. Together the detectives logged more than 400 hours in the first three days after ZeZe's body was found. The investigators assumed she had been raped but the pathology lab tests were inconclusive. The girl obviously had sex before her death but it could have been consensual. The information was critical since consensual sex would suggest that ZeZe and her murderer were in a positive relationship, however brief, before things went bad.

The report also showed she had massive skull fractures from blows with a blunt instrument and 12 stab wounds, including one in the chest and another that partially severed an artery in her left arm. At least three of the knife wounds and any of the skull fractures could have been fatal. The inside of one thumb and several fingers had superficial cuts indicating she was trying to defend herself against a slashing knife. The combination of apparent consensual sex and vicious knife wounds indicated the relationship went seriously sour, obviously triggering an overwhelming psychotic attack by the murderer.

Near her body and in various parts of the gravel pit were identical sets of tire tracks. Leading from one set of tire tracks to the woman's body the investigators found drag marks and blood stains, suggesting that ZeZe may have been killed and her body dumped under the tree by her murderer. The tracks had a distinctive tread mark used on four-wheel vehicles for extra traction. But three of the tires were mounted backward. The task force made plaster casts of the tracks and took samples of the blood. They also went looking for matching tire tracks at pullouts within several miles of the gravel pit. They found similar tracks at various spots, one of them beside Campbell Creek more than two miles away.

The task force put out a request for information from the public, a pro forma plea for which they held little hope. They had sent such requests in the two most recent murder cases, those of Celia Van Zanten and Shirley Ann Jones, both 18 years old when they were brutally murdered. Celia Van Zanten had been gagged and raped, then thrown into a ravine south of Anchorage. She died of exposure while struggling to climb out of the ravine. Shirley Ann Jones left an Anchorage night club with an unidentified man. She was found the next morning in a truck yard where she had been raped and beaten, then left in the cold. She never regained consciousness.

Neither of the past requests resulted in useful information. This time the investigators included the fact that the victim may have had consensual sex with her killer. Coroner Ronnie Bray was furious. She angrily told a reporter that ZeZe Mason apparently died the night she disappeared; she had been savagely beaten and repeatedly stabbed. The cause of death was given as severe head wounds and loss of blood. "I am mad," she said. "I have received no police report and no autopsy report. The coroner's job is to find out how a person died, and it's the troopers' job to find out who is responsible." She said the troopers' press release "was in very bad taste and wholly unnecessary. I can just imagine how upset that poor girl's family is since the troopers released that information this afternoon. I just don't let things like that out of my office. One must have concern for the living as well as for the dead in a situation like this."

The investigators were chastened by the coroner's angry outburst but they were determined to break the case and encouraged by the response they were getting to their announcement and the evidence they were collecting as a result. "We got really good prints at the scene," one trooper told a reporter, referring to the tire tracks from Zieger's truck.

While that evidence was being studied, tips from the public began to come in, apparently motivated by the coroner's well-publicized fury. One tip came from Hiram Matthews, a gravel truck driver who said he saw a young woman who fit ZeZe's description climbing into a pickup occupied by two men. He said he later saw the same pickup at the gravel pit but by then there were only two people in it—and they appeared to be making out.

Another tip came from Ralph Keiner, another of Gary Zieger's co-workers. Keiner said he had been riding around with Gary on the day of ZeZe Mason's murder when Zieger stopped to pick up a female hitchhiker. Gary dropped him off near a South Anchorage fire station and drove away with the girl. Keiner said Zieger had a large knife on the dashboard of his truck. Gary's boss at Arctic Pipelines reported that one of his other employees told him he saw Zieger washing his pickup that day in Campbell Creek, a spot where detectives made casts of tires matching those found near the young woman's body.

Gilmour was then surprised when a woman called to complain that her biker boyfriend was being persecuted by police. He was not the murderer, she said. Gilmour had never heard of her boyfriend and had never had anyone come forward with an alibi for a suspect before he even became a suspect. She was convinced police were just days away from arresting her lover, whose only offense was often driving his pickup truck in the gravel pit where ZeZe Mason's body was found. The woman said she knew who the real killer was.

Her boyfriend turned out to be an employee of a tire station and had helped another young man mount a set of all-weather tires on a truck he often drove to the gravel pit. She said she couldn't remember the other man's name but she'd seen it in a newspaper recently when he was rescued from a disabled boat in Cook Inlet southwest of Anchorage. Investigators checked copies of the Anchorage newspapers and saw that Gary Zieger had been assisted in getting to shore from a boat with a blown engine.

———·———

GILMOUR'S INVESTIGATORS DROPPED IN ON the woman's boyfriend, who admitted that he and Zieger had stolen a set of tires and inadvertently mounted three of them backward. Since the back-mounted tires would not cause a driving problem, Zieger had elected to leave them that way. They would cause weird-looking tread marks but Zieger assumed nobody would notice.

Several of the team members went to Zieger's home and searched the pickup. They pulled out the floor mats and swabbed samples from all parts of the truck. The back-mounted tires matched the tread samples left at the crime scene. Zieger had washed the truck's interior thoroughly but the officers found traces of what looked like blood, including a dime-size smear on the inside panel of the driver's side below the armrest.

The investigators arrested Zieger and impounded the truck. The warrant charged first-degree murder, murder during an attempted rape and murder during a robbery. The robbery charge was based on the fact that ZeZe's ring, wallet, checkbook, some clothing and a small amount of money were missing. Zieger was assigned a cell at the State Jail and held for $75,000 bond. The detectives kept quiet about their findings but the Anchorage Daily News found an unnamed source who said the blood in Zieger's truck appeared to be a match for ZeZe Mason's blood. Though interesting news, it would prove a difficult case to make at the time since DNA testing was still years in the future.

At a bail hearing on September 8, Superior Court Judge C. J. Occhipinti ordered Zieger's public defender, the district attorney's office, the police and the coroner to put a lid on their public comments about the case. Zieger's lawyer asked for a lower bail amount and argued that the evidence didn't even point at his client. He said one witness reported seeing ZeZe get into a truck with two men, both of whom had dark hair.

Zieger's hair was light blond. The lawyer said Gary was a hunter and the blood in his truck was probably from an animal he had killed.

A secretary/bookkeeper from Gary's office testified he had been at the company for a year and was a responsible, dependable and careful employee. She said Gary impressed her so much that she co-signed for the loan on his truck because his parents were unwilling or unable to. She said his job required him to drive through the gravel pit where ZeZe's body was found on virtually a daily basis.

Judge Occhipinti decided that the evidence was circumstantial but certainly not weak; the public deserved to be protected. He held fast on the $75,000 bail requirement and Zieger stayed in jail awaiting trial.

———————

INVESTIGATORS TALKED TO A NUMBER of other people about Zieger, including more of his friends and fellow workers. Unlike the aging bookkeeper, those his age considered Zieger dangerous and potentially violent. He was quick to anger; they didn't trust him and were cautious around him. He had a reputation for enjoying violent sex and forcing himself on women, and sometimes men. One of Gary's former hunting partners said he wouldn't turn his back on him.

Despite his reputation, Zieger had only a minor criminal record for assault and battery. But Zieger's lack of court convictions did not deter investigators from considering him for what he almost certainly was: a sociopathic killer, a very dangerous young man who had no regard for human life.

Because of the publicity in the Anchorage news media, including the troopers' announcement that the victim might have had consensual sex with her killer—and the hope of selecting a jury that hadn't been exposed to the story—Zieger's trial was moved to Kodiak, an island fishing community 200 miles southwest of Anchorage. The jury was sequestered and boarded at a local hotel for the duration of the trial. One local resident told a reporter that Kodiak people were unlikely to be influenced by anything they read in an Anchorage newspaper. He said they were very independent and tended to think for themselves before making up their minds. "Most folks here tend to not believe things unless they see them," he said. "We're pretty isolated here."

When the trial opened Zieger's new lawyer, Jon Larson, told the jury that Gary did pick up a young woman on the day of ZeZe Mason's murder and drove around with her in his truck. But he dropped the woman off and was busy for the rest of the day with other matters. He said it was unclear whether the woman was ZeZe and pointed out that when Gary's co-worker looked at photos of ZeZe he couldn't be sure she was the woman he saw in Zieger's truck.

An expert witness testified that the substance on Zieger's truck panel was human blood but matching it to ZeZe Mason was impossible. Other blood spots were found on the armrest, kick panel and window on the passenger's side of the truck and on a yellow hardhat found in the truck. The witness said he could only be certain that some of the blood came from a human and the rest came from a human or other high primate. The chances that an ape had been bleeding in Gary's truck seemed ridiculous but the information was duly entered into the record. A pathologist said some of the blood could have been in the truck for up to a year. He said he couldn't determine either the blood type or the sex of the individual that bled in Zieger's truck.

When prosecutors called Ralph Keiner, Gary's co-worker, Keiner undermined the statement by their boss, Michael Beaver, who said Keiner told him of seeing Zieger washing his truck at Campbell Creek. He said what he told Beaver might not have been true.

An expert from the FBI's Crime Lab in Washington, D.C., testified that the tread design of the tires on Gary's truck appeared to match that found at the murder scene but he couldn't be certain they were made by the same vehicle—despite the mismatched mounting of three wheels.

The jury heard five days of testimony and looked at 125 exhibits but there was no conclusive evidence that Gary Zieger was the murderer. On the sixth day of the trial Zieger was called to testify and his lawyer asked him: "Did you kill ZeZe Mason, Gary?"

Zieger replied firmly, "No, I did not."

The prosecutor showed Gary bloody photos of ZeZe Mason's dead body. Later Zieger told a reporter: "I agree they were super gross. But what do they want me to do, plead guilty so the public will be happy? Sure it was bad and everything. I'm sorry it happened, but I'm a lot sorrier that I was arrested."

———————

THE JURY FOUND GARY NOT GUILTY on all counts. He slumped in his chair and the judge declared the case closed. His parents ran to the defense table and tearfully showered him with hugs, handshakes and congratulations.

Alaska newspapers decreed that Zieger was found innocent, though that was hardly the case. He was found not guilty because the prosecution was unable to prove its case; the necessary evidence just didn't exist. One juror told a reporter for the Anchorage Daily News "We just didn't think they proved he did it. He may have done it, but it wasn't proved to us."

When Zieger went to recover his pickup truck at the police impoundment lot he found the seat covers, door panels and floor mats lying in a pile. He was furious that the police hadn't put the truck back the way they found it but the disgusted officers couldn't bring themselves to perform such a courtesy. They were certain Zieger had gotten away with murder.

Colonel Ed Dankworth, director of the Alaska State Troopers, told the public that the recent murders of three young women were difficult to investigate and prosecute. He said such crimes are easier to prevent than they are to prosecute. He said drivers are at risk from picking up dangerous hitchhikers and hitchhikers—especially young women—were at risk from getting into cars with strangers. "A person standing beside the road with his thumb in the air is really inviting trouble," he said. Dankworth's message resonated with the public and hitchhiking became notably rarer in the months and years after ZeZe Mason's murder.

Zieger was then interviewed by a reporter at the home of his former boss, Michael Beaver, where Gary was house-sitting. He complained about being in jail, losing wages, his legal bill and being in arrears on truck payments. "I don't know what I'm going to do," he said. "They jerk you off the street for five months and then they open up the door and say, 'Here you go. Have a nice day.'"

Gary went back to work at Arctic Pipelines. His boss said the company had two years of training invested in Zieger; he was a good worker and they didn't want to lose him.

———

IN THE FALL OF 1972, while Gary had been still awaiting trial, his friend Benny Ramey made friends with Wesley Ladd, a former Cordova fisherman and cannery operator. Ladd was trying to buy Cindy's Massage Parlor, a popular Spenard whorehouse owned by John F. "Johnny" Rich, a handsome young crime figure, gun dealer and owner of several marginally legal businesses. Johnny's co-owner in Cindy's was Ferris Rezk, a 28-year-old hard-charging businessman and heroin dealer. Rezk agreed to sell his share of the business for $10,000. Ladd made a down payment of $7,000 and agreed to come up with another $3,000, but was having trouble finding the additional three.

Rezk was unwilling to wait for the last $3,000 and warned Ladd he was in danger of losing the $7,000 already paid if he didn't come up with the rest of the money, due on November 26. A day after that deadline passed a snowplow operator at Angelus Memorial Park called police and said he had found a body at the cemetery, one that did not belong there. This one was sprawled on the back seat of a 1968 Plymouth. It was Ferris Rezk with a .38 caliber bullet in the back of his head, his sweater pulled up over his head and shoulders, and his pockets empty.

Word was on the street about Wesley Ladd's dealings with Ferris Rezk for Cindy's Massage Parlor so police went looking for him. Ladd was interrogated and arrested the next day, and charged with first-degree murder. When the case went to trial several months later, testimony indicated several people were with Wesley Ladd when Ferris Rezk died. They included Cindy Bennett, the woman for whom the massage parlor was named, Jack Anderson, who was a friend and fellow fisherman of Ladd's, and a man named Larry who was reportedly a mysterious mob killer.

Ladd's lawyer was Edgar Paul Boyko, a former Alaska attorney general known as a colorful character and one of the state's best-known defense attorneys. Boyko gave a classic performance after which people in the courtroom were scratching their heads, wondering who killed Ferris Rezk and why. At one point Boyko told jurors that the real killer had been in the courtroom during the proceedings, causing everyone in the room to look around at their neighbors.

In testimony, two witnesses said they saw Wes Ladd with the gun in his hand when Rezk fell to the floor and Ladd himself said his gun was used in the killing, but he said the mysterious Larry had fired the shot and he wound up with the gun in his own hand after struggling with Larry. Boyko said Larry had been sent by a mob in the Lower 48, a group that was trying to take over Alaska's massage parlors for the coming boom years of pipeline construction after the big oil discovery at Prudhoe Bay.

———·———

THERE WERE A FEW MOMENTS OF HUMOR in the trial. One young woman described being interviewed as a prospective employee of Cindy's. Prosecutor William L. Mackey asked, "Did the interviewer explain that it was a house of ill fame?"

"No," the woman replied. "She said it was a whorehouse."

When Boyko suggested that the Rezk killing was a mob hit, the prosecutor said that if the murder took place with three witnesses, with just one bullet in the gun, and if Wesley Ladd wound up with the pistol in his hand, the jury "should include in your verdict a recommendation that the organization get its money back from the hit man."

The all-woman jury deliberated for 15 hours and decided none of the evidence proved anything definitive. Some believed Boyko's claim that the mob was moving into Alaska but none considered the evidence sufficient to find Wes Ladd guilty. He was set free.

When the trial ended on April 8, Boyko told reporters he thought a special grand jury should be convened to investigate whether the mob was in fact moving into Alaska. The district attorney responded that the regular grand jury was meeting frequently and Boyko was welcome to submit any evidence he had of mob involvement in Alaska. The invitation went unanswered.

———————

In May, 1973, Trooper Director Dankworth transferred Sergeant Jim Vaden, a promising investigator in the Ketchikan Trooper post, to Anchorage. There Vaden was assigned to the Major Crime Unit of the newly formed Criminal Investigation Bureau. Vaden left Ketchikan reluctantly but was very interested in working with the Major Crime Unit and its chief investigator, Don Church. Shortly after Vaden's arrival in Anchorage, Church was promoted and Vaden was assigned to take his job as the unit's lead detective.

Vaden had a unique way of doing things. For one, he liked to get to know those he was investigating. Since Gary Zieger was the talk of the department, Vaden called Arctic Pipelines and invited Zieger to have coffee. The call surprised Zieger but he was curious and accepted. Zieger thought the invitation might be a sign of respect on Vaden's part even if Vaden considered it more of an adversarial occasion. The cop and his criminal target met at a restaurant at Fireweed and C Streets, a place popular with off-duty police officers.

By the time they met, Zieger was extremely suspicious and borderline paranoid. He was convinced Vaden had a hidden agenda and would be arresting him for something. He insisted that Vaden drive in and out of the restaurant's parking lot several times before parking and coming into the dining room. He wanted to see if anyone was following Vaden.

Both men ordered coffee and Vaden told Zieger he liked to get acquainted with people he was likely to arrest. Since Zieger was widely feared, Vaden considered him especially interesting. The two men hit it off fairly well despite their adversarial relationship. When they were about to part company, Zieger asked Vaden what he thought might happen to him. Vaden replied that since he was feared by both police and his own peers one or the other would probably kill him. He said Zieger would likely either die in a shootout with police or be murdered by his friends.

———

WHILE WESLEY LADD WAS STILL IN JAIL waiting for his trial for the murder of Ferris Rezk, local gun dealer and nude photo studio owner Johnny Rich picked up the expired lease on Cindy's Massage Studio and took ownership. He remodeled the little whorehouse and changed out its furnishings, transforming it with gaudy signs, mirrored ceilings and other accouterments for a night of illicit passion. By the time Ladd was released, Johnny was fully in charge at Cindy's and had made it his own. Ladd was furious. He had given Rezk $7,000 for what he considered to be the rights to Cindy's even though he had never paid the last $3,000.

On August 22 Johnny Rich left a topless bar and headed for an auction house. Wesley Ladd, Benny Ramey and Virginia Pinnick knew he would be there and drove up to the auction house in a rented vehicle. They wanted a car that Johnny wouldn't recognize. The three had been looking for Johnny for several weeks. Ramey walked into the auction house, found Rich and said he knew somebody who wanted to buy two shotguns. Ramey was carrying $400, which he flashed for Rich to convince him the inquiry was serious. Rich asked him to meet for a drink at PJ's bar at 11, after the auction. Ladd, Ramey and Pinnick then drove around for a time before stopping to pick up Gary Zieger just before 11. When Johnny Rich drove up, Zieger and Ramey, both carrying weapons, stepped out of the Matador tavern. Ramey followed Rich into the auction house and asked him to step outside. There he asked if Johnny would come with him to Eagle River, where the buyer of the shotguns was waiting. Johnny declined saying his gun-dealing license only allowed him to sell weapons within the City of Anchorage. Ramey then pulled his gun and Zieger stepped from behind Johnny's Cadillac. They forced Rich into the back of the Cadillac, took his keys and drove off with Ladd and Pinnick following behind.

They went to Caye Mason's cabin in Eagle River, led Johnny inside and ordered him to sit on a bunk bed. Ladd had stopped for a drink but arrived about 20 minutes later. Johnny asked Ladd what they wanted, what the forced trip was all about. Ladd told Johnny, "I feel you owe me some money. You and I know that you did tell some lies and you could have helped me by telling the truth at my trial."

Johnny answered that he "got confused" in his testimony. He was terrified, afraid he would be killed and virtually begging to be freed. Ladd later testified that he wasn't angry with Rich. Johnny had tried to bargain his way out of the problem. "I know I beat you out of the massage parlor," he told Ladd. "I paid quite a bit through my nose myself in a roundabout way. I will give you the massage parlor back and I'll give you $5,000 that I have got in the checking account if you will just let me go."

Ladd testified that he was having second thoughts about killing Johnny and asked Zieger to step outside with him. "Let's take the deal," Ladd told Zieger. "It's what we want. That's all we want is the massage parlor." Johnny's captors had legal papers filled out by their lawyer, Duncan Webb, and they needed to have Johnny sign them. The papers included a bill of sale and a power of attorney.

They also had a letter they didn't show Johnny, one written by Caye Mason, addressed to Wesley Ladd and supposedly signed by Johnny. The letter said Johnny was leaving town and wanted to make things right with Ladd. It said Johnny wanted to sell everything he owned to Ladd.

Johnny said he was afraid to sign any of the papers because he assumed they would then kill him. He said the papers would be worthless since Cindy's was nominally owned by his girlfriend, a dancer who went by the name of Angel Dust. Ladd said Johnny was stalling but told him they had a plane waiting at an airstrip in Palmer that would fly him out of Alaska after the papers were signed. Ladd and Rich argued until Ramey walked over and slammed the side of his gun against Johnny's head. "Just sign the damn papers," he said. "We don't want to hear any more crap."

Ramey went to hit Johnny again but Ladd stopped him, went outside and grabbed a bucket and towel. He dipped the towel in cold water, wrung it out and gave it to Johnny to place on the side of his battered head. Zieger then put a clamp on Johnny's testicles and tightened it until Johnny was howling in pain. "Hey, this ain't necessary," Ladd said. Johnny stumbled to his feet, walked to the sink counter and signed the letter and the power of attorney.

Virginia Pinnick began to panic about what might be about to happen. She seemed ready to cry when Ladd approached her outside the

cabin and said everything was going to be OK. He told her they were going to set Johnny free. As he turned to go inside they heard a shot. When
they went inside, Ramey told them Zieger had tried to force him to shoot
Johnny. Ramey refused, so Zieger fired the shot. Johnny lay on the floor
pleading for his life. He had a bullet wound in his chest, but the round
had bounced off a rib without hitting any vital organs.

Ramey pulled his own gun and walked behind Zieger, afraid the
wildman might shoot him. Zieger suggested somebody shoot Rich again.
When no one moved, Zieger pointed his gun at Ladd and said, "Shoot
him. We are in it, you get into it too. We are all into it."

Ladd took the .45 from Ramey's hand, pushed Johnny's reaching
hand away and said, "This is for snitching on me in court." Then he whis-
pered, "Forgive me God" and fired a second shot into Johnny, killing
him.

Zieger then went through Johnny's pockets, taking his watch for
himself. Caye Mason kept $500 in cash and the others divided up the
keys to Johnny's Cadillac, a .22 automatic pistol, two derringers, some
fishing equipment and a painting Johnny had bought at the auction.

They stuffed the body into an old sleeping bag offered by Pinnick,
backed Mason's car up to the cabin and stuffed the bag into the car's
trunk. Mason stayed at the cabin to clean up while Ladd, Ramey and
Zieger got into Mason's car and Pinnick climbed into her truck. She led
the others out of Eagle River and down the Glenn Highway to Jonesville,
site of an old coal mine. On the road to the mine they selected a wide
spot in the road and stopped to dig a shallow grave. Ladd stood with his
arms around Virginia Pinnick while the others dug the grave.

———————

THE NEXT DAY MASON AND PINNICK drove Ramey in Johnny's Cadillac
to Anchorage International Airport. Ramey was decked out in new
clothes they bought him for the occasion. He boarded a flight to Seattle
with a ticket issued under the name John Rich. Mason gave him a return
ticket on Western Airlines issued under the name "Robert Stanford."

Mason and the lawyer Webb signed Johnny's sale documents to witness his signature. They later convinced a third person to sign as a witness, saying they had seen Johnny sign them himself. A few days later
Webb, Ramey, Mason and Ladd made the rounds of Johnny's businesses
and stopped at his home, showing the signed and witnessed papers as
they went.

———————

JOHNNY'S 16-YEAR-OLD PREGNANT WIFE, Bridget and 15-year-old daughter Kim were worried. His criminal enterprises and seamy associates were a constant concern and his dropping out of sight was even more worrisome. The two girls reported him missing and immediately launched their own search, checking out all of his usual haunts. Police were searching too but there were few clues and many rumors. Nobody had seen Johnny since he left PJ's.

Wesley Ladd's lawyer Duncan Webb told investigators he understood Johnny was out of state on a business trip and had been calling to see how things were going in Anchorage. Webb said he didn't know where Johnny was but was confident he was doing fine. One of Johnny's friends told investigators he had known Rich for 12 years and had never known him to leave Alaska. Johnny liked to stay close to his massage parlors to make sure the girls didn't steal from him. And since Johnny's wife was just days away from childbirth the likelihood of his leaving the state just then was low.

A newspaper article about Johnny Rich's disappearance mentioned that he had been arrested multiple times on gambling charges. Johnny's daughter Kim Rich was infuriated by the reference. She called the reporter and demanded to know why, in a three-paragraph article about her father's disappearance, the reporter saw fit to mention his gambling arrests. She was especially infuriated since by that time many people suspected Johnny was dead and Kim thought the article was disrespectful. The reporter answered that Johnny Rich was one of Anchorage's most notorious underworld figures and he thought her dad's gambling activities might have something to do with his death.

A few days later, Kim was approached at the Tesoro service station where she worked by lawyer Duncan Webb and his assistant, Caye Mason. Webb gave Kim an envelope containing a copy of a power of attorney signed by her father and stating that Caye Mason would assist Kim in making payment on the lease on Johnny's home. Webb told Kim that Johnny had gone to Seattle on business and would return in a few days and that Johnny had asked Webb to look after things in his absence. Webb said Johnny wanted him to go to the house and inventory what he found there. He said someone had filed a lien against Johnny's property and he wanted to make sure Kim didn't lose the rights to her father's new boat, his Cadillac or household furniture.

Webb said that when he went to the house, Johnny's roommate, Al

Bennett, had told them to ask Kim about permission to enter. Johnny's daughter took the envelope and wrote, "Al let them in. Kim" on the back.

Webb and Caye Mason headed for the house a few blocks away and a few minutes later Al Bennett came running up to the Tesoro station. He shouted to Kim from across the parking lot: "What the hell did you let them in for? Wesley Ladd is with them." Bennett then turned and ran away.

Kim was terrified. Wesley Ladd was her father's enemy, the last man he would want to enter his house. After work she took a cab to a ticket vendor where she bought tickets for a concert coming to Anchorage that summer. The cab waited and took her home. As they pulled into the driveway she saw her father's Cadillac driving away. She asked the taxi driver to catch him but the Cadillac disappeared into the traffic. Back at the house she stepped to the porch and found the door bolted. Al Bennett opened it with a rifle in his hands. Bennett said Duncan Webb and Caye Mason told him the same story they told her, but he also mentioned that they were driving her father's Cadillac and had his large ring of keys. No one should have had Johnny's car or his keys. Something was very wrong.

Bennett had reluctantly let them in and watched as they inventoried Johnny's belongings. They spent most of their time developing a log of the many guns Johnny owned. Before they left they told Bennett that he would have to pay rent to Duncan Webb if he wanted to stay in the house. He said they would be back in a few days to make arrangements for Johnny's belongings.

———

AFTER THEY LEFT, BENNETT CALLED CINDY'S and warned them that Ladd, Webb and Mason might be on their way. The manager of the massage parlor quickly gathered up all important paperwork and money and loaded it into a trailer, which one of the masseuse's boyfriends then towed away. After Cindy's, the group drove to FiFi's to try again. Then Johnny's lawyer, Jim Johnson, called police. Johnson called the massage parlor and told an employee there to have a locksmith change all the locks and said that if Ladd and the others came back to give them nothing.

Police were skeptical of the entire transaction on Johnny's two massage parlors. Duncan Webb told police he had driven Johnny to the airport and knew Johnny had plans to return on August 29. When Webb returned to his office he instructed his secretary to write an appointment in his datebook for a meeting with Johnny Rich on August 29. She was suspicious and refused, so Webb did it himself. Shortly afterward Webb told the secretary that he believed Wesley Ladd had killed Johnny. The secretary called attorney Bob Wagstaff, who took her to police to give a statement.

Webb later told investigators that he only participated because he was afraid Zieger would kill him. He said Zieger told him he had already killed three people and if Webb didn't help with the murder and money scheme, he would "blow him away." Caye Mason said she participated for the same reason.

While the search for Johnny Rich was still on, Caye Mason, Virginia Pinnick and Virginia's brother faked a phone call from Caye's home, supposedly talking to Johnny Rich in New York. The phone call was intended to throw off any investigators who might be tapping the telephone.

Wesley Ladd was then in jail after being arrested on a weapons charge. He called Vaden from the jail and asked the trooper to visit him there. Vaden was preparing to file murder charges against Ladd and his co-conspirators in the Rich murder case. Ladd said he was ready to tell all. Trooper Vaden arrived hoping to get more information about the involvement of Duncan Webb. Ladd tried to convince Vaden that Zieger had fired both shots into Johnny's body. He failed to understand that modern technology would show that the second and final shot, the one that ended Johnny's life, came from Ladd's gun.

GARY ZIEGER'S LUCK TOOK A TURN for the worse when he was stopped on the Seward Highway and arrested after police found stolen dynamite and 12 pounds of illegal marijuana in his truck. He was tried and convicted in October and the judge set sentencing for November 29. Zieger knew his conviction would put him back in jail and wanted the lightest sentence possible. He dropped his public defender and asked Duncan Webb to file an appeal for him. Webb said that because of Zieger's record and the evidence against him, a successful appeal would be difficult and expensive. He wanted an advance of $10,000. Zieger told him not to worry; he knew where he could find the money.

Jimmy Sumpter was a successful businessman and owned two of Anchorage's most successful topless clubs, the Kit Kat Club and the Sportsman Too. Because of his businesses, Sumpter kept a large amount of cash and a collection of expensive jewelry at his house, sometimes flashing both the cash and the jewelry at his clubs. Sumpter worked odd hours and often visited his properties in the middle of the night.

Around 2 a.m. on the night of November 26, 1973, Sumpter heard the sound of glass breaking. It was actually the sound of a window being broken in the rear of his house but Jimmy decided he had imagined the sound and that it might be a premonition of something bad about to happen. He decided to check his clubs just in case. Sumpter was in a war of sorts with the Brothers motorcycle gang, which wanted to control the flow of topless dancers into Alaska and to organize the girls at Sumpter's clubs. The Brothers were a constant problem.

As Jimmy left the house, Zieger unlocked the broken window, climbed into the house and went looking for cash and jewelry. When the burglar reached the master bedroom, Sumpter's 40-year-old wife Marguerite heard him and screamed. The intruder shot her, set the bedroom on fire and ran to the basement where Marguerite's 13-year-old son, Richard Merck, was sleeping in his bedroom. Richard's 16-year-old sister had heard her mother's scream and ran from the house before the burglar saw her. After the intruder left the house the girl returned, kicked in a basement window and tried to rescue her brother from the burning building. She found him shot dead in his bed. Investigators later said that the burglar/killer had stolen $20,000 in cash and jewelry from the house.

The murders devastated Jimmy Sumpter and put him in the mood to get revenge. He offered a reward of $10,000 in $20 bills. The reward was nominally for information leading to the arrest of whoever killed Sumpter's wife and son, robbed his house and set it afire. But the word on the street was that Sumpter was convinced his tragedy was the work of The Brothers. The reward could be claimed, so went the street rumor, by anyone who killed a Brother, any Brother. He simply wanted revenge.

The next day Trooper Sergeant Gilmour and Anchorage City Detective Ron Rice went to Sumpter's house and were standing outside when they noticed a curtain move in the house across the street. They walked over and rang the bell. A frightened woman came to the door and invited them in. She said that shortly before the fire broke out at Sumpter's she noticed a pickup truck with a camper shell parked outside. When the fire broke out a man ran from the house, jumped into the truck and tried to drive off. The truck spun out of control and swerved into her yard, damaging a fence. The woman wrote down the truck's license number and gave it to the investigators. The license number was for Gary Zieger's Dodge. Gilmour's team obtained a search warrant for the truck.

Rice asked the Anchorage Police Department to issue a bulletin alerting all units to be on the lookout for the Dodge pickup, which many officers already knew was owned by Gary Zieger. One patrol car reported the truck was parked behind PJ's, a strip club in the Spenard neighborhood. Rice ordered up a tow truck and drove to PJ's to watch as Zieger's pickup was hooked up to be towed to the police garage. There it would be searched and the tires removed to have its treads matched against the tracks in the yard of Jimmy Sumpter's neighbor.

While Rice and Detective Stan McCartney watched, Zieger arrived with his public defender. Zieger and the lawyer climbed into the back of Rice's patrol car. Rice and Zieger knew each other. The last time they clashed Zieger had told Rice something like "The next time I see you will be through the cross-hairs of a rifle." Rice said later he was unsure of Zieger's exact words but when Zieger and the lawyer climbed into his cruiser, he turned to them, put his hand on his pistol and told Zieger, "If you put a hand in your pocket you are a dead man." The lawyer's mouth fell open. The four men then sat silently while the tow truck driver finished his work.

The regular members of the motorcycle gang considered Zieger dangerously crazy and had no intention of making him a full member. Zieger was attractive to women and had numerous girlfriends, so Trooper Vaden interviewed several of them. He concluded that Zieger was either a conflicted homosexual or bisexual and was impotent. His sexual problems sometimes brought him to homicidal rage. He wanted to prove to his friends that his attitude about murder was casual, that he was ready to kill at any time. Vaden once told a reporter "he wanted to become the premier hired gun in Alaska, a hit man."

Detective Rice said he suspected Zieger killed Jimmy Sumpter's wife and stepson because he thought it would win him acceptance with The Brothers. When Zieger heard about the reward he grew terrified; he knew the motorcycle gang might kill him to placate Sumpter. Zieger's friends said the last time they saw him his hands were trembling and he was crying. He called one friend and asked for a ride. The friend refused saying Gary was dangerous to be around right then. Zieger called his lawyer and asked that police place him in protective custody. The lawyer tried but the request was denied.

———

ZIEGER'S BODY WAS FOUND on the Seward Highway near Potter Marsh, a shotgun blast to his chest and a .357 pistol stuffed down the front of his pants. The investigators decided that the .357 was a message saying that Zieger had been the killer of Marguerite Sumpter and her son. They had been shot by a .357 but ballistics tests showed it was not the pistol found in Zieger's trousers. Jimmy Sumpter was in the company of friends at the time of the killing.

Zieger was just 20 years old when he died. One of The Brothers later approached a relative of one of Zieger's victims and told her that Gary's last words were "Tell my mother I love her." The gang wanted the individual to know that they had killed the murderer and that Gary Zieger was no longer a threat to her, to themselves or anybody else.

———

HOWARD WEAVER, THEN A REPORTER for the Anchorage Daily News, noted in his book "Write Hard, Die Free" that Zieger's death inspired him to write one of the best leads of his journalism career: "Gary Zieger lay dead alongside the Seward Highway Tuesday, his life of 20 troubled years ended by the shots he waited for all day."

After Zieger's killing, police received a tip that his buddy Benny Ramey was trying to sell some jewelry, including expensive pieces that prospective buyers recognized as items they had sold to Jimmy Sumpter. The investigators found Ramey hiding with friends in Wasilla in the Matanuska Valley north of Anchorage. Ramey had with him a wad of cash, numerous pieces of jewelry and at least one gold nugget known to have been stolen from Jimmy Sumpter's house. Ramey told the troopers that Zieger had given him the jewelry and asked him to sell the pieces, keep a portion of the proceeds and give him the rest of the money.

Ramey was charged with receiving and attempting to sell stolen property. He denied having anything to do with the Sumpter robbery but he became talkative and told investigators that he knew where Johnny Rich was buried. He told the officers about Johnny's last days, his treatment by his kidnappers and his shooting by Gary Zieger and Wesley Ladd. He led them to Johnny's gravesite near the Jonesville Mine.

Trooper Vaden went to the Jonesville Mine site and watched as a front-end loader excavated a half-acre of mine tailings in search of Johnny Rich's grave. They had no luck until lawyer Duncan Webb's assistant, Caye Mason, and her daughter Virginia Pinnick came forward and offered to pinpoint the grave location. At the mine site, they pointed Vaden's equipment operator to a spot where Johnny's body was found a foot beneath the surface.

While awaiting trial on the various charges, Ramey asked to be set free on bail. Police and the prosecutors worried that turning Ramey loose might be an invitation for one of his enemies to kill him. Assistant District Attorney Mick Hawley told the judge that, if freed, Ramey might be unavailable on account of "being extinguished."

Ramey continued talking and told about the night of Johnny's murder and of Duncan Webb's drawing up of the power of attorney to be signed by Johnny, the one putting Webb in charge of Johnny's affairs and turning ownership of Cindy's Massage Parlor over to Wesley Ladd. Among the items Webb drafted for Johnny's signature was a letter that started "Hi Wes" and offered Johnny's apology for having taken advantage of Ladd's incarceration to take over ownership of Cindy's.

In May 1975 Webb was convicted of being an accessory in the murder of Johnny Rich. He was given a two-year probation and disbarred from practicing law. Ladd and Ramey were charged with kidnapping and murder. Ramey pled guilty and got a minimal 10-year sentence as a reward for testifying against the others. He was released after six years. Ladd received two life sentences but was set free on parole after serving eight years.

Kim Rich, Johnny's daughter and later author of "Johnny's Girl," a notable book about growing up with a father who was a notorious criminal, later wrote that her father ignored warnings about getting into the massage parlor business. She said Johnny once tried to open a massage operation in their house but the city denied him a license.

Kim wrote in an article for The Anchorage Daily News, where she was a reporter, that when her father acquired Cindy's Massage Parlor and later opened a second place several miles away he told her he thought about naming it Kim's Massage. When Johnny learned that there was already a Kim's massage parlor in Anchorage he named his own place Fifi's. Young Kim was disappointed.

Detective Ron Rice is skeptical that Zieger robbed Jimmy Sumpter's house and killed his wife and son for money to pay a lawyer. He is convinced that Zieger thought the robbery/murder would win him acceptance with the motorcycle gang that seems to have killed him.

Trooper Vaden concluded that Gary Zieger came from a very strange family when Zieger's father showed up at the Criminal Investigation Bureau and tried to claim the pistol that Gary used to kill Jimmy Sumpter's wife and son. The elder Zieger said it belonged to Gary and he wanted it as a family souvenir for Gary's younger brother.

CHAPTER 3

The Baker - 1983

ROBERT CHRISTIAN HANSEN was a uniquely Alaskan murderer. He was also one of the most prolific killers ever to run loose on the Last Frontier.

Hansen was born in Estherville, Ohio in 1939, the son of a baker. He was thin, painfully shy and had a pronounced stutter and a severe case of acne that left his face and psyche deeply scarred. His shyness and stutter made it difficult to express himself, a problem that elicited snickers from his classmates, both male and female. And that instilled in him a commitment to getting revenge, especially with the girls whose rejection doomed him to a life of quiet rage.

Hansen was a loner. He learned baking from his domineering father but had a dysfunctional relationship with him, adding intensity to his simmering anger. In 1957 he enlisted in the Army Reserve and served a year before being discharged. After basic training he was assigned to Fort Knox, Kentucky, where he attended Military Police School and often cavorted with prostitutes in the nearby community. His military experience later helped him get a job as an assistant drill instructor at the police academy in Pocahontas, Iowa.

In the summer of 1960 he met and married a young woman. The marriage ended early when his endless fury caused him to burn down a Pocahontas school bus garage. Hansen was angry at the school superintendent, who disciplined him on several occasions, and wanted to get even. During the investigation the fire chief got a call from a youth who worked with Hansen at the bakery. The 16-year-old said Hansen bragged to him that he planned to burn down the bus barn and recruited his help. Hansen led the boy to the barn, climbed into the loft and spread gasoline around. Then the two lit a match, threw it and ran back to the bakery. There, they began painting an oven, pretending they had been doing it all along. While the barn was burning, a fireman attempted to drive a bus out of the building. The vehicle's fuel tank exploded and the fireman was blown out of the bus onto the ground, suffering extensive cuts and burns.

Hansen was arrested for arson and sentenced to three years in prison. He served 20 months in Anamosa State Penitentiary and his wife divorced him while he was behind bars. Over the next few years he was arrested several times for petty theft, a larcenous hobby he indulged throughout his life.

While he was in prison, a psychiatrist diagnosed him as having an "infantile personality" and said Hansen engaged in fantasies of getting revenge on the women who rejected him. Hansen told the psychiatrist he wanted to blow up the town water tower and shoot out the lights of a police cruiser. He wanted to get even with many people.

The psychiatrist reported on Hansen's statements at a parole hearing so Hansen decided it had been a big mistake to confide in the doctor. He decided that in the future he would say he couldn't remember such things. He was learning from his mistakes.

———

HE ALSO DECIDED TO DO AT LEAST A FEW GOOD THINGS in hopes of impressing others that he was a nice person at heart. While at the penitentiary he assisted a staff counselor, typed letters for prisoners who couldn't read or write, took a correspondence course on the Bible and helped his fellow prisoners with religious counseling. A staff counselor helped him get into speech therapy at the nearby University of Iowa, nearly eliminating his frustrating stutter.

In late 1962 a prison psychiatrist reported that Hansen still had an infantile personality but his antisocial attitude was greatly diminished. Hansen's hard-earned duplicity would serve him well in the years ahead.

———

ROBERT'S PARENTS WERE GREATLY EMBARRASSED by his arrest and imprisonment so they left Pocahontas and bought a small resort on a lake in northern Minnesota. When he was released, Robert joined them and went to work painting boats and cabins and rigging docks for fishing. He began guiding fishing parties and gained a new love for the wild country.

At the lake, Hansen met Darla, a young woman from Pocahontas whom his parents had hired to clean cabins. Darla was then a student at the University of Iowa. They made plans to marry after her graduation. Hansen got training in cake decoration and held jobs in Minnesota, North Dakota and South Dakota. His jobs usually ended when his employers discovered he was a thief with an explosive temper. At one bakery, Hansen took to hiding stolen goods around the shop—radios, small appliances and sporting goods. One suspicious co-worker took his boss out to the parking lot to show him that Hansen had two bicycles in the back of his truck, both with somebody's anti-theft locks still attached to their wheels.

In 1965 Hansen was arrested for stealing from a sporting goods store but Darla prevailed on the Lutheran pastor to intervene on his behalf and the charges were dropped. A few months later his boss caught him with the cash drawer, which Bob had pried open with a knife. The boss threatened to fire him but Hansen said he was quitting and taking another job.

Their time in northern Minnesota instilled in both Hansen and his wife a love of the outdoors so after her graduation in 1967 they loaded their belongings and a tent into their new Pontiac and headed for Anchorage. There he got a job as a baker and cake decorator at a Safeway store; wife Darla took a teaching job at Government Hill Elementary School.

Darla became active in the Anchorage Lutheran Church and together they went hiking, climbing, camping and fishing. When Darla gave birth to a daughter she became preoccupied with motherhood. Hansen made up for the loss of his wife's companionship when he discovered bow hunting and the prestige of taking trophy animals. He began collecting animal-head trophies including record-class mountain goats, caribou and Dall sheep. And, most importantly, he befriended a fellow hunter, insurance salesman John Sumrall.

In 1971 Hansen killed a large Dall sheep and claimed it as a world record for bow-hunting. But his claim was challenged when a tipster reported to Pope and Young, the hunting trophy experts who arbitrate such things, that Hansen had used a rifle and took the sheep in a closed area. Hansen signed an affidavit that the sheep was killed with an arrow and

John Sumrall vouched for his claim. The world record was allowed to stand.

On November 15, 1971, Hansen came to the attention of authorities for a more frightening violation. An 18-year-old woman named Susie Heppeard stopped at a red light on Northern Lights Boulevard and noticed a man in the next car wearing an orange hunting hat and looking her way. Susie smiled reflexively and drove on. At her apartment she undressed and was about to step into the shower when her doorbell rang. She wrapped her body in a towel and went to the door. Waiting outside was the man she saw at the traffic light. He asked to use a phone book saying he was looking for a friend in the apartment complex. Susie pointed to the book on a table by the door. The man flipped through the phone book, said his friend must be unlisted and tried to strike up a conversation. He asked for a date and Susie told him she was engaged. He left.

A week later Susie pulled into her driveway after midnight and saw a man wearing an orange hunting cap scurry behind an adjacent building. When she stepped out of her car the man approached, put a gun in her face and said: "Shut up, sweetheart, or I'll blow your brains out." Susie screamed. The man cocked the gun and muttered: "Scream again and I *will* blow your head off."

Susie's roommate, Susan Scott, peered out an apartment window and saw a man holding a gun against her friend's head. She yelled: "What's going on, Susie? Are you alright?"

While Susan frantically dialed police, their other roommate, Frances Lake, came to the living room window. "What's going on," she said, "I thought I heard a scream."

"You did," Scott replied. "I think that guy may be going to rape Susie."

Frances opened the door and shouted, "Susie, get away from that jerk! We've called police."

The man pushed the gun into Susie's back and tried to force her toward the street, then he heard the wail of police sirens and quickly disappeared into the dark. When police officers jumped from their cruiser Susie fell to the ground and shrieked: "He said he was going to blow my head off!"

At that point Hansen's luck took a nasty turn for the worse. His pursuers included Alaska's first canine police unit. The dog found Hansen walking through the snow in his shirt sleeves. Hansen told Officer Archie Hutchins he had been driving, felt woozy and pulled over to get some fresh air. Another patrolman found a loaded .22 pistol under a seat in Hansen's car. Hutchins and the dog followed Hansen's trail backward and found an orange hat in the snow and a .357 magnum revolver in the wheel well of an abandoned car.

Hansen admitted that the hat and the handgun were similar to ones he owned. The tips of the bullets in the .357 were creased by a knife, creating what are known as "dum-dum" shells, lethal missiles that expand on impact and have a devastating effect on their target.

Hansen told police he might have been involved in the incident with Susie Heppeard and suggested that if he was, "I need help." He was charged with criminal assault. Hansen hired a defense attorney, prominent Anchorage lawyer Jim Gilmore, who asked that Bob be examined at the Langdon Psychiatric Clinic and released on his own recognizance. The prosecutor objected, arguing that Hansen had threatened Susie Heppeard's life and should be released on $2,000 bail. Hansen was set free on his own recognizance, a personal obligation involving no cash, but he was prohibited from making contact with Susie.

HANSEN'S BIZARRE BEHAVIOR with Susie Heppeard and his improvised dum-dum bullets won him a place in what Anchorage Police called "the asshole book," a catalog of misbehaving locals that was often referred to when bad things happened in the city. Keeper of the asshole book was homicide investigator Ron Rice, a seasoned officer who was then learning the art of criminal profiling and decided Hansen was potentially dangerous and deserved a prominent listing in the book.

In mid-December a grand jury indicted Hansen for assault with a deadly weapon. Just three days later he kidnapped an 18-year-old prostitute known as Patty. She had stopped for an early morning cup of tea at the Nevada Cafe in Anchorage. He tried to pick her up outside the cafe. When she spurned him, he pulled out a pistol and ordered her into his Pontiac. As they were driving through South Anchorage, Hansen spotted a police cruiser with two officers. "There goes your help," he told the girl. "If we get stopped, don't do or say anything or I'll have to shoot them. Understand?" She nodded in terror.

Hansen tied her hands and feet with shoelaces, then shoved her to the car floor. He drove down the Seward Highway to the turnout at the small community of Indian and parked on a secluded dead-end road. Hansen noticed that she had black lace on her bra and asked politely if he could rip it off. The girl asked him not to tear it because it had been expensive. He removed her bra and her dress carefully, saying she couldn't run away if she was naked.

Patty asked Hansen to stop at a roadside store in Portage and buy cigarettes, which he did. He then drove onto the Kenai Peninsula, rented a cabin at the Sunrise Inn, took her inside and raped her. On the drive back to Anchorage he suddenly reversed direction and headed south again saying he wanted to visit a cabin where he had taken a woman the week before. The cabin was on Cooper Lake Road, which was by then blocked by snow, forcing him to turn back. Midway down the steep road he stopped the car, pushed the girl out and cocked his pistol. "Start running," he said.

Patty pleaded with him, saying that he was handsome, good in bed and they could date. She also told him she had a baby son who would lose his mother if she died. Hansen hesitated to free her, assumed that she would go to police if he did. He found a court document in her purse, an order giving custody of her son to her parents. It included her parents' name and address so Hansen wrote them down telling her he would kill both of them and her son if she said anything to anyone about their encounter.

Hansen dropped the terrified woman off in Anchorage a few blocks from her car. She ran to it, leaped in and sat trembling, shuddering with the thought that if her attacker had looked deeper into her purse he would have found a business card for her father, an Alaska State Trooper.

The frightened dancer was at first determined not to involve police in her case but changed her mind on Christmas Day when two young men found the half-naked body of a college freshman in a ravine near McHugh Creek Campground south of the city, a few miles from one of the places Hansen had driven her. The young woman's hands had been lashed behind her back with wire; she had been raped and her chest slashed. Detectives concluded she must have been alive when she fell or was thrown into the ravine, was unable to climb out and froze to death.

Patty confided to her father that she had been kidnapped and raped by Hansen and she suspected the McHugh Creek murder might have been Hansen's work. Her father went to fellow officer Walt Gilmour and said he had an informant who could provide information about Hansen. He said the informant was his daughter and she was willing to tell her story but hoped publicity could be avoided. Patty went to State Trooper headquarters and identified Hansen from file photos.

Hansen was re-arrested and new charges lodged against him. While in the booking process he was checked in by a rookie officer. The inexperienced jailer went through Hansen's wallet and logged its contents. Hansen asked to see his wallet for a minute, saying there might be additional money in it. The booking officer handed Hansen the wallet, was distracted briefly and turned back in time to see the prisoner pocketing a piece of paper.

When the officer's co-worker returned, the rookie mentioned the palmed piece of paper and suggested they should search Hansen again. They found the wadded paper in his pocket. Hansen said it was the name of someone who could bail him out. The officer hand-copied the two names and address from the paper and handed it back to Hansen. By the time they realized that the names were the girl's State Trooper father and his wife, the parents Hansen had threatened to kill, their prisoner had already eaten the original piece of paper and they couldn't prove the booking officer had copied it from the one in Hansen's pocket.

On December 29, Hansen was arraigned and ordered held for $50,000 bond. At a hearing on January 7, Hansen's lawyer, Jim Gilmore, attacked the credibility of the victim and offered three character witnesses for the baker: Hansen's family pastor, the Rev. Albert L. Abrahamson, pastor of Lutheran Central Church, and his two hunting buddies, insurance salesman John Sumrall and Gerald Goldschmidt, an environmental health officer for the Alaska Native Health Service.

Hansen did appear to be a solid citizen. Besides the people vouching for him, he was a business owner and family man. Most importantly, the computer system used by investigators was still being developed and many records had yet to be entered. It did not yet contain anything on Hansen's criminal record.

And Patty was a poor courtroom witness, nervous and uncertain. When police asked her to take a polygraph test, she had refused, leading them to believe she was lying. Gilmore emphasized both her work on the streets and her experimentation with drugs, leaving her credibility in tatters. All three of Hansen's character witnesses testified they were sure he would never harm anyone. Goldschmidt insisted the young woman must be mistaken. All said their friend and parishioner should be returned to his family.

Of the two people involved in the incident, Hansen seemed to be the most credible citizen, a man with respectable friends. A few months after the trial, the charges in the young dancer's case were dropped in plea bargaining. Hansen was sentenced to five years for the earlier assault on Susie Heppeard. The judge ruled that he could be considered for parole once he was deemed psychologically fit. A psychiatrist reported he considered Hansen to be schizophrenic and capable of committing violent acts without remembering them. He said he considered Hansen's problem treatable and recommended twice-a-week counseling and close supervision.

Hansen had figured out how to game the system and soon convinced his jailers he was a model prisoner. In less than three months he was transferred to a halfway house, given psychiatric treatment and placed on work release.

Years later he told investigators that while on work release he would drive to downtown Anchorage, park on the street and watch prostitutes work the area. "I'd get a tremendous gosh dang," he said. Watching the women interact with customers gave him a "sexual blow-up charge."

———

ANCHORAGE WAS UNDERGOING AN ECONOMIC BOOM in the early 1970s as companies geared up to build the trans-Alaska oil pipeline. Most of the companies involved in the pipeline project had major offices in Anchorage The city bustled as their employees, contractors and other workers arrived looking for work. The jobseekers included many single men who were attractive targets for the city's growing force of dancers and prostitutes. Since many such working women stayed in the area only briefly and often left without notice, the disappearance of girls in the trade was not considered cause for alarm. It was generally assumed they had simply left town. The fact that many such young women were sent to Alaska's largest city by Seattle mobster Frank Colacurcio and his agency, Talents West, added to the lack of accountability or concern. The easiest assumption was that the girls simply moved on or were transferred to a new area. In some cases they were rescued from the life by friends or family.

The city was growing rapidly as suburbs sprang up and the business heart of Anchorage migrated southward to Midtown, leaving behind the seedier areas of Downtown. The city's fast-changing geography switched responsibility for policing much of Anchorage from the relatively sizable Anchorage Police Department to the Alaska State Troopers, who had fewer officers and were responsible for a large portion of the entire state. The Troopers were a well-trained professional organization but their smaller numbers were a disadvantage in protecting such a large area. The situation, including parallel growth in other parts of Southcentral Alaska, was ripe for a predator like Robert Hansen.

Hansen moored his 36-foot cabin cruiser in Seward, 125 miles south of Anchorage in prime sport fishing and hunting country. He used it for trips with his buddies and occasional outings with wife Darla.

On July 17, 1973, 16-year-old Megan Emerick was doing her washing at the Seward Skill Center when she folded her clothes, ran a brush through her long blond hair, left the dormitory and disappeared. She was never seen again but police believe her body is in a shallow grave marked by an X on a map of Resurrection Bay, a map later discovered among items Robert Hansen kept hidden in his home. Two years later, Mary K. Thill accepted a ride from friends from her home at Lowell Point to the city of Seward. Her friends dropped her off and Mary Thill was never seen again. Police believe her grave is marked by another X on the map of Resurrection Bay, the map found in Robert Hansen's house.

A few weeks after Mary Thill disappeared, Hansen dropped in for a few drinks at the Kit Kat Club on Old Seward Highway. He flashed a roll of bills and told people he was new in town and came to work on the pipeline. A dancer agreed to meet him. When she climbed into his car he roughed her up, put a pistol to her head and drove to the edge of Chugach State Park on the city's south side. There he raped her, then let her go.

The woman told her story to Sherryl Messer of the Anchorage Rape and Assault Center, saying she was afraid for her life. Messer said she wanted to pass the information on to police and the victim agreed provided her name was kept out of it. Messer passed the information on to Trooper Sam Barnard who showed her a photo of Hansen. The victim said the man in the photo was her attacker. She had memorized the man's license plate number but declined to press charges. She was a schoolteacher from another state, had come to Alaska to make money during pipeline construction and didn't want the embarrassment of court proceedings, afraid the news might reach her hometown.

Barnard ran the license number through police files and learned that the vehicle was owned by Robert Hansen. The Trooper notified a parole officer who called Hansen in for questioning. Hansen claimed that he and the dancer had been on a date. He said she asked for money, he refused to pay and she got mad and hollered rape. Barnard didn't believe Hansen but since the dancer refused to testify and had already disappeared he couldn't take action against him.

Hansen had learned a lot during his imprisonment, among other things how to tell both jailers and psychiatrists what they wanted to hear, suggestions that his mental health was improving. He also became convinced he was making a mistake by letting his victims live to testify against him.

"We taught the guy to kill," said Trooper Major Walt Gilmour in an interview after publication of a book he co-authored on the Hansen case, Butcher Baker. "Now he is back on the streets and he knows he needs to kill."

IN DECEMBER OF 1976 a security guard at the Fred Meyer store caught Hansen trying to steal a chainsaw. He was charged with larceny from a building and told Judge James Singleton that when he walked past the saw in the store he thought about his elderly father, who was ill but wanted a chainsaw to use when he got well. Hansen said he didn't have enough money to buy the chainsaw so he left the building, then he ran across an elderly man lying in the parking lot. The man had suffered a heart attack and was being treated by paramedics. The scene made him think about his father, his dad's ailing heart and upcoming birthday, so he went back into the store and took the saw. "I know what I did was wrong," he told the judge, "and I'm sorry for it."

SINGLETON SENTENCED HANSEN to five years in prison. He was sent to Juneau Correctional Institute and released 16 months later after the Alaska Supreme Court reviewed his case. The court shortened his sentence based on the fact that his previous offenses had been five and 15 years before and Hansen had "maintained steady employment, been a good provider and has earned the reputation of a hard worker and a respectable member of the community." As in the past, a psychiatrist's report suggested that Hansen was disturbed and potentially dangerous but his antisocial behavior seemed to respond to drugs like lithium.

JUDGE SINGLETON ORDERED HANSEN'S RELEASE but noted angrily that "I'm absolutely convinced that Mr. Hansen is going to commit additional crimes. But in this case the Supreme Court has indicated that as long as the crimes are against property, not crimes of violence, the community is just going to have to tolerate it."

Singleton ordered that Hansen undergo psychiatric and drug treatment but the assistant district attorney responsible for the case didn't follow through and Hansen never received the treatment. He was released on unsupervised parole and a few weeks afterward murdered a woman at Summit Lake on the Kenai Peninsula. Hansen later told investigators he killed that woman because he had come to realize he was making a mistake in letting his victims live to testify against him. That disappearance was followed by a series of abductions, rapes and murders. Most were reported as dancers and prostitutes who dropped out of sight. They generally left belongings behind but those were minimal and inexpensive, reinforcing speculation that they had just left town for parts unknown.

HANSEN THEN OPENED A BAKERY near Downtown Anchorage. The venture was successful and he was able, with the help of an insurance settlement, to buy a small airplane perfect for wilderness adventures, a SuperCub. He did not have a pilot's license, couldn't get one because he was taking lithium, but he learned to fly illicitly, probably with the help of one of his buddies. He became a skilled back-country pilot, what Alaskans call a Bush pilot, and added an exciting new dimension to his adventures.

At first Hansen flew primarily in spring and summer, but as his skills improved and his lust for blood increased he began stalking women every few weeks. His new air mobility expanded his options for adventure.

His early list of murders included an unidentified prostitute who was believed to have come from Kodiak and whose body was discovered near the village of Eklutna. Hansen picked her up in the fall of 1979, made a deal for sex and drove her to Eklutna Road. There his truck became stuck in the mud and she tried to help free it. She grew worried about Hansen's aggressive behavior and tried to run away but Hansen chased her down, threw her to the ground and stabbed her in the back. He buried her beneath a power line in a shallow grave that was discovered the following July. Investigators were unable to identify the woman and dubbed her "Eklutna Annie." The officers could find no clues to her murderer.

ON MAY 19, 1980, CANNERY WORKER JOANNE MESSINA met Hansen on a dock in Seward while walking with her dog. He bought her dinner at the Harbor View Restaurant and afterward in his camper she propositioned him. He drove to the Snow River on the highway north of Seward. She grew worried and asked him to take her back to Seward. They fought and she jumped out of the camper. He chased her with a .22 pistol and whacked her in the head. Messina fought back so Hansen killed her with two shots from the .22. He dragged her body to a gravel pit and covered it with sand and rock. Hansen shot the dog, threw its body into the woods, dumped Messina's camping gear nearby and tossed the pistol into the Snow River. By the time police found her body a month later it had been dug up and half-eaten by bears.

Anchorage Police were becoming increasingly worried about the number of young prostitutes and topless dancers gone missing in the city. Because the women lived in unstable domestic arrangements and many were drifters who moved from city to city, state to state, it was difficult to be sure for a long time that anything really was wrong. One of those who took an early interest in the shrinking shady-lady count was Detective Maxine Farrell. With a booming economy and the city filled with newly prosperous oil and construction workers, young sex trade amateurs were flocking to Anchorage to make a nest egg before they returned to their homes. With both professionals and amateurs active in the trade, keeping track of who might be missing was a forbidding chore. But Farrell noticed a repeating pattern in the reports on many of the young females. Often a topless dancer would make a date with a man she didn't know who offered her $200 or $300 for a nude photo session or a lunch date. When the woman failed to return, a friend would report her missing.

On the evening of September 12, 1982, two Anchorage police officers on an off-duty moose hunting trip noticed a boot and a jacket on a Knik River sandbar. They started digging and unearthed the shallow grave of a partially clothed woman whose eyes were covered by an Ace bandage. The gravesite was in a remote area 25 miles north of Anchorage. At first light next day the two men headed back to their vehicle and drove to the Palmer office of the Alaska State Troopers to report their grisly discovery.

Leading the investigation into the murder was Sergeant Rollie Port, a decorated Vietnam War veteran who studied his cases and was known to his colleagues as a man who could spot evidence that others had overlooked. Before the body was removed, Port had the gravesite photographed from multiple angles and ordered a thorough examination of the body, which had been in the grave for months and emanated a strong smell that repulsed those doing the examination. Port had gravel shoveled from the grave and sifted through a large wire screen. Soon. a spent

.223 rifle cartridge bounced on the top of the screen.

Identification of the body proved difficult both because of its condition and the fact that the list of missing women included several with similar descriptions. Two weeks after the grave was discovered the victim was identified as Sherry Morrow, age 24, who had been a dancer at the Wild Cherry Bar and disappeared 10 months earlier. Her boyfriend had reported her missing when she failed to show up for a doctor's appointment. The night before she was reported missing, Sherry told a girlfriend she had a date with a man who offered her $300 to star in a photo layout.

At that point the news media got wind of the discovery and linked it to reports of three other dancers gone missing. Detective Maxine Waters worried that the information might start a public panic and tried to assure people that there was no reason to worry. She said investigators did not believe there was a mass murderer running loose in the community. State Trooper Lieutenant John Shover told reporters there was no reason to think that the number of disappearances were anything more than a coincidence.

Investigators were then searching for bodies all along the Knik River, laboriously drilling test wells in the gravel. Sherry Morrow's grave had been found in a sandbar on the river below Pioneer Peak. The spot was accessible by motor vehicle, airplane or riverboat, so the killer had a lot of options for getting there and other victims might be found anywhere similar transportation could be used. They considered the fact that the killer might have left Alaska but the fact that the victim was buried in a sandbar on the Knik River suggested he was a local and might still be living nearby.

———

HANSEN KEPT ADDING TO HIS LIST OF MURDERS but his luck began to run out on June 13, 1983 when he picked up 17-year-old Cindy Paulson. Hansen met her walking near Fifth and Denali, a frequent strolling spot for hookers. He lured her into his car by offering $200 for oral sex, then slapped handcuffs on her and drove her to his home. There he dragged her into the basement and raped her. (Hansen's wife Darla and their two children were in Arkansas visiting with Darla's parents. Afterward they planned to spend time in Europe.)

"Tell me you want it," Hansen demanded of Cindy. She began to cry.

"Tell me you want it, baby." She didn't answer.

Hansen finished quickly while Cindy's mind churned, trying to think of a way to escape. She considered crawling out a bathroom window and told Hansen she urgently needed to use the toilet. Hansen tied a thick nylon rope around her neck and held it like a leash while she went into the bathroom. When the rope went slack, she leaped to the bathroom window but found it nailed shut.

Outside the bathroom door she heard the sound of heavy chains being dragged across the floor. She stood silently in the small room thinking he was going to kill her for sure. Cindy decided to take an aggressive approach, stripped naked, threw open the door and stepped into the basement room.

"Go back in," he ordered.

"No," she replied.

"I said go back in."

Cindy stood her ground so Hansen grabbed her, dragged her to a heavy post in the middle of the basement room and tied her with the chain, wrapping it four times around her neck.

"If you cooperate, I won't hurt you," he said, tightening the chain. His acne-pocked face, framed by horn-rimmed glasses, pressed close to hers. The terrified girl thought she saw warts, adding to his frightening appearance. Then he surprised her by grabbing a brown, yellow and orange afghan and wrapping it around her.

"I'm tired," he said. "I haven't slept for a long time. I'm going to go to sleep on the couch. D-d-d-don't wake me up", he said, stuttering, "or you'll make me mad. And you don't want to see me mad." With a gun still in his hand, Hansen walked to a television set and turned it on, saying she could watch it while he slept Then he spread out on the couch.

While Hansen slept, Cindy's mind churned furiously. She looked around the room, which was dimly lit by the television and the weak rays of June's midnight sun filtering through the windows. She saw a broken clock, a computer, a rack of women's clothes, a pool table, a foosball table and many hunting trophies. On the floor was the bearskin rug on which he raped her. Wolf pelts lay stacked in a corner. The wall was lined with caribou and wild goat heads. Tables were covered by mounted ducks, other game birds and a stuffed fish. The thought occurred to her: "*This guy likes to kill things. I've got to get out of here.*"

Cindy saw a pool cue leaning against a pool table and considered grabbing it and whacking Hansen on the head. She quickly abandoned the notion, writing it off as a stupid idea that would only get him angry. But she was convinced he was going to kill her. Hansen awoke and came to her side. Cindy pleaded with him, asking to be let go, to see her parents again.

Hansen tried to calm her, saying everything would be OK. He said he had brought seven girls to the basement room before her. "Usually I keep them a week," he said. "But I really like you, so I'm going to treat you special." His words terrified Kitty, convincing her he had killed all seven of the women.

"Why do you do this?" She asked.

"I used to work on the North Slope," he replied. Hansen said he had been paying $200 to women for 10 or 15 minutes of pleasure. Now he was going to get his money's worth by bringing girls to his house and doing as he pleased with them for as long as he wanted.

Hansen told Cindy she was so special that he would take her to his remote hunting cabin, make love to her one more time and get her home by 11 in the morning. Hansen said he had a plane at a local airport and they could use that to fly out to his cabin.

"Okay, good," she said. "That's fine." She pretended to go along with his plan, thinking she needed to get out of that basement and make a run for freedom or she would never live through the night.

"Even if you do tell on me," Hansen said, "I'll have an alibi. My friends will say I went to the lake with them."

She thought Hansen was going to kill her right there but he put the key in the padlock, released the chains and told her to get dressed. Cindy decided to run as soon as they got outside and, since she wouldn't be able to run in her pumps, carried the shoes in her hand. But there would be no going outside, with its opportunity to flee while screaming for the neighbors. Hansen led her from the house into an attached garage, forced her to lie down on the car floor and covered her with a green army blanket, then opened the garage door. Soon they were driving toward Merrill Field on the east side of Downtown Anchorage.

Cindy had another thought. She was staying at the Big Timber Motel down the street from Merrill Field, a small municipal airport. If she could get there her friends could protect her and she would be safe. Hansen parked beside his SuperCub and began pulling things from his car trunk and loading them into the airplane.

Cindy noticed the driver's side door was ajar and decided to make a break for it. She waited until he was leaning into the airplane and she could see only his legs, then leaped through the car door and ran barefoot through the gravel parking lot, the bottoms of her feet aching. Hansen raced after her, gun in hand and running furiously.

She slipped into a used-car lot and tried to hide behind a car, then saw Hansen racing toward her. Cindy ran into the street and jumped in front of a truck. The driver's eyes went wide and he slammed on the brakes. He opened a door and asked: "Are you alright?" She leaped in beside him saying "No, he's going to kill me."

"Who's going to kill you?" The driver looked out to see Hansen running toward them with pistol in hand. He put the truck in gear and quickly drove away. "Take me to the Big Timber motel," she told him. The driver was reluctant. "I think we ought to go to the police station," he said. "That guy has got a gun."

"No, just stop," Cindy shouted.

"No way," the driver answered.

"Then just stop right here," she ordered. "Just stop and let me out, man."

Hansen by then had turned around and was jogging back to the airport and his vehicle. The truck driver pulled up at the Mush Inn Motel, a short way down Fifth Avenue. Cindy ran to the front desk and asked the clerk to call her pimp. The pimp showed up in a taxi a few minutes later and tried to calm Cindy down. The truck driver headed for the Anchorage Police station and told officers what he had just witnessed. He said Cindy's attacker wore a green coat and drove a green car. He had written down the vehicle's license number and gave that to the officers.

Cindy and her pimp walked to the Big Timber Motel, where he tried to stop her shaking and flooding tears. She asked him to take the handcuffs off but he had no key and no tools. He tried to quiet her while racking his brain for a solution.

"Stop it, please," he ordered. "Please."

Cindy said OK but the tears still streamed down her cheeks. The pimp slapped her in frustration, then ran down the motel hallway to his brother's room. When he returned he had a gun in his hand and muttered "I'm going to kill that motherfucker." He left Cindy still in handcuffs and headed for the airport, looking for Hansen.

APD Officer Gregg Baker rushed to the Big Timber Motel and found Cindy alone in her room, still wearing the handcuffs. He removed the cuffs and listened as she told her story. Baker took her back to Merrill Field where she identified Hansen's airplane. He called the airport tower and gave them the SuperCub's tail number. The aircraft was registered to Robert C. Hansen, who lived at a South Anchorage address.

While Baker and Cindy were sitting in his cruiser, an airport security guard rushed over and told them that he had seen a white man in a green coat running to a green vehicle with Alaska license number BJZ-775, also registered to Hansen.

Several officers were dispatched to Hansen's house while Baker took Cindy to Humana Hospital. When a doctor examined Cindy he found sperm on a tampon she had been wearing. When two APD officers arrived at Hansen's house he wasn't there but showed up a few minutes later. They noted that he fit the description Cindy had given of her attacker.

Police searched Hansen's home and the airplane but nothing revealing. Hansen had removed Cindy's shoes from the airplane and disposed of them somewhere. He denied having done anything wrong and said the woman was just trying to get even with him because he refused to pay her exorbitant demands simply for a night of sex. When Investigator Will Dennis told Hansen he was suspected of raping a prostitute, Hansen smiled and said: "You can't rape a prostitute, can you?"

"In this state, you can," Dennis replied.

"Well, I didn't pick up any prostitute last night." Hansen said he didn't rape anybody and his friends would testify he was with them at the time Cindy claimed she was being attacked.

"From 5 p.m. to 11:30 p.m. last night I was at the home of John Sumrall fixing an airplane seat. You can ask him. And then, from there, I went to John Henning's house and stayed until about 5 a.m. this morning talking about fishing. After that I went to Merrill Field and put the seat in my airplane." He said he then drove home and found two police officers waiting for him.

Sumrall managed one of Anchorage's largest insurance company offices and lived in a large house on the Anchorage Hillside. Henning was a private contractor and boat builder. Both were respected businessmen whose testimony would have been given great credibility if called before a jury.

Hansen agreed to allow investigators to search his home, car and airplane. Their search of the car turned up a box of center-fire rifle cartridges under the front seat, bullets that looked to be either 30.06 or .223 caliber. They didn't confiscate the bullet box and later couldn't pin down which they were. They also found an Ace bandage.

At the house they found a scene much like the one Cindy described. There were animal traps and trophies but no ropes or chains. In a basement wall they found a false panel covering a stash of rifles, pistols and ammunition. One of the pistols was a Thompson Contender, a lightweight single-shot weapon popular with marksmen. It came with interchangeable barrels in varying calibers usually associated with rifles, 30-30, .223 and .222.

THE NEXT DAY CINDY RECOGNIZED Hansen's pockmarked face from a lineup of unidentified men. But Hansen's two friends, John Sumrall and John Henning, both told police their buddy couldn't have attacked the girl because he was with them during the hours of her ordeal.

Hansen's prior run-ins with the law and his listing in the asshole book made him a prime suspect for the attack on Cindy, but her profession combined with his seemingly meek demeanor and regular employment, backed up by good references from his respectable friends and a lack of evidence, made it difficult to bring charges against him. The case had gone cold.

Since the second Knik River victim disappeared from the city and her grave was found in a rural area, both Anchorage City Police and Alaska State Troopers worked on the case. The two-agency team started with a list of 15 men with whom Anchorage prostitutes had reported worrisome encounters with prospective johns.

Trooper Sergeant Lyle Haugsven was assigned to work both the Cindy Paulson and Sherry Morrow cases. Haugsven was a hard-working, determined man who dug deeply into both cases. He re-interviewed Sherry's friends, including her boyfriend Dale Yonkoske. That interview turned up the fact that Sherry always wore a gold necklace with a gold arrowhead pendant. Dale had given it to her as a gift. The necklace was not on Sherry's body and had not been found. Perhaps the killer had kept it as a memento.

Haugsven also asked for a report from Merrill Field Tower on flights by Hansen's SuperCub, hoping the information would point toward a flight to Sherry Morrow's gravesite on the Knik River. That didn't work because, though the tower operators were unaware of it, Hansen had re-painted his aircraft's tail numbers in a smaller type size that the tower had difficulty seeing and recording. When an operator would call to ask for his tail number, Hansen would give another aircraft's number, usually one parked near his airplane. Hansen didn't even have a pilot's license. If asked about the license he would lie about that too.

On September 2, 1983, another body was found in a grave on the Knik River, a spot close to the site where Sherry Morrow's body was found buried. Haugsven was away on leave so Sergeant Edward Stauber took over the investigation. Since the spot where the second body was found was accessible by both boat and light aircraft, Stauber and several troopers got a boat and motored down from the Knik Highway bridge. At the gravesite, they found decomposed remains in another shallow grave on the riverbank. It appeared the murderer had been in a great rush and did a poor job of covering his victim. The corpse was wearing unbuttoned and unzipped blue jeans, a striped sweater that had been cut up the front, a bra that had been cut in half and tan boots. Like the first, this grave also contained a .223 shell casing. They removed the remains hoping that the jawbone might identify the woman by matching it with dental records. But there existed no file of dental images to simplify the search. They sent the .223 casings found in both graves to the FBI to determine if they were fired from the same weapon. When the report came back, it confirmed that the same weapon, and presumably, the same killer, fired both shots. One of the casings appeared to have been reloaded.

The autopsy showed the woman had been in her late twenties or early thirties. She had been killed by one shot in the sternum; the bullet passed through her heart. Her name was unknown.

<hr>

FIVE DAYS AFTER THE SECOND GRAVESITE was found, Trooper Lieutenant Bob Gent added Trooper Sergeant Glenn Flothe to the team working the case. Flothe was a crack investigator who had sat in on Haugsven's weekly briefings on the case. Flothe was an unusual man, a well-trained police officer with the mind of an engineer. His supervisor, Major Walt Gilmour, said Flothe was "what you want a police officer to be." Flothe was a quiet man who once intended to be a teacher but changed his mind after enrolling in a few police science classes at Anchorage Community College. He met some of Alaska's top police officers there, became enchanted with their stories and decided to become one himself. One of those he met was Walt Gilmour, who told Glenn that if he wanted to become a State Trooper he should attend a police academy in Anchorage. Flothe later studied engineering at the University of Alaska Anchorage, attended the police academy and ultimately began to use the approaches he learned in the engineering classes for his police work.

As he dug into the case of the missing women, Flothe laid out all the evidence on a large wall grid with a timeline for each piece, photos of the women, the dates they were last seen and everything collected by the investigators. Some of the women had presumably left town on their own but a number, at least seven, had left to meet a man who offered big money for dates. Those seven were almost certainly murdered.

Flothe also started to read books about history's serial killers, including the notorious Ted Bundy who kidnapped, raped, robbed and killed a long list of women in several states during the 1970s. Most interesting to Flothe was a killing in Colorado where Bundy kidnapped a young woman, put her in handcuffs and tried to drive away with her in his Volkswagen. The woman had escaped and identified Bundy as her attacker. Her testimony resulted in his being jailed for the first time. Flothe was fascinated by the information, both because the incident was so much like Robert Hansen's attempted abduction of Cindy Paulson and the victim's description was very similar to Cindy's.

When Flothe interviewed Cindy he found her—unlike Hansen's other living victims—to be one of the best witnesses he ever worked with. Among other things, she had memorized the tail number of Hansen's SuperCub, the location of his house and everything in its basement.

Flothe studied his wall-grid intensely, working his keen mind to determine where it all led. The grid pointed to Hansen but when he delved into the state's computer system he could find nothing about Hansen. Gilmour stopped by one day, looked at the matrix and asked of Cindy Paulson. "Is she a dancer?"

"A hooker," Flothe said. "Works Fifth and Denali."

"And she's identified a suspect?" Gilmour asked.

"A guy named Robert Hansen."

"Is he a pimply-faced guy with a stutter?"

Flothe said the description fit.

Gilmour asked about Hansen's prior arrest record. Flothe said the only thing that came up in the computer was the 1977 arrest for stealing the chain saw from the Fred Meyer store.

Gilmour said the computer system was wrong, that there should be lots more. When Flothe checked further he learned that Hansen's record had been in the system but was dropped out due to a lack of recent complaints. (Hansen's recent victims weren't living to tell their tales and computer storage space was limited.)

Gilmour was convinced Hansen was the killer, especially since he knew Hansen had told one of his rape victims that he had killed people and gotten away with it. Gilmour urged Flothe to dig out the old paper records in the Susie Heppeard case and anything else he could find. Flothe did, found multiple reports on complaints about Hansen and moved his name to the top spot in his list of suspects.

Then Associated Press editor Paul Jenkins heard about an unusual weekend search on the Knik River. Haugsven, by then back on duty, told Jenkins that investigators were trying to put together a psychological profile on the killer of several women. Jenkins did his own digging and got a list of seven possible murder victims from Flothe. On September 20 he distributed an article to Associated Press member media with the headline: "Authorities Fear List of Women May Grow."

Police put a round-the-clock surveillance on Hansen and Flothe's list of presumed victims grew to 22. Flothe sent a request for assistance to the FBI's Behavioral Sciences Division in Quantico, Virginia, the nation's leading experts on serial murderers. Quantico sent two agents, James Horn and John Douglas.

The FBI men's report to Flothe, as detailed in Walt Gilmour and Leland Hale's *Butcher Baker*, was: "The man you want probably stutters. Is likely an excellent hunter. His wife is probably religious, and not totally aware of her husband's activities. He's known as a good provider and hard-working businessman. He's successful, or at least we wouldn't be surprised if he is. He probably stashes things. Like maybe rings or jewelry or drivers' licenses or maybe clothing. He likes to keep it close to him, so he can review it in private. He takes it out and relives the killings. It's a movie in his brain and the objects he's taken from the scene turn him on. If he's really into it, the killings are all he thinks about 24 hours a day. Everything else is just a motion to him. His work, his normal routine, is just a motion. Everything is wrapped up with murder. His whole life, his whole thinking. He probably plans the kills far in advance."

Flothe wanted to look for any souvenir items in Hansen's house and asked the district attorney's office to issue a new search warrant, but since there was no new evidence they turned him down. So Flothe called an old friend in the Fairbanks district attorney's office, Pat Doogan, who flew south to Anchorage at his own expense and drafted the warrant. Together they went to Judge Victor Carlson, who approved the warrant, ruling that it was justified as a search for evidence of a continuing criminal enterprise.

Flothe worried what his supervisors might think about his circumventing the system to get the search warrant, but Gilmour told him: "It's like being the point man in a jungle patrol. If things go wrong, you're the first one to get shot—and everybody else is mad at you." Flothe knew he had done the right thing; he was convinced that Hansen was the murderer. He shrugged off his concerns and focused on finding evidence.

Troopers searched Hansen's bakery and took him to their office for an interview. In the meantime other officers were conducting a more detailed inspection of Hansen's home. Behind the headboard of his bed they found an aviator's map containing 24 X-marks, some of them at spots where bodies had been found.

When Flothe and his team asked Hansen about the map he said the X-marks indicated places where he had practiced touch-and-go landings. He also kept asking "Why is everybody picking on me."

Flothe decided the map by itself meant little. If Hansen could land at those spots, so could any skilled aviator. Flothe wanted to find Hansen's stash of murder mementoes, which the FBI profilers had convinced him must exist. His enthusiasm spread to other officers who wanted to help. Lieutenant Pat Kasnick volunteered to search the attic of Hansen's house, a difficult and arduous chore due to the attic's high temperature, low ceiling and the sticky fiberglass insulation blown into the space between the rafters. Crawling on his knees and carrying a flashlight, Kasnick, his eyes watering and his body sweating, worked his way through the uncomfortable space for hours, methodically lifting up insulation and running a hand through every possible hiding place.

After searching about 200 square feet of the attic, Kasnick reached under a chunk of fiberglass and felt a hollowed-out cache containing metal, the barrel of a weapon. Lifting the fiberglass he found the cache contained a .22 rifle, a 7 mm single-shot pistol, several newspaper clippings and a bag of jewelry. One piece in the small jewelry sack was a gold arrowhead necklace.

On September 28, 1983 the second body found on the Knik River was identified through dental charts as Paula Goulding, 31, from Kona, Hawaii, a dancer at the Great Alaska Bush Company and an inexperienced prostitute. Her roommate, who reported her missing, said she had gone to meet a man who offered her $200 to meet him for lunch, then disappeared. When Hansen later confessed to the Goulding murder he said he flew her out to a cabin, a low-sided log structure with a canvas top. He made the mistake of referring to the cabin as his *meat shack*, a hunter's term for a place to hang and age big game. Goulding panicked at the words, assuming they referred to her, and began to struggle against her restraints.

He said after they landed and were walking toward the cabin an airplane flew over and began circling the area. Hansen grabbed Goulding by the arm and told her that if the plane landed and she said anything he would shoot both the pilot and her. He took her inside, handcuffed her to an iron post and went back outside. When the aircraft dipped low over the cabin, Hansen waved to the pilot in a way that suggested everything was OK. The plane waggled its wings, turned and left the area.

By that time Paula was totally losing her cool. Hansen released her, trying to calm her down. She ran, he chased her down and shot her, then dug a grave, threw her in it, tossed the empty .223 cartridge in with her and covered her up.

Such details were still unknown to Flothe but he was determined to build his case against Hansen. He told Sumrall and Henning what his team found at Hansen's house and they admitted they had been lying to protect their friend. The investigators interrogated Hansen for several days, showing him the condemnatory evidence they found. Flothe talked to Hansen's wife Darla, Cindy Paulson and others involved with Hansen and his grim life. Then lawyer Jim Gilmore called and said his client wanted to "clear the decks."

When Hansen was reinterviewed he admitted to 17 rapes and murders over a 12-year crime spree. All the killings were of dancers and prostitutes, people he considered beneath him. But Flothe and the investigative team were convinced that there were likely more, perhaps many more, and Hansen was omitting them from his victim list because they were not from society's lower echelon.

———————

HANSEN WAS CHARGED WITH THE 17 MURDERS and admitted to them in court. At his sentencing hearing, which lasted just two and a half hours, Assistant District Attorney Frank Rothschild told Judge Ralph Moody: "Before you sits a monster, an extreme aberration of a human being, a man who walked among us for 17 years serving us doughnuts, Danish, and coffee with a pleasant smile. His family was a prop; he hid behind decency."

"This hunter who kept trophies on the wall, now has trophies scattered throughout Southcentral Alaska. And while he doesn't talk about or admit to it, it's obvious from looking at where things started and where women ended up, he hunted them down. He'd let them run a little bit, then he enjoyed a hunt, just like with his big-game animals. He toyed with them; he got a charge out of it."

Judge Moody sentenced Hansen to 461 years in prison plus life, a legal nicety that means "and throw away the key." He died in 2014 at Spring Creek Prison in Seward, Alaska, with 430 years left unserved in his sentence.

CHAPTER 4

A Scheming Man - 1976

NEIL MACKAY WAS A BITTER and angry man, one who somehow made friends as well as enemies. To many of those who disliked him, one frustrating thing about the man was he seemed to get away with murder.

Mackay was born in Canada but his family moved to California when he was only two. His father died two years later and Neil's mother married a man who proved to be a strict disciplinarian, one who enforced his rules with severe beatings. His mother took him to church and tried to help him avoid his stepfather's wrath by following the family rules. Neil grew up a bitter boy who yearned for a dead father he barely knew. He was certain his dad was a better man than the severe relative who raised him.

When the Japanese attacked Pearl Harbor in 1941, Neil was completing his senior year in high school. He enlisted and became a Marine fighter pilot and instructor. He was seriously injured during service; his military records indicate he was hurt in a plane crash though he told a friend it was a Jeep accident. The crash, whatever its nature, resulted in back and shoulder injuries and left him with a steel plate in his head.

At war's end, Neil married his high school sweetheart Barbara and attended law school near Los Angeles. In 1951 he earned his law degree and moved with Barbara to the Alaska Territory. Neil disliked California

and was convinced he could make his fortune in the Far North. He landed a job as a vice president at the First National Bank of Anchorage. He
worked in mortgage lending and learned the finer points of real estate
speculation. The job put him in position to learn what properties were
in or near foreclosure, and which property owners were in financial difficulty. He used that information to buy land and buildings at bargain
prices, then sold them at a tidy profit.

Neil passed the Alaska bar exam in 1954, quit the bank and opened a
law practice. He used his real estate expertise to manage his fast-growing
holdings. While in high school he had worked as an ambulance driver
and driving for a mortuary. He often said his job was to race to the scene
of accidents, deliver survivors to the hospital and the rest to the under-
taker. That experience led him to open a mortuary on Fourth Avenue,
one of Anchorage's main thoroughfares. In the back of the mortuary he
opened a law office. His rapidly expanding business interests soon made
him a millionaire.

Neil's friends considered him an astute businessman who could be
generous when so inclined, though most said they didn't often see that
side of him. He was a hard-working man so both his law practice and
real estate businesses were successful. Mackay's critics considered him an
amoral and unethical man who worshipped money. One former friend
said he was "obsessed with money." Neil became an alcoholic but traveled
to Seattle for treatment and quit drinking.

———————

IN 1961 THE ALASKA BAR ASSOCIATION tried to suspend his law license for unfair treatment of a real estate client. The ABA board tried
to overturn a committee decision to suspend his license but the Alaska
Supreme Court ruled against Neil. Its decision noted: "We find him
unfit to continue as a member of the profession and as an officer of the
courts of Alaska."

Later that year the court rethought the decision and reduced Neil's
disbarment to a one-year suspension of his law license. And some years
after that the court decided even the lesser penalty was excessive and
cleared his record. Fellow lawyer Edgar Paul Boyko felt Mackay had
been unfairly treated and the court action was politically motivated.
"It's a black stain on Alaska justice," Boyko told a reporter. "I think that
kind of got Mackay started on a spiral down, and he's never been the
same since."

———|———

MACKAY BECAME CLOSE TO THE PFEIL FAMILY, German immigrants who moved to Alaska after the war. Emil worked at the Alaska Railroad and his wife Muriel was a teacher. After retiring from the railroad, Emil became a successful real estate investor and active in local politics.

Neil and Barbara lived in a penthouse atop a 14-story office tower on the edge of downtown Anchorage. Called the Mackay Building, it was then the state's tallest office building. In 1965, after 20 years of marriage, Barbara filed for divorce, though she continued as Neil's bookkeeper and property manager. Neil fought the divorce but it was approved and finalized by the court in 1968. Barbara then married an Iranian-born doctor and Neil married Muriel Pfeil, 33, daughter and namesake of Emil Pfeil's wife, who had financed a three-story annex to Neil's office tower. Mackay was then 45 and his new wife was a hard-driving and successful travel agent.

Neil's marriage to young Muriel was troubled from the start. His wartime injuries kept him in constant pain, making him difficult to live with. He suffered severe headaches and seizures, and took a variety of drugs, both legal and illegal. They stayed married for five years, living apart for half that time, and separated permanently in 1973, a few months after the birth of their son, Neil Pfeil Mackay, who became known as Scotty.

A Supreme Court justice and friend of the Pfeil family presided at the divorce hearing and drafted a settlement. He wrote of their marriage and courtroom behavior: "Each of the antagonists had extremely short temper fuses and almost daily there were demonstrations of temper tantrums manifested in bitter reproaches toward each other during recesses and other breaks, anger at the judge . . . anger at opposing attorney. It seemed as a result of their temperaments that this marriage was doomed from the beginning and the only good thing that came from it was a marvelously likable child."

Things got worse as the divorce trial proceeded. Muriel claimed Neil abused her physically and blew his top when she suggested that Scotty might not be his son. Neil called her a pathological liar and the two got into a fistfight in a hallway of the courthouse. A judge ordered them both to undergo psychiatric examinations. The results were never disclosed. Neil refused to return to the courthouse and barricaded himself into his apartment.

Muriel estimated Neil's net worth at $5 million, including real estate,

and she wanted half. When settlement hearings began, the judge barred
the two combatants from his courtroom, insisting on meeting only with
their lawyers. He awarded Muriel $757,000, roughly $1,000 a day for
each day of their marriage, plus $500 a month for Scotty's support.

Mackay was furious and tried to avoid paying Muriel, but eventually gave in. Even worse to him than the money was Muriel's attempts
to keep Scotty out of his father's life. She argued that Neil was a chronic
drug abuser given to violent outbursts and a potential threat to the child's
safety. The courtroom battles brought memories of Neil's own childhood
flooding back along with the constant agony he endured after the death
of his own father and his mother's remarriage.

The judge had his doubts about Muriel's claims but he was aware of
Neil's history of drug abuse—and the animosity between the two combatants was common knowledge. He limited Neil's visitation rights with
Scotty to part of one weekend each month. Neil tried to get the visits
expanded to a full weekend a month and asked to take Scotty to Hawaii
for one month each year. Muriel argued against both of Neil's requests
and asked the judge to rule that Neil's suitability as a parent be reviewed
and he be denied any visits with the boy.

THE RELATIONSHIP BETWEEN NEIL AND MURIEL came to a dramatic
end on September 30, 1976, when she left her travel agency in downtown Anchorage, a block from the offices of The Anchorage Times, and
walked to a parking lot across the street. Muriel was wearing a new coat
and had been showing it to her employees. She opened the door of her
Volvo station wagon, slipped behind the wheel and was blown apart by
a powerful explosion under its hood, apparently triggered remotely by
someone with an electronic detonator.

A witness said the car's hood was blown 100 feet into the air. The explosion shattered windows in nearby buildings and shook the ground for
blocks around. A mechanic ran to the car and tried to open the door. He
saw the bloody mess inside and backed away in shock. At The Anchorage
Times office down the street, Managing Editor Bill Tobin craned his neck
from a second-floor window as his reporters, editors and a photographer
ran to the scene.

Observers speculated that the blast was triggered when Muriel put
her key in the ignition. Detectives concluded that was unlikely because
Muriel had driven to the spot just 90 minutes earlier after dropping

Scotty at his babysitter's house. Her car was parked in a busy spot and it would have been difficult for an intruder to approach the vehicle, put a bomb under the hood and wire it to the ignition. That meant the bomb had probably been placed in the car earlier, perhaps the previous night, and the explosion was triggered by somebody nearby who watched her climb into the Volvo, someone who then slipped away as people ran toward the wreckage. Muriel's keys were found on the floor of the Volvo, which detectives interpreted as evidence that the keys were not in the ignition when the bomb went off, thus the explosion was indeed triggered remotely.

The investigators combed the wreckage, gathered parts of the vehicle from the parking lot and adjacent street, and checked nearby offices and portions of the Captain Cook Hotel facing the blast scene, asking people what they had seen. Other detectives collected and dug through airline passenger manifests to see who might have left town shortly after the explosion.

Because of the bitter divorce and the couple's violent track record, Neil was the immediate focus of the investigation. He was the primary suspect. Fifteen detectives worked on the case, including officers from the Anchorage Police Department, Alaska State Troopers and the U.S. Bureau of Alcohol, Tobacco, Firearms and Explosives. Pieces of Muriel's Volvo were sent to the FBI's crime laboratory in Washington, DC, but no useful evidence developed. Anchorage Police Chief Charles Anderson said his office was "considering using a polygraph to test certain people who may be involved." Whether Neil ever underwent a lie-detector test is unknown, though it was obvious he was one of the people Chief Anderson was referring to.

———

THE INVESTIGATION WAS INTENSIVE and suspicions focused on Neil, but there was little evidence, nothing pointing to him or anyone else. After months of hard and thorough work, the detectives reluctantly moved the case to the back burner. Despite their best efforts, they had nothing to work with on a solution to Muriel's murder.

The most frustrated of all was Robert Pfeil, Muriel's brother and Alaska Airlines' most senior pilot. Muriel left a million-dollar estate to her son Scotty, and her will appointed her brother as its executor. Muriel's will expressed the wish that Bob adopt Scotty. Shortly after her violent death, Neil petitioned for full custody of the boy. Muriel's brother was determined to keep that from happening and to carry out his sister's wishes. He hired lawyers to fight Neil's petition and placed newspaper and television ads offering $20,000 to anyone who could provide information on Muriel's murder. No information offers came forward.

In December, 1977, with the custody battle still unsettled, Mackay won court approval for a visit with Scotty, then five years old. Neil and Scotty boarded a plane for Hawaii, then hopped on a second plane bound for Micronesia, an unauthorized diversion. Mackay vacationed briefly with Scotty, then returned to Hawaii leaving the boy with friends on the atoll of Likiep in the Marshall Islands. Neil was arrested in Honolulu but refused to say where he'd left his son. Bob hired private detectives who tracked the boy to Likiep and returned him to Alaska.

Mackay was able to convince a judge that he was a loving father and, despite the virtual kidnapping, was awarded custody of Scotty a year later. The judge overlooked the unproved rumors that Neil paid for Muriel's execution. Mackay then moved to Hawaii and lived with the boy in a penthouse suite of a resort hotel on Waikiki. He told his Alaska friends he had been driven to live in tropical seclusion by unfair and unrelenting suspicions about his ex-wife's death.

Bob Pfeil was indeed unrelenting. He was convinced that Neil had arranged for the bomb to be placed in Muriel's car and detonated when she climbed in. He was determined to prove it. Neil's fury grew worse when he learned that Muriel's brother was using money from her estate—money that should have gone to Scotty—in his search for the boy. Those expenses included $53,000 for the detectives who found Scotty in Likiep and $90,000 in legal costs. Mackay felt Bob was stealing from Scotty.

Neil hid his anger from Scotty though their Waikiki apartment was littered with books and papers related to the custody battle and his legal wrangling with the boy's uncle. Paperwork covered virtually every available space, including Scotty's bed, leaving the boy to sleep wherever he could. Mackay was an embittered recluse. Concerned neighbors often brought food to make sure the boy ate properly.

———

THE DISPUTE TOOK A NEW TURN on October 12, 1985, when Bob Pfeil was returning home after an Alaska Airlines flight to Kotzebue and Nome. He taxied the jetliner to the Anchorage terminal and shut down the engines as his passengers left the airplane. Pfeil closed out his log and headed to the employee parking lot for his silver Mazda. From there he headed for his home on Campbell Lake. As he neared home, Pfeil slowed for an intersection as a tired-looking Lincoln Continental pulled alongside. A young man leaned out of the Lincoln's window with a .45 caliber pistol in his hand. The young gunman fired five times; two bullets lodged in the vehicle and three tore into Bob's body. One caused a flesh wound, another struck his lung and a third lodged in his spine. Two spent casings fell to the pavement.

A neighbor heard the shots, saw Bob slumped in his vehicle and called police. An ambulance carried him to Providence Hospital where doctors tried to ease his pain. He told police he was sure his brother-in-law was behind the shooting. "The son-of-a-bitch finally got me," he said. Bob gave the officers a rough description of the shooter and the old Lincoln he rode in.

The detectives posted a heavy guard around Bob's room and renewed their determination to bring Neil Mackay to justice. Pfeil's friends were angry and offered a $50,000 reward for information leading to the arrest of Bob's assailants. Since Mackay was a suspect and the attack seemed to involve people in two states, the FBI joined in the Alaska police effort. Bob's wounds were life-threatening so he was flown to a medical facility in Minnesota. His wife Marianne told reporters the outlook was grim. "We can always hope for miracles," she said, "but I don't know. He's in good spirits, though. He is a fighter."

———————

THE ANCHORAGE POLICE HOMICIDE RESPONSE TEAM began checking with their sources in the city's underworld. Several of Pfeil's neighbors told investigators they had seen a mustard-colored Lincoln shortly before the shooting. The vehicle contained two men and parked backward on the street, apparently to watch for approaching traffic.

The team issued a description of the vehicle, saying it was a 1960s Lincoln sedan with triple tail-lights and rust spots on its right side. Within days the team's leader, Detective Sergeant Mike Grimes, learned that an 18-year-old punk named Tyoga Closson bragged to his friends that he knew something about the shooting of the Alaska Airlines pilot. Closson reportedly admitted to one friend that he had done the shooting himself. Grimes interviewed the boy, who at first claimed to know nothing about the crime. He eventually said he was asked to drive for the shooter, whose name was John Bright. Closson said Bright asked him if he was interested in making money for doing something illegal.

"How illegal?" Closson had asked.

"Well, I need a driver cause I need to shoot somebody."

Closson said he told Bright to "get fucked."

Closson told Grimes that another of his friends, 19-year-old Bob Betts, had taken the job as Bright's wheelman. Closson said Betts asked him about a nickel-plated .45 Colt automatic stolen from a lawyer's home where his girlfriend was house-sitting. Later, Closson changed his story and said his girlfriend had stolen the pistol and given it to him in trade for a gram of cocaine. Closson said Betts wanted the gun for what he had in mind because it was more powerful than most pistols available on the street.

Several days before the shooting Betts said he wanted to use the .45 and offered Closson $75 to rent it for a day. He assumed Betts wanted it for a robbery and would need it for just that day. Then Betts asked to keep it for another day. When Closson asked why, Betts said nothing had happened; he said he had thrown a rock through someone's window but nobody came out and he'd need to try again.

Closson told Grimes that Betts later returned the pistol and suggested he get rid of it. He said he traded it to a drug dealer for a small amount of cocaine. The detective told Closson he was in big trouble and was facing a long jail term because he knew about the shooting ahead of time and participated in it by supplying the gun. Closson was terrified and agreed to talk to Betts while wearing a hidden microphone and transmitter. Police and prosecutors agreed that if he cooperated Closson would be charged only with theft of the pistol, which would involve a relatively short jail term. Afterward he would be placed in the witness protection program.

Detective Grimes and his team worked with Closson on the approach he should take with Betts and the questions they wanted him to ask. Closson met with Betts and immediately launched into an argument, saying Betts had used his pistol to shoot the pilot. Betts grew angry and claimed Closson was playing games with him. "You knew exactly what I was going to do with the gun," he said. As the conversation continued, Betts grew more cautious in his remarks. The listening detectives concluded Betts drove the Lincoln for the shooting. When the conversation ended, Closson told Betts that he had been caught and was offered a deal by police. He said if Betts also cooperated they might offer him a deal as well.

LATER POLICE WENT TO BETTS' HOME and convinced him to work with them. Betts told them he, his friend John Bright, 21, and Larry Gentry, 33, were hired for the hit by Gilbert "Junior" Paoule, 38, manager and part-owner of The Wild Cherry, a topless-bottomless club in Anchorage. Betts and Gentry were former Wild Cherry employees. Gentry was a part-time drug dealer and sometimes filled in for Paoule. Bright was a former club bouncer whom Paoule had fired for using a baseball bat on a pimp.

Betts told Grimes that Bright was the shooter. He said Gentry helped plan the shooting and supplied the car plus a .12 gauge pistol-grip shotgun as a backup weapon. He offered to testify against the others and agreed to wear a wire while talking to them about the crime. Betts and Gentry had never met so Betts went to Gentry's home and demanded $700 he said was owed him for driving the old Lincoln used in Bob Pfeil's shooting. Gentry was surprised and confused by the claim and told Betts to go away and not bother him again or he would regret it.

"I'll see what I can do for you," Gentry fumed at Betts. "You know what I feel like doing right now? Next time you remember your fucking manners."

The principal owner of The Wild Cherry was Frank Colacurcio, a Seattle mobster whom Junior Pauole had met while both were serving time at McNeil Island, a federal penitentiary on an island near Tacoma. Pauole was serving a 10-year sentence for possession of heroin. Colacurcio was in prison for racketeering and interstate transportation of gambling equipment. Pauole was sent to McNeil from his birthplace in Honolulu, where he had been engaged in drug possession, armed robbery and burglary.

Pauole and Colacurcio became friends. After Junior's release, Colacurcio hired him as a bartender and doorman at one of his Seattle nightclubs. When Colacurcio learned of trouble at one of his clubs in Waikiki, the Crazy Horse Lounge, he sent Pauole to investigate. The club manager told Colacurcio that Hawaii mobsters had beaten him up and demanded a 30 percent share of club proceeds. When Pauole talked to his friends in the Hawaii underworld he was told that the manager was lying in hopes he could claim he solved a problem himself and win a promotion from Colacurcio.

Pauole's success in Honolulu convinced Colacurcio that he should send his new friend to Anchorage to deal with The Brothers motorcycle gang which was trying to take over the topless dancer circuit. Pauole hired the gang's leader as a doorman and, since Colacurcio was primarily interested in skimming profits from liquor receipts at the clubs, he worked out a deal for The Brothers to manage and recruit the dancers. The Brothers took a proprietary interest in Colacurcio's clubs and went to work discouraging any competition. They found they could make more money in enforcement and driving away competitors, including burning down one competing nightclub, Moby Dick's.

Colacurcio was encouraged by Pauole's creative approach and made him manager of all his topless clubs in Anchorage. Among other things, Pauole skimmed up to $60,000 a month from club receipts, burned the cash register tapes and delivered the unreported cash to Colacurcio.

One of the clubs was a few blocks from the Mackay building. Neil Mackay owned the building housing the club and became a frequent visitor when he was in Anchorage. Mackay was impressed by Pauole's connections with the Seattle mobster. Though Mackay no longer drank, Pauole helped him with the club's other offerings and introduced him to the most attractive dancers. If Mackay was in the mood to talk, the dancers would talk to him all night. If he wanted sex, Pauole would deliver the women to Mackay's penthouse and pick up their tab. That discretion, which distanced Neil from the club's seedy activities, also impressed Mackay.

———

MACKAY WAS THEN TRYING TO DETERMINE if Pauole could help with his troublesome brother-in-law, Bob Pfeil, and mentioned that his ex-wife had been giving him grief and that he had taken care of that problem. Mackay told Pauole that an old military buddy planted a bomb in Muriel's car and detonated it from a half-block away. Mackay said because of the bombing his ex-brother-in-law was giving him problems and he was sure the man was stealing from his son Scotty's estate.

Mackay and Pauole talked intermittently for two years about ways to end the Bob Pfeil problem. Then Pauole ran into difficulty when the Alaska Beverage Control board learned of mobster Colacurcio's connection to the Anchorage topless clubs and revoked their liquor licenses. Pauole closed the clubs but reopened the Wild Cherry as a topless/bottomless club that didn't serve liquor. He wanted to get back into the liquor trade and hoped Neil might be able to get him restarted in Hawaii. In early July, 1985, Pauole flew to Hawaii, met with Neil and they struck a deal. Later Mackay handed Pauole an envelope containing $10,000 in $100 bills. The money was to be used to hire a Hawaiian hit squad to kill Bob Pfeil.

But Pauole had exaggerated his Hawaiian underworld connections and was unable to deliver an assassination team. And since Colacurcio had severed his connections with Alaska, Pauole no longer had any clout with the underworld there. So Pauole hired Larry Gentry, an old night-club employee who knew a few people that might be up to the job. One of Gentry's connections was John Bright, a man the detectives learned wanted jobs as a hit man. Pauole knew Bright but didn't want to deal with him directly so he asked Gentry to be a go-between. Pauole thought Gentry was the more intelligent of the two; he was trustworthy and therefore the one he wanted to deal with. Pauole asked Gentry what he thought Bright might be capable of.

"He told me he was capable of anything," Pauole told the detectives. "and one day I just asked Larry if John Bright would do this. He says, 'Yes, he'll do it. He would shoot somebody.'" Pauole gave Gentry $7,500 to be shared with Bright, with $1,000 to go to the driver.

Bright went to the library and found a photograph of Bob Pfeil. He checked the pilot's flight schedules, followed him home and studied Pfeil's house. He considered shooting him with a rifle from across the street, but Pfeil's flight schedules changed frequently, his movements were unpredictable and staking out his house would be problematic. By early October, Pauole was becoming impatient. Pfeil was still alive and John Bright was sleeping all day instead of tracking Pfeil's movements. Pauole worried that Bright might be keeping the money without doing the job. Gentry said he'd get after Bright and make sure it happened.

Several days later Bright and Betts borrowed Closson's .45 and Gentry's rusty Lincoln, then waited near Pfeil's home. When the pilot drove past they pulled up beside him, Bright leaned out a window and opened fire. Afterward, Gentry called Pauole to tell him the job was done. Pauole called Mackay and told him that Pfeil had been "taken care of."

Mackay answered: "Good, I was just getting ready to fight him in court."

———

THE FOLLOWING DAY'S NEWS REPORTS indicated Pfeil was still alive and being treated under guard at Providence Hospital. Bright told Pauole that if he could have another $300 he'd buy plastic explosives and finish the job. Pauole said no. "I don't want to have nothing to do with that now." He said he told Bright, "You're crazy."

Pauole asked Bright if Bob Pfeil had seen his face at the shooting.

Bright said he thought Pfeil saw him so Pauole decided to get the gunman out of town. He bought a plane ticket to Florida and gave the ticket and $5,000 in cash to Gentry for Bright. Deciding not to waste an opportunity, Pauole used his own name on Bright's ticket so he could get the frequent-flier miles.

Sergeant Grimes' team was then hard at work gathering information and used witness statements to develop a description of the Lincoln Continental. Pauole decided to get rid of the car; he and Gentry took it to a junkyard and gave the operator $100 to crush it and dispose of the resulting scrap. They didn't want to rouse the man's suspicions by asking him to hurry and he didn't get around to it before police came by a few days later.

Eight days after the shooting, Pauole called Mackay and told him that Pfeil was still alive. "He's a very tough man," Pauole said. "He's hit five times."

———

Tyoga Closson's bragging about being involved in the shooting caused the plot to unravel. When he implicated his friends, police began to put the scheme together and developed detailed reports. Gentry soon realized that Betts had been wearing a wire during their conversations; he admitted his part in the plot and identified Bright as the shooter. He said Pauole hired the team at the request of Neil Mackay.

Gentry agreed to wear a wire in his conversations with Bright and Pauole. The nature of the discussions convinced the listening detectives that Bright had been the triggerman and Pauole the paymaster. Shortly afterward, Betts talked to Pauole, who answered cautiously but managed to implicate himself.

Betts and Pauole were arrested on November 8 and ordered held on bail of $5 million apiece, cash only. Both demanded to see lawyers. When Pauole's lawyer arrived, police showed him the evidence and played portions of the audiotapes. The lawyer advised Pauole that his best bet was to work with police in developing evidence against Mackay. He said that would involve the lightest sentence. Pauole agreed and was offered a 20-year sentence if he would draw Mackay out and testify against him when the case went to court.

Police were worried that Mackay might hear about the arrests, so they moved quickly. At 3 a.m. the next morning Detective Grimes asked a judge for permission to record conversations between Pauole and

Mackay. The judge approved and the authorization was signed within the hour. Pauole called Mackay at 4:30 a.m. with detectives listening quietly as Neil answered.

Mackay didn't want to talk, afraid his phone might be tapped. He gave Pauole the number for a phone in the lobby, took the elevator down and the two began a series of phone calls.

Mackay was nervous and cautious, but his nervousness caused him to make serious mistakes. Pauole told Mackay that police were after him and he was hiding in Anchorage. "I'm scared," he said, "because, you know, I never do that crime. All I did was get the money from you and give it to this guy . . . I don't want to go down, Mackay. If I go down, you going to go down with me because that $10,000, you know, I never got nothing out of this whole thing. I'm a three-time loser. I'm going to go to jail for life."

Mackay was evasive and tried to avoid talking. Pauole said, "I need some help. Please help me. Don't dummy up on me."

Mackay replied: "Well, see, here's the situation. I don't know nothing about nothing. They're trying to lay something on you, trying to tie you in with me . . . you know it's not right, but OK, I'll see what I . . . I'll do everything I can. Don't say too much, you know. You're going to implicate yourself."

Near the end of the third call Mackay asked questions related to items the two men discussed immediately after the shooting. "You mentioned something about a metal thing. Is it ground up?"

"What?" Pauole responded. "The car? You mean the car?"

"Yeah," Mackay replied.

Then, to the amazement of the listening detectives, Mackay asked: "What about the G-U-N?"

"I don't know nothing about that," Pauole answered "Those two guys got that, that uh, the G-U-N."

Later that day two Honolulu police detectives went to Mackay's penthouse and took him into custody. A judge ordered Neil held on bail of $25 million, cash only.

On November 11, two days after Mackay was arrested in Hawaii, Robert Pfeil died while undergoing surgery at the Mayo Clinic. While his doctors were removing bullets from the pilot's spine and lungs, a blood clot lodged in his heart and ended his life. The case against Neil Mackay, John Bright, Larry Gentry and Robert Betts was elevated and all were charged with first-degree murder. Gilbert Pauole, under his plea agreement, was charged with attempted murder.

On February 11, 1986, the four defendants accused of first-degree murder, plus Tyoga Closson (who like Pauole had a plea agreement based on his cooperation) were in court for an evidentiary hearing. Because the ages of all but Mackay ranged from late teens to early 30s, many of the spectator seats were filled with their grandmothers, mothers, wives and sisters. All were angry because the young defendants had told their families they expected to receive immunity from prosecution in return for their assistance to investigators. Closson and Pauole, however, had formal agreements for reduced charges and shorter sentences.

The judge decided that the five defendants would be tried separately and, as a safety precaution, the Mackay and Bright trials would be held in Fairbanks. Larry Gentry was the first to be tried and faced a jury in March, 1986. In his opening remarks, Gentry's lawyer warned the jury that the prosecution "is going to take us on a glass-bottom boat ride through the sewers of Anchorage." His caution proved justified and the jury heard tales of drug-dealing, prostitution, pimping and beatings, as well as the planning and execution of a murder. Junior Pauole testified that Gentry was involved in the conspiracy to kill Bob Pfeil from the beginning and was an active and willing participant.

Gentry's lawyer tried to discredit Pauole and argued that his testimony could not be trusted because he was simply trying to steer suspicion away from himself. He said Pauole was a known liar and admitted to perjuring himself while testifying before both Alaska's Alcohol Beverage Control Board and a federal grand jury in Seattle, as well as a second grand jury in Portland, Oregon. Pauole had also admitted to involvement in a murder-for-hire, to lying to his girlfriend, cheating on his frequent-flier mileage account, lying to the Internal Revenue Service, and lying to investigators in the killing of Robert Pfeil. Pauole had also told detectives that if the Bob Pfeil murder had worked out he might have taken on a few more contract killings.

But Gentry's accomplices and the evidence against him convinced jurors that he was one of the planners in the Bob Pfeil murder and supplied both the car and the backup gun. Gentry, then age 33, was found guilty of first-degree murder and sentenced to 40 years in prison, with 15 years suspended. He would become eligible for parole 15 years from his conviction.

Two weeks after Gentry's conviction, Tyoga Closson was sentenced to 18 months in prison for stealing the .45 caliber pistol used to shoot Pfeil. Judge Mary E. Greene told Closson he should "thank his lucky stars" that he hadn't been charged with murder and that his cooperation with police had won him a short sentence.

The wheelman in the Robert Pfeil murder, young Robert Betts, was tried in August, 1986. His lawyer said Betts thought he had an immunity deal because Closson told him he could probably get one if he cooperated and, on the basis of that statement, Betts had told the officers what he knew. When she sentenced him, Judge Greene said he could have gone away for 99 years but she was reducing it to 50 years because Betts had assisted the investigators. He could become eligible for parole after the first 20 years and was released . . . .

The triggerman, John Bright, was convicted of murder on October 17, a year and five days after Robert Pfeil was ambushed outside his home. Judge Greene gave Bright a sentence of 99 years in prison, with parole eligibility after serving 40 years.

———

JURY SELECTION FOR MACKAY'S TRIAL in Fairbanks began in January. Mackay was a multi-millionaire and could afford the best legal talent. In addition to Anchorage lawyer Bill Bryson, Mackay hired Milwaukee lawyer James Shellow, known nationally for defending American Indian activists involved in the deadly shooting siege in Wounded Knee, South Dakota, in 1973. The Mackay/Shellow team's advantage in the Pfeil murder trial was that though there was an abundance of evidence against the other defendants, Mackay's ties to the case were relatively tenuous. There was plenty to raise suspicion but the information came from other defendants whose motives made them untrustworthy.

All of the other defendants were intimately involved in the plot. But Mackay's only direct connection to the case was through Junior Pauole, the only one to talk to Neil about the murder either in person or by telephone. Police had heard Mackay make suspicious comments to Pauole about disposal of a vehicle and the G-U-N, but there was no direct evidence.

As the trial began, Judge Greene ruled that Pauole would not be allowed to testify about his conversation with Mackay in which, Pauole said, Neil told him about having his wife blown up. She ruled out recorded conversations between Mackay and Pauole the night Pauole was arrested. She also ruled out documents on the legal battle between the pilot and Mackay, documents supporting the argument that Neil might have a motive to kill his ex-brother-in-law. Judge Greene decided the documents could be prejudicial without proving anything. The jury did get to hear the taped conversation between Pauole and Mackay in which Neil had asked whether "the metal thing" had been destroyed and what happened to "the G-U-N."

Mackay's lawyer argued that Neil was simply playing along with what he considered an extortion attempt by Pauole, an attempt to force Neil to pay money or face being accused of murdering Pfeil. Lawyer Shellow portrayed Pauole as a desperate man who had fallen out of favor with a mob boss who wanted cash to buy a nightclub in Hawaii and start a new life. He said Pauole knew Mackay would be a suspect because of his long battle with Pfeil. He argued Mackay would not have wanted to get involved in such an act because the only thing he wanted was to continue his life with Scotty and the boy was already living with him. Getting involved in such a plot would just jeopardize that life.

Shellow called Scotty, then 14, as a witness. Until the boy saw his father that day and got a quick embrace, he had not seen Neil since the day he was arrested 17 months earlier. The courtroom embrace was an emotional moment for spectators.

Mackay's trial was abruptly ended after three months when a two-inch stack of documents, exhibits and other evidence was found in the jury room, some of it never authorized for review by the jury. Judge Greene declared a mistrial. The presence of the unauthorized records in the jury room was never explained to the public. At least seven jurors said they had read the materials and talked about them with each other. A newspaper reporter interviewed several jurors and was told the materials were unconvincing in the case against Mackay and that they would have voted to acquit him.

Mackay was freed, retried in November and found not guilty. The jury foreman told the reporter that none of the jurors, including two who argued that Mackay should be found guilty, believed Junior Pauole.

After Mackay's trial, Pauole's sentence was reduced from 20 years to 18 as a reward for his cooperation in the various proceedings in Alaska and for assisting federal investigators looking into mob activities in Seattle and Arizona. He would be eligible for parole in nine years, when he would be age 50.

———

IN APRIL THE MULTI-MILLIONAIRE Neil Mackay asked to be repaid the $501 he spent for his return flight to Honolulu after the second trial. An assistant attorney general reluctantly agreed, but only after Alaska

Governor Steve Cowper endorsed Mackay's request.

Scotty stayed in Anchorage to finish high school and attend college, then went into banking. Mackay became a recluse in his penthouse atop Honolulu's Ilikai Hotel and was found dead there on September 24, 1994. A coroner said his death had gone unnoticed for four days.

CHAPTER 5

New Ways to Track A Killer - 1979

THOMAS RICHARD BUNDAY became a serial killer at a time in the late 1970s when the concept was virtually unknown. He started murdering women near Fairbanks when investigators there were just starting to solve crimes with computers.

To work the groundbreaking case, Alaska law enforcement had to come up with creative solutions to unfamiliar problems. In the end, even when Bunday was caught, it took an elaborate scam to make him confess.

Bunday's first victim was Glinda Sodemann, age 19, newly married and the daughter of an Alaska State Trooper. She disappeared near her home on August 29, 1979, and was reported missing by her husband, Jerry. The initial investigation turned up no useful information, nothing that would suggest anything unusual was going on in her life other than adjusting to her new role as Jerry Sodemann's wife.

Glinda's decomposed body was found several months later in a gravel pit off the Richardson Highway near Eielson Air Force Base, 22 miles south of Fairbanks. She had been shot in the face, apparently with a .38 caliber pistol. The decomposed nature of Glinda's body made it impossible to determine if she had been raped. Husband Jerry was questioned and quickly cleared, leaving the Fairbanks community wondering what in the world happened to her.

Ten months later, on June 11, 1980, 11-year-old Doris Oehring was riding her bicycle on Badger Road in North Pole, a suburb of Fairbanks.

Doris' older brother Thomas saw her sitting on the bike and talking to a man in a light-colored pickup truck. The man wore blue clothing that looked a lot like an Air Force uniform. Two days later Doris disappeared. Her bicycle was found hidden in bushes beside Badger Road, a spot where a driver told police he saw a small bluish car come racing out of a roadside turnout around the time she disappeared.

Doris' brother talked with a police sketch artist who developed a composite likeness of the man he saw talking to his sister. The sketch was widely distributed to police agencies and the news media. Investigators were thinking she might have been kidnapped or murdered, though at that time there was no evidence suggesting either possibility. State Troopers asked for the public's help in the investigations. The request brought a raft of ideas but nothing concrete, nothing that would point to a suspect.

The troopers asked Eielson authorities for a list of automobiles permitted to drive on the base and roughly matching the description of the vehicles spotted by Doris' brother and the other witness. The Air Force came back with a list of 550 civilian cars and light trucks and their license plate numbers. One of the vehicles was registered to Thomas Bunday, a resident of Moose Creek who went by his middle name, Richard. His home was just a few miles from the spot where Glinda Sodemann's body was found, though at the time there was no reason to connect him to the murder or even to raise suspicions.

————

THEN ON JANUARY 31, 1981, the family of 20-year-old Marlene Peters reported her missing. She was last seen trying to hitchhike from Fairbanks to Anchorage where her father was undergoing cancer treatment. A state trooper investigator looked into the case and could find no evidence of foul play. Whatever happened to her could have happened anywhere along the 350-mile route.

Just five weeks later, 16-year-old Wendy Wilson disappeared. She was last seen hitchhiking and getting into a light-colored pickup truck near Moose Creek between North Pole and Eielson on the Richardson Highway. At that point, investigators began to suspect that the disappearances of young women might all be linked and that they could have a serial killer on their hands. Three days later, Wendy's body was found on Johnson Road, near the trans-Alaska oil pipeline and 32 miles south of Fairbanks. She had been strangled and her face obliterated by a shotgun blast.

Nine weeks after Wendy Wilson's body turned up, the remains of Marlene Peters were found two miles away on Johnson Road. She had also been strangled and her face destroyed by a shotgun blast. Then, just two days later, Fairbanks Police were notified that 19-year-old Lori King was missing. She too was last seen walking in Fairbanks and may have been hitchhiking.

Initially, each of the cases was being investigated by different officers whose experience levels and approaches varied widely. Technical Sergeant Sam Barnard of Alaska State Troopers handled the investigation of the Wendy Wilson killing. Barnard went to the spot where Wendy's body was found and took photos of the scene. He then put her body in a bag, loaded it into the trunk of his car and drove to the Boondocks Bar near Eielson Air Force Base. There he asked the bar clientele to come outside and see if they recognized her. The results of the bizarre effort are unknown.

By that time the news media were referring to the various cases as the Fairbanks Serial Murders, a type of crime beginning to get attention in the national media. Police, the military and volunteers mounted a massive search of the Johnson Road area, looking for bodies of the still-missing women, Lori King and Doris Oehring. The investigators again asked for information from the public, any clues or suspicious activities they spotted, any strangers they noticed showing up in their neighborhoods. They also asked the public to write down and save the license plate number of any vehicle seen picking up hitchhikers.

ON SEPTEMBER 2, 1981, FOUR RABBIT HUNTERS found the body of Lori King in a wooded area near an old Nike missile site off Johnson Road. Lori had been strangled and her face ruined by a shotgun blast. Since the body was found on federal property, both the FBI and the Eielson Office of Special Investigations entered the case to support the efforts of Alaska State Troopers. The team of skilled investigators, then working on the various cases, became known as the Areawide Homicide Task Force. The task force was staffed with representatives of those agencies as well as the Army's Criminal Investigation Division from Fort Wainwright, the Fairbanks Police Department and the North Pole City Police Department.

The national news media were then focusing on a series of murders of young black men in Atlanta, Georgia. The Alaska State Troopers sent Sergeant Barnard to Atlanta to see what he could learn from state and federal investigators who were trying to solve what became known as the Atlanta Child Murders. The Atlanta task force was looking into a flood of leads and tips, and they were using new computer techniques to sort and make sense of the mass of information arriving daily. The computers were giving valuable direction on which leads were worth following and which were probably useless or pointed in unhelpful directions.

Barnard then flew to the Behavioral Sciences Unit at the FBI Academy in Quantico, Virginia. There he spent two days with its behavioral experts, laying out all the evidence the Alaska task force had accumulated on the Fairbanks cases. The FBI men developed a profile of the likely murderer. They decided the killer was most likely single, lived alone, had a hard time holding a job and was a civilian. Barnard took the FBI profile back to Alaska and distributed it to other members of his task force.

Though they were then looking at the possibility that the murders were committed by a member of the military, the FBI-developed profile suggested that was unlikely, that the killer was almost the opposite of anyone in the military. The FBI profilers were considered accurate in their conclusions 85 percent of the time, so the Alaska investigators excluded military personnel from their possible suspects—for the time being.

The investigators assumed there was a sex angle to the Alaska cases. Most of the victims had been strangled and shot in the face—but there was no sign of rape. They contacted a psychologist who suggested that the murderer might have shot his victims in the face to erase their identities, perhaps to obliterate the memory of someone else, a person whose face came to mind when he was pulling the trigger. The shootings had been unnecessary since the victims were already dead from strangulation.

Police requests brought in 7,000 comments, suggestions and bits of information, some of which seemed almost certainly relevant to the investigation. Many were from Fairbanks area residents who thought they knew someone weird, someone who might be involved in bizarre activities. Some were their neighbors. Those added 1,000 names to the 550 already included in the OSI list of drivers authorized to drive on base.

One major problem was that the overwhelming bulk of the information needed to be evaluated, sorted and separated to determine which pieces pointed in a useful direction and which could be ignored or set aside for later consideration. Those were the days of mainframe and mini-computers so data entry sometimes required a massive effort. The success of the Atlanta Task Force in using computers to sort the large volume of tips, clues and hard data in the search for their child murderer suggested the Alaskans should try something similar. The Alaska Task Force acquired a data-sorting program and made arrangements to operate it from Fairbanks on a mainframe computer located at the State Data Center in Anchorage.

———

TROOPER SERGEANT CHRIS STOCKARD was a self-described techno-geek and had training in computer technology. He was then working in the troopers' Judicial Services unit and was returned to the investigative unit because his interests and special training made him a good match for Trooper Sergeant Jim McCann, a hard-working and dedicated investigator who was already compiling an impressive record of confessions from criminal suspects. McCann's specialties were crime-scene investigation and suspect interrogation. Though the task force was heavy with skilled investigators, McCann and Stockard were selected as a two-man team with unmatched abilities and techniques that often brought results.

Using computers to focus on a single investigation was then on the leading edge of police work. At that time the mainframes and minicomputers were used almost entirely for department-level record-keeping. Using them to analyze and solve cases was breaking new ground.

To provide Stockard with a searchable database, the massive amounts of information volunteered by the public and developed by the task force needed to be entered into state computers. Traditionally the investigators would have worked with white boards and file cards, but developing technology suggested the information needed to be assembled into a computer database. The old manual sorting was not up to the task.

Skilled clerks were brought in to take as much of the load as possible but inevitably the job required having Stockard, McCann and others spend grueling hours at keyboards. The full data-entry project took three months, operating around the clock, and exhausted all who worked on it. Stockard cross-referenced items in the new database and sorted them into useful pieces that could be evaluated for value and relevance to the case. The really important leads floated to the top and were turned over to the task force members. In the end their effort showed results.

Stockard found that developing computer technology enabled entirely new approaches to information management, especially valuable text search capability. That made it possible for officers to call up historic material that had been previously entered into the database and to draw on reports filed months before when their relevance was not yet appreciated.

And McCann concluded that while the FBI profile of the Fairbanks Area murderer didn't point directly to a suspect, it did include valuable information such as the likelihood that the first murder was probably committed within a mile of the killer's home, that he might have brought the victim to his home and, most importantly, each victim would be found progressively farther away from the killer's home. McCann charted each of the killings on a map and rapidly narrowed down the area in which the killer's house was likely to be found.

Since the concept was just becoming understood and little information was then available for research on serial murders, Stockard mined one of the few sources published on the subject, a book by author Ann Rule on the string of murders by Ted Bundy in 1974-78 and entitled "The Stranger Beside Me." Bundy killed more than 30 young women and girls in seven states. Stockard wanted to know how a person could kill one person after another and still live among others without being suspected, as Ted Bundy obviously had.

———————

ONE OF THE POSSIBLE SUSPECTS WHO FLOATED to the surface quite early was Technical Sergeant Thomas Richard Bunday, a 33-year-old airman working at Eielson Air Force Base. In February, 1982, Special Agent Mike Kohn of Eielson's Office of Special Investigations notified the Task Force that he had flagged Sergeant Bunday as one of three people working on the military base who behaved strangely toward women. Kohn said Bunday had shown what one investigator described as "inappropriate behavior around female co-workers and had generally showed disrespect for members of the female sex." One of Bunday's co-workers reported that he was verbally abusive and she was afraid of him. But Bunday didn't fit the FBI profile. He was certainly weird enough, but he was married, had two children and was a career member of the Air Force. Bunday was kept on the suspect list but the task force turned its attention to others who fit the suspect profile more closely. Those were men who behaved bizarrely but were single civilians who seemed more likely to commit such awful crimes. Those prospects appeared far more promising than Richard Bunday.

Since the last known murder had been committed on May 16, 1981, by November of 1982 the task force concluded the lack of new victims suggested the killer was then either dead, in prison somewhere or had moved away. Those who moved away, they figured, would include members of the military reassigned to posts outside Alaska. The investigative team began an intensive review of each of the four known murders, plus the disappearance and presumed murder of Doris Oehring, whose body had still not been found.

The team included in the list of possible murders by the Fairbanks serial killer a sixth case in which a 22-year-old woman was found dead. Her body turned up on September 16, 1980, off the Parks Highway near Hurricane Gulch. The victim's name was Cassandra Goodwin. The details of the murder were somewhat different than the others but the investigators decided it should be considered some of the Fairbanks serial killer's work. They asked the Air Force for a list of all Eielson military personnel who were transferred elsewhere after Lori King was strangled and shot in the face in 1981. They also asked 50 police agencies and the Air Force Office of Special Investigations to report any murders similar to those in Alaska that took place near military reservations anywhere in the world.

The Alaska task force's request for information turned up the fact that Air Force Technical Sergeant Bunday had been reassigned to Sheppard Air Force Base near Wichita Falls, Texas, during that timeframe. And not long after his arrival there a young woman's body was found in much the same condition and circumstances as the Fairbanks Area victims. Trooper Sergeant McCann wanted to fly to Texas to interview Bunday but his supervisor decided to send Sergeant Barnard because of his previous work with the FBI.

Barnard flew to Wichita Falls, met with Bunday and interviewed him at length. Bunday seemed cooperative and initially answered Barnard's questions. He agreed to take a lie detector test but then backed out saying he didn't trust the Air Force polygraph operators. He also refused to provide samples of his hair or allow a search of his home. Barnard felt Bunday's refusals were not necessarily indicative of guilt since both Bunday and his wife were confrontational people and obstinance was in their nature.

While Barnard was in Texas, the Alaska Task Force asked Doris Oehring's older brother Thomas, the young man who had seen his sister talking to the man in the truck, to look at a photo lineup that included a picture of Richard Bunday.

"That's him," he said.

There was no doubt in the boy's mind that the man in the photo was the guy he had seen talking to his sister two days before her disappearance.

————|————

BUNDAY HAD A DIFFICULT CHILDHOOD growing up in Tennessee. His father often beat him and gave him one last whipping the day before his death. Richard skipped his father's funeral and went to a band concert in Nashville instead. Bunday and Marcia met when both were in high school and got married after graduation. He then joined the Air Force and served for 16 years, including a hitch in Asia, following which he was assigned to Eielson Air Force. While he was in Southeast Asia, Bunday had an affair. When Marcia found out about Richard's dalliances she had an affair of her own and became pregnant by her lover. One of the Bundays' two children, a boy, was the product of Mrs. Bunday's illicit encounters.

In their investigation the team members learned that Bunday's son's bedroom was spartan and looked almost like military quarters. His other child, a daughter, had a room that was colorful, decidedly messy and definitely a child's bedroom. While the Bundays were living near Fairbanks, Marcia experimented with various religions, trying each for a few months before switching to another. The investigators also learned that Richard had two vehicles registered in his name, one a white pickup truck, the other a small bluish-green sedan.

One high school friend said Bunday enjoyed practical jokes and had a mean streak. He often sneaked up on people and pinched them on the chest, hard enough to leave black and blue marks. While living in North Pole he got into a months-long feud with a neighboring farmer. Bunday claimed the farmer had hurt one of his pets so he lit a fireworks cherry bomb, dropped it into a small jar and threw it at the farmer's pigs, spraying them with glass shrapnel.

While the Fairbanks area murders were still ongoing, Bunday went to a military psychologist to discuss his marital difficulties. The psychiatrist was Clarence Williams, chief of the Eielson mental health clinic. Later, Williams himself went to prison. He had hired a hit man to shoot his wife in the face, hoping she would be considered one of the Fairbanks serial killer's victims. He didn't know that the serial killer was his patient, the technical sergeant with the marital problems, but the idea somehow made sense to him.

———

WHEN SERGEANT SAM BARNARD RETURNED from his Texas interview, he said he was convinced Bunday was not their guy and—especially since the FBI profile suggested Bunday was the opposite of their suspect—suggested they concentrate on others who fit the profile more closely.

Trooper Lieutenant Bob Jent asked McCann what he thought about the case and McCann told him he was confident that Bunday would prove to be the murderer. Jent showed a printout of Barnard's interview with Bunday to McCann, asking what he thought. McCann reviewed the interview transcript and told Jent he didn't think Bunday's responses in any way eliminated him as a suspect, that the FBI's profiles were considered right 85 percent of the time, but that left a 15 percent failure rate. "I thought you would say that," Jent replied. Jent then decided to send McCann and Stockard to Texas to work on Bunday and try to elicit a confession, their specialty.

Stockard had worked with McCann on an earlier murder case and the two made an excellent team. Many experts didn't like two-officer interrogation teams, but McCann and Stockard found they could be much more effective together than by using the one-man approach. The two questioners could then take different approaches and go forward with whatever method seemed most promising. Each could observe and play off the responses of the individual being questioned, taking cues from his answers. If a suspect reacted negatively to one interviewer, the other could take over and the first man would watch the suspect's facial responses and body motions for "tells" about when he was being truthful and when not, and when he was likely holding back critical information. The second officer also had an advantage in observing the suspect while the first was concentrating on formulating questions and deciding where to go next. If the interview was handled by phone, the second officer could listen in and offer suggestions to the first by jotting them on a pad or giving hand signals.

McCann was also persistent. If a suspect stopped talking or got too evasive, McCann would break off contact, leave the individual to stew for a while and then approach him again. At that point McCann would suggest that he knew much more than he had when he last talked to the suspect and wanted to clarify a few things, just to "clear up" some interesting matters the individual had mentioned in their previous conversation.

The two Alaska troopers flew to Texas, rented rooms in a LaQuinta hotel near Sheppard Air Force Base and set up shop. They spent three

days with investigators from Texas state and federal investigative agencies, including the Air Force Office of Special Investigations. They shared
information and arranged for OSI agents to place surveillance on Bunday
while they were in the area. McCann and Stockard wanted to know how
Bunday was reacting to their presence and what he did after he left their
hotel rooms.

———————

The FBI's Behavioral Science Unit profile on serial killers suggested their suspect would not confess no matter what they did. That told
McCann and Stockard they would need an innovative approach to dealing with Bunday. Among other things, they decided to play on his natural
paranoia about being a suspect in such a string of murders—and to make
him think the investigation was all but over. They staged the LaQuinta
rooms to look like a long-active stakeout facility with borrowed filing
cabinets, calendars marked off with days of activities logged, waste bas-
kets filled with crushed cardboard coffee cups and fast food wrappers,
bulletin boards with distant surveillance photos of Bunday and his vehicles, and notes to nonexistent colleagues. Most of the materials were on
a far wall of one hotel room, too distant for anyone to see clearly without
stepping close. Then McCann called Bunday, told him they were investigators in town from Fairbanks and invited him to drop by. They never
mentioned what they were investigating and Bunday didn't ask but he
agreed to meet them that evening after he got off work.

When Bunday showed up, the two troopers introduced themselves,
gave him their business cards and sat down. They waited for Bunday to
ask what they wanted with him but he never did. They reminisced about
his time in Fairbanks but initially avoided mentioning their interest in
the murders. After a half hour in which Bunday never asked why they
were there, never showed any curiosity about why they wanted to talk
to him, they volunteered that they were the latest in a long line of investigators who had been looking into "these things" that happened near
Eielson Air Force Base while he was stationed there. They were the "big
guns" who were stepping in to close out the cases, to bring "this business" to a close. McCann's approach called for avoiding use of the word
"murder." Later Stockard said they found Bunday's seeming total lack of
curiosity an indicator of his guilt, perhaps recognition that his run was
nearing its end. "Most persons being questioned by the police, especially
innocent ones, want to get to the point," Stockard wrote in one report.

"Bunday definitely was in no hurry to get to the point."

The Alaskans discussed their investigation in very positive terms and told Bunday they thought he could be helpful. They said they were in town to clear up a few things, to tie down a few details of the Alaska killings that were still unclear. Bunday stayed for several hours that day and promised to come back the next day. McCann was a master at striking up casual friendships and indicated he was hoping his new buddy Bunday could be helpful in figuring out what happened. Bunday's answers to questions were vague but he notably did not deny involvement in the murders. He acknowledged that he "had troubles with girls" while he was living in Alaska.

The next day, Bunday arrived almost exactly at the agreed hour. This time McCann and Stockard stepped up the pressure, becoming more accusatory. They told Bunday they knew he had committed the murders and were just in Texas to wrap things up, to bring the cases to a close. They said they knew how, when and where he killed the young women but they just didn't know why. They recounted the details of the murders and told him why they were convinced he was the killer. They said they also knew he had now killed a Texas woman and suggested he might be more comfortable in a cool Alaska prison than if they left him to be caught by Texas Rangers and he was locked up in a penitentiary in the hot Texas climate. They said either they would take him into custody or the Rangers would. The choice was his. Bunday once again listened quietly and gave short answers but did not deny being the Alaska murderer. By the end of the session he was crying and seemed close to confessing, but never quite took the last step. When McCann tried to get him to talk about what was bothering him, Bunday said he couldn't discuss such things as effectively as he could when he wrote them down. McCann told him to write down his thoughts before they met again.

Bunday agreed to return the next day and arrived almost exactly on time once again, but this time he didn't stay. He handed McCann a folded note, avoiding eye contact. McCann pocketed the note and invited him inside but Bunday declined and left. The note mentioned how much he respected the two Alaskan investigators and contained what they considered a weak denial that he was the Alaska killer. The Alaskans decided it was time to turn up the heat and search Bunday's home and vehicles. The next day, Sunday, March 13, 1983, McCann and Stockard showed up at Bunday's home with search warrants and accompanied by an FBI agent, a representative of the Wichita Falls district attorney's office and observers from the Sheppard AFB Office of Special Investigations. After serving the warrants the Texas officers backed off, telling Bunday that McCann and Stockard would conduct the search because they knew how much he distrusted the local authorities.

The Alaska troopers spent 12 hours at Bunday's home searching all its rooms and yard spaces, and the suspect's two vehicles. They collected hair and fiber samples and left with bags of material including ammunition of the type used in the Fairbanks area shootings, packaging for a pistol like the one used to kill Glinda Sodemann, clippings from Fairbanks newspapers about the killings and the investigation, and surveillance photos of young girls. By the time they left, McCann and Stockard were exhausted and inadvertently took Bunday's key ring, which had become mixed with their collection of materials.

An hour after they left Bunday's home, he called the LaQuinta rooms asking about his keys. McCann stepped dripping from the shower, talked to the suspect at length and quickly found his keys in the materials they collected from his home. McCann apologized for the error and said they would give him the keys next time they met. Bunday kept talking and, from his tone, McCann felt sure he was almost ready to confess. Still standing near-naked at the phone, McCann kept the suspect talking and asked again about the Alaska murders. Bunday came very close to admitting that he had done them. Though vague in his comments about most of the cases, he emphatically denied having killed Cassandra Goodwin. He said they should be looking to someone else for that murder, then agreed to meet with them again the next morning.

On Monday, Bunday was early, for the first time. He had agreed to be at the LaQuinta at nine a.m. but showed up at eight, taking the troopers by surprise and not quite ready. They wanted to record the conversation so Stockard surreptitiously turned on a recorder hidden under a bed, but Bunday declined to enter the room. He stood in the doorway and admitted he had killed the five women in Alaska, including the still-missing Doris Oehring. Stockard noted that Bunday seemed to feel killing Doris had been a mistake but showed no remorse about the other murders. He said Doris' body could be found in a remote section of Eielson Air Force Base.

Bunday lingered by the door, still declining to come in. Eventually he turned and left. McCann and Stockard had no authority to arrest anyone in Texas and there was no Alaska warrant for his arrest so they couldn't stop him. They suggested they would soon be taking him back to Alaska with them. Bunday agreed to return that afternoon, which would have allowed the troopers time to obtain their arrest warrant before he returned, but fate got in the way.

The Alaskans finally received their warrant the following morning but Bunday still hadn't shown up. They called his house and Bunday's wife said he was out riding his motorcycle. She said he would be meeting her that afternoon at the H&R Block office in Wichita Falls to work on their tax return. The OSI surveillance team staked out the H&R Block office but mistakenly followed Marcia Bunday's vehicle when she left, allowing Bunday himself to drive off in a different direction on his motorcycle. McCann and Stockard waited at the LaQuinta, hoping their suspect would stop by one more time or they would receive word on his whereabouts. When the call came, the news was awful.

Bunday had driven into Oklahoma, then turned back toward his home. By that time he was into a heavy Texas rainstorm and stopped under an overpass. There he placed the Alaska troopers' two business cards on a rock, then raced off down the road until he spotted a large dump truck coming in the opposite direction. He swerved across the centerline and bore down on the truck. The startled driver tried to avoid a collision but Bunday chased him across the highway and smashed into the truck just behind its cab, killing himself instantly.

———————

WHEN THE MATERIALS COLLECTED from Bunday's home and vehicles were examined, the investigators determined that hairs in the pickup truck came from Wendy Wilson and the shotgun shells were from the same manufactured batch as the shells used to destroy the faces of Lori King and Wendy Wilson. Multiple searches were conducted on remote areas of Eielson AFB and after two years the bones of 11-year-old Doris Oehring were finally discovered, scattered by animals. Bunday had apparently strangled her at one of his favorite spots, then drove onto the base with Doris' body in the trunk of his car, getting waved through by a sentry, before dumping her in a remote location only he would know about and could visit.

Despite the evidence and the circumstances, a Texas coroner refused to rule that Bunday's death was a suicide, apparently hoping that would help Bunday's family. Texas Rangers told McCann and Stockard that the Wichita Falls woman they originally believed was killed by Bunday was a drug dealer and the prime suspect in the case was her boyfriend. No arrest was ever made in the case and, because it so closely resembled the Alaska murders, the Alaskans remained convinced that Bunday had done it. They thought Bunday denied the murder in hopes of spending all of his prison years in Alaska and his decision to commit suicide came later.

Sometime afterward, Stockard was called back to Texas to testify in a lawsuit filed by Marcia Bunday against her insurance company. Mrs. Bunday had decided that since the coroner ruled her husband's death was apparently accidental, she should ask his insurance company to pay double indemnity.

The company refused to pay on the grounds that Bunday was a serial killer who appeared to commit suicide after investigators elicited his confession. The insurance company apparently prevailed and the double indemnity was denied.

CHAPTER 6

Protector of the Wild - 1983

LOUIS HASTINGS LOVED WILD PLACES and wilderness creatures and harbored a simmering fury toward those who harmed them. He especially hated the trans-Alaska oil pipeline, which he saw as an industrial intrusion on a great unspoiled natural area.

Hastings was a balding, bushy-bearded man who once worked at Stanford University as a computer programmer. While there he often volunteered to clean and care for seabirds whose feathers were matted by oil spills off the vulnerable California coast. He was an intelligent, quiet man, a thoughtful person who couldn't live with what humans were doing to the natural world.

Working on the oiled seabirds and other injured wildlife took a growing emotional toll so he decided to get as far from the civilized world as he could. Louis and his wife Lennie both worked at Stanford but grew disillusioned by California, decided to quit their jobs and moved to Alaska. They bought a home in Anchorage, which allowed him to run a computer business from his house when he was in town. They put the rest of their small savings into a vacation home in the remote village of Kennicott, a tiny settlement at the edge of one of Alaska's most beautiful natural areas, the Wrangell-St. Elias National Park. The area has a harsh climate, with temperatures of 50 below in winter and 90 degrees above in summer. In winter, total snowfall averaged more than four feet.

When they arrived in Alaska, they found the state in a strong growth

cycle. Its economy was bolstered by massive volumes of oil transported to the Port of Valdez on the Gulf of Alaska by the pipeline from the
distant North Slope. The pipeline was built across the heart of the state
and was then moving two million barrels of oil a day, nearly a quarter of the nation's oil production, and generated growth in much of the
United States. Alaska's thriving economy and growing population made
Hastings feel he couldn't escape from civilization. Even his dream environment was being encroached on by voracious humanity. It wasn't the
pristine retreat he longed for.

When Hastings' fury finally boiled over, he tried to wipe out the entire winter-time population of McCarthy, a tiny unorganized community
near Kennicott.

———————

LOUIS D. HASTINGS WAS BORN JANUARY 1, 1944, in Leewood, Kansas, a
small suburb of Kansas City. After his arrest Louis' mother and sister told
a judge that his childhood had been difficult. His father returned from
World War II with what would be diagnosed today as post-traumatic
stress disorder. Though Louis was less than a year old, his father already
disapproved of the infant. His sister described the man as a master of
psychological abuse. The father eventually left the family to try his luck
at being a gigolo. Whether he succeeded is unknown.

In his youth, Louis was a warm and caring person, kind to the elderly, loving and patient with children—and gentle with animals. The
boy suffered from chronic depression though his condition seemed to
respond to treatment. He served in the Air Force and afterward became
a computer programmer, though he wasn't all that good with computers.
A friend said his colleagues did not consider Louis' work to be all that
professional or capable. "He was like all computer programmers," the
friend said, "a little weird. But you have to be that way to be a programmer. You have to be into yourself. He seemed to do better with machines
than with people."

Hastings worked at Stanford for five years and was known as an in-
trovert who told colleagues nothing about his personal life. His co-workers said he was obsessively worried about his safety. In June, 1979, he
married Lennie Stovall, a librarian at the university. The couple honey-
mooned in Alaska and stopped for a time at Kennicott Glacier Lodge
near McCarthy. They decided to quit California life and move to Alaska.
The following spring they resigned their jobs at Stanford.

In Anchorage Louis tried to join the community's computer programming subculture, but his personality problems got in the way of acceptance by his peers. The couple purchased a long-unoccupied mill-worker's house on property that was formerly part of the old Kennecott Copper Corporation mine operation five miles from the village of McCarthy. ("Kennicott" is an alternate and inaccurate spelling for the property.)

Louis and Lennie used the remote house as a weekend getaway but Louis began spending much of his time there, neglecting his part-time business in Anchorage. By January of 1982 Hastings' life was disintegrating. He was in poor health, his marriage falling apart and his little business was failing. Louis tried to kindle a romance with Ann Kelsey a woman he had been writing to in Palo Alto, California. He flew to Palo Alto, checked in at the Mayflower Hotel, called Ann and told her he needed to see her. The two had previously talked about suicide and Hastings told her he was thinking of killing himself and wanted the event to be a twosome. Kelsey declined to see him, saying she wasn't ready to die. She later described the conversation to investigators. Kelsey said he wanted to see her "before February."

Louis spent more and more time in McCarthy and began planning in detail how he could get even with the world. His wife Lennie rarely visited. He began hoarding guns, ammunition and commando gear, even fashioned a silencer for one of his pistols and kept a list of 200 Alaska civic and political leaders. His list included the home phone numbers and addresses of members of the Anchorage Police Department's Crisis Intervention Response Team, highly trained and heavily armed officers.

One of the things Louis resented most was his failure to find a pristine wilderness in Alaska. The trans-Alaska pipeline was carrying oil that filled much of the nation's needs and fueled the economy of many countries around the Pacific Rim. The Alaska economy was thriving, people were moving into the state and Louis Hastings was thinking about how he could interrupt the pipeline and get the world back to what it was supposed to be.

He decided that one winter day he would kill everybody in McCarthy and Kennicott, starting with those waiting for the weekly mail plane. He would kill the pilot and fly the plane to a pipeline pump station 80 miles away. There he would steal a fuel truck and, shooting all the time, crash it into an oil-laden pipeline facility, blocking the oil flow. Louis calculated that, with wintertime temperatures, the oil would congeal and cause minimum damage to his beloved environment. The fuel truck would catch on fire and he would perish in the inferno. Since his body would be incinerated and everybody in the two villages would die, his family wouldn't know that he was a murderer and had committed suicide, which was important to him.

———————

THE KENNECOTT COPPER LODE was discovered in 1900 by prospectors who noted a distinctive green patch in the rocks above Kennicott Glacier. The miners climbed the cliff and took samples of what proved to be an ore vein 10 to 20 times larger than most of the world's other big copper deposits. They named the mountain Bonanza Peak. The find became one of the world's largest copper mining operations and once employed 1,000 workers. The Bonanza Peak discovery came just a few years after gold was discovered on the Klondike River in the nearby Yukon Territory. As a result, the world's mining interests were already primed to spend big money on mineral deposits in the Far North. The wealthy Guggenheim mining and smelting organization and J. P. Morgan, a financier and banker, bought the rights to the Bonanza Peak deposit and called it the Alaska Syndicate. The syndicate's properties included the new Kennecott Copper Corporation and the Alaska Steamship Company.

The Alaska Syndicate built a 198-mile railroad to a port at Cordova and the mine produced for 30 years, bringing thousands of tons of copper worth hundreds of millions of dollars into the world's marketplace (billions in today's dollars). McCarthy was established at the mouth of one of the four deep shafts sunk to produce the copper and at one time had a population of about 650. It was the sin city of the mining-shaft communities, offering the incoming miners hotel rooms, restaurants, brothels and illegal whiskey.

The mine closed in 1938 when the Depression dropped the price of copper to a level too low to support the high-cost Kennecott operation, which closed. In the ensuing years the area was mostly occupied by wilderness enthusiasts trying to escape civilization. The area drew a unique group of residents—some year-round, some temporary—who valued their privacy but recognized that the people of any community are interdependent, especially in remote areas. They respected each other's desire to be left alone but each kept a watchful eye on his neighbors' welfare. When Louis Hastings started living part-time in Kennicott, the area's few residents could recognize each other's boot tracks. Said Nancy Gilbert: "You walk out to get water and you say, hey, so-and-so has been by on the path." As the Chicago Tribune once noted, "They don't make towns much tinier than McCarthy."

The big event each week was the arrival of the mail plane, when pilot Lynn Ellis flew in mail and packages from the airstrip at Glennallen 100 miles to the west. Most of the few members of the community would gather to wait for the mail plane at the home of Les and Flo Hegland, an elderly couple who had a powerful radio they used to send weather reports to the Federal Aviation Administration. Their radio was the only one in McCarthy, powerful enough to reach the outside world. The local people used their rustic cabin as the unofficial post office and thereby a gathering place. The Heglands took their postal duties seriously and built a heated porch on the cabin so packages could be left without freezing before their recipients came by to get them. Their home was the virtual town square.

Maxine and Jim Edwards had lived for 25 years on a homestead in a grove of spruce trees on the west side of the Kennicott River, raising and homeschooling their children there. Maxine was considered especially well-suited for the life; she could drive a bulldozer during the day and serve dinner on laundered table linen in the evening. The mail plane arrived on Tuesday and everybody looked forward to that. It was rare contact from outside the remote community. The community usually gathered at the Edwards' place to await its arrival. As a State Trooper later described it, "You can have Easter, and you can have Thanksgiving, you can have Christmas, but it's not as important as Tuesday."

———

ON MARCH 1, 1983, MAXINE CROSSED the frozen river pulling a small plastic sled to hold packages dropped at the airstrip by pilot Lynn Ellis. She walked to the Hegland cabin just off the airstrip and dropped in for her weekly visit with Les and Flo. Their cheery cabin, less than 100 yards from the airstrip, was a comfortable place to wait for the mail. The Heglands were also good company.

Neighbor Bonnie Morris drove in on a sled towed by her dog team. She dropped off her outgoing mail but didn't stay. One of her dogs was going into heat and the team was getting difficult to manage. Bonnie invited Maxine to stop in for cookies when she was near her cabin, then gave the command "Hike." Her dogs lurched forward in their harnesses and headed for home.

Harley King and his wife Jo lived at Long Lake, 20 miles up the valley. He was a hunting guide and former commercial fisherman. The Kings had made the area their home for 17 years. In the 1950s Harley hunted wolves with fellow guide Jay Hammond, who later became what Hammond himself called "Alaska's bushrat governor."

Harley usually waited until after the mail plane arrived and dropped by when convenient to see if any mail had arrived for him or Jo. Their friend, Donna Byram planned to fly out on the mail plane next day to visit Anchorage, so Harley planned to pick Donna up at her cabin and take her to the airstrip on his shiny new snowmobile, a Ski-Doo.

Newlyweds Tim and Amy Nash lived their idyllic life in a cabin four miles from McCarthy. They generally preferred to be alone and weren't expecting any mail. They were married the year before after Amy came to McCarthy as a tourist. Tim was living alone following a divorce. The two fell in love and were married that Christmas. They were settling in after returning to the village on Valentine's Day, two weeks before, from a long honeymoon in the East. When they returned, their neighbors gave them as a gift, a quarter of a moose and a mincemeat pie with a heart carved into the center.

Lynn Ellis was warming up his small airplane that morning at Glennallen Airport, an hour's flight from McCarthy 100 miles to the southeast. He was the owner and chief pilot of his air charter service and McCarthy's only direct link to the outside world. McCarthy had no electricity, telephones, water system or television. Lynn knew all the isolated residents of the community; they were his friends and customers, and he looked after them.

An unpaved road provided a surface link to McCarthy but the road ended at the river in summertime. A bridge had washed out 10 years earlier so when the ice melted, the river was crossed with an elevated cable car that travelers pulled hand over hand. The state tried to rebuild the bridge, then offered to install a footbridge, but its efforts were fought by the people of the area, who valued their privacy. The McCarthy area residents cut logs for support towers and salvaged unused cable from the mines for a tram. When the state sent a foreman to direct local people working on the project, he soon quit because nobody would follow his orders. The tram was eventually completed the summer after the murders. The remaining villagers decided it would be a better alternative than a bridge, which would have brought in too many people and ruined the atmosphere of McCarthy. They decided a tram would attract fewer people and worked hard on the project, in part as group therapy. "It's not like we are cutting down the old cable and putting up signs saying, 'Go home, we don't want that influence anymore,'" one resident said. "It's just the opposite. We're opening our arms to the world."

———————

Louis Hastings was a loner, but that didn't set him apart from his neighbors. They all had somewhat similar feelings. He stayed away from the others and that fit right in with community expectations. His neighbors were mostly great storytellers, their skills honed at gatherings in Heglands' cabin and midwinter visits with each other. Hastings was the opposite, but little else about him stood out.

Loy Green, a resident of the McCarthy area since the 1960s, recalls a conversation he once had with bush pilot Gary Green. "You know that Lou?" Loy said. "He's kind of strange."

"Well, so are you," Gary replied. "We all are. So what?"

Judy Miller recalls encountering Hastings at the airstrip a few weeks before the murders. Miller said her earlier impression of the man was that of "a walking computer . . . Such an emotionless person." When she saw him at the airstrip that day he asked the location of her cabin, which is hard to find. The question coming from such a weird man made her cautious, so she answered vaguely.

Louis spent the evening of February 28 having a few drinks and playing a game of Risk by lamplight with one of the neighbors he knew best, Chris Richards. Chris didn't really like Hastings but decided the two of them should try to get along since they were neighbors.

At 29, Chris Richards was a summertime construction worker who owned a large and friendly husky named Mix. He and the dog lived in a hillside cabin with a close-up view of Kennicott Glacier. He once told a reporter he could hear the beating of a raven's wings a quarter of a mile away. During their board game that night Richards casually mentioned that two of their neighbors were away on a skiing trip; Hastings seemed disappointed.

Hastings had already decided that when the time came to kill everybody he would go after Richards first because his friend's cabin was isolated and just a mile down the glacier from his own. Hastings wanted to try a few tactics on Richards before he tackled the rest of the village. The two discussed plans to meet the mail-plane next day at the airstrip four miles away.

On the morning of March 1, Hastings got dressed and headed down the glacier toward Richards' place. Chris saw him approaching, pushed the door open and shouted an invitation for Louis to come in for coffee. As he entered the cabin, Chris heard Hastings take a deep breath. Chris was reaching for a coffee cup when Hastings raised his silenced pistol and shot him in the side of the face. The bullet smashed Chris' eyeglasses and lodged in his cheekbone, then another bullet cut a furrow in his neck. Richards turned, screamed at Hastings and demanded he stop shooting.

Chris fell to the floor, bleeding, stunned and in shock. "You should see yourself," Hastings said. "You're down on the ground. You're already dead. Stay there and I'll make it easy on you."

Richards' shock turned to fury. He leaped to his feet, grabbed a kitchen knife and stabbed it into Hastings leg, then his chest, and ran outside in stocking feet and one slipper, wearing a tee shirt and light corduroy pants, still bleeding from his wounds. He churned through the snow, expecting at any moment to get a bullet in the back. Hastings fired several shots after him, wounding him once more, but Chris managed to drop into a ravine and wade through waist-deep snow to a nearby tourist cabin known as the Kennecott Lodge. There he found boots, snowshoes and a parka, put them on and ran down the trail toward Tim and Amy Nash's place. Hastings followed Richards' tracks to the Kennecott Lodge. Finding it empty, he set it afire.

Since Richards had been able to get up and run away despite being shot twice with a pistol, Louis decided he needed to step up his firepower. He pulled a .223 semiautomatic rifle from his gear and hurried four miles through the cold to the cabin of Les and Flo Hegland, who were having breakfast with Maxine while waiting for the mail plane. Louis kicked in the door and entered the room spraying bullets from the .223. Les, Flo and Maxine all fell mortally wounded. Hastings methodically put a bullet into each of their heads.

Louis wanted to ambush anyone else coming to the Hegland cabin to await the mail plane so he hid the bodies. He dragged the corpses one by one to a rear bedroom and stacked them neatly on top of each other. The cabin's door hung by a hinge and both the floor and Louis' clothes were heavily bloodied but he decided to just sit down and wait.

When Chris reached the Nash cabin, Tim came outside, took one look at his damaged eye and asked what happened. "Goddamn it, I've been shot," he said. "Lou shot me." Richards thought Hastings might be coming right behind him and told Tim, "As soon as you see him, start blasting."

Tim assumed Chris and Louis had been fighting and urged Chris to relax. He couldn't see anyone on the trail and thought the battle must be over. But Richards was sure Hastings was coming toward them. "I'll calm down when you load all your guns," he said.

Tim and Amy gave Chris first aid for his wounds, then loaded him into a sled hooked to their snowmobile and headed for the McCarthy runway. There they found pilot Gary Green cleaning snow from the wings of his airplane. Green quickly finished his work and offered to fly Chris to the hospital at Glennallen. He said he had just seen Hastings headed toward the Hegland cabin.

———

WHILE GREEN AND THE WOUNDED CHRIS HASTINGS climbed into the aircraft, Tim left on his snowmobile to try to warn the Heglands that Lou Hastings had flipped his lid and was shooting people. When he arrived he found the cabin door hanging from its hinge and the smell of gunsmoke in the air. He entered the cabin, shotgun at the ready, and found the three bodies stacked in the bedroom. When he turned to leave, Hastings jumped out of hiding and shot him in the leg with his .223. Tim pointed his shotgun at Hastings and fired a round, lightly wounding him.

Tim then ran limping back to the airfield, where he urged his wife Amy to climb into Green's plane and fly to Glennallen with Keith Richards. She refused to leave and told Tim they should both stay at the airfield and wave off Lynn Ellis, who would soon be landing with the mail.

Amy backed away from the aircraft and Gary took off down the runway. As his plane climbed out above the airstrip, Hastings circled quietly behind Tim and Amy, climbed a small hill about 250 yards away, then fired a volley of shots from hiding, killing them both. He walked to their fallen bodies, put a bullet in each of their heads and dragged them down the runway. He tried to hide the bodies behind a snow berm to avoid having Lynn Ellis see them too soon.

———

WHEN HARLEY KING SHOWED UP at Donna Byram's place, Donna looked at the snow machine and told Harley the seat wasn't big enough for both of them. Harley was towing a sled behind the Ski-Doo and suggested she ride on the back of it. Donna assumed he meant sit in the dog sled and said she thought it would be a cold ride. He told her to just stand on the runners. Moving to keep her balance would keep her warm and he said he'd keep the speed down to minimize windchill, as well as avoid low-hanging branches.

Harley asked her if she could walk part of the way if she had to because the Ski-Doo had been performing erratically and it might die sometime before they completed the two-mile trek to the airstrip. She said she walked a lot and was in pretty good shape. Donna decided the arrangement would work, stepped on the runners and off they went.

As they approached the airstrip Donna heard a few shots, which wasn't unusual around McCarthy, but it got her attention since stray bullets were always a concern. Donna saw the bloody snow and wondered which of her neighbors might be shooting animals so close to the runway. The amount of blood was also large, the red pools a stark contrast to the white snow.

She wondered which of her neighbors would do such a gross thing so close to their homes. "You'd think they'd have a little more pride in their community not to make a mess like that," she thought, "especially on the airstrip." She was an animal lover and the thought of killing creatures virtually in the middle of town was especially inappropriate. Donna decided she wouldn't be judgmental about people and turned her mind to the trip ahead.

Donna and Harley both had poor vision and, as they traveled down the runway, saw several figures lying motionless in the snow. They assumed the figures must be animals, perhaps moose or caribou, and rode toward them.

Donna saw a figure walk over and duck behind a large snow berm, disappearing from sight. She thought it might be that recluse Louis Hastings and that he was avoiding them because he was anti-social. "I figured if he wanted to be friendly, he wouldn't have walked off the airstrip up over the bank because he had to climb up over the snow to get there. I thought if he wanted to talk to us he would have stayed on the runway and probably waved or spoke to us."

Donna looked up as they approached the snow berm and was shocked to see the bodies of Tim and Amy. Beside them stood Louis Hastings, who was then pointing his .223 rifle at her and at Harley. She watched terrified as a line of bullets kicked up snow in front of them. "I saw them hitting the ground and the snow pinging up and I'm thinking 'Oh, God they're crazy over here' and I'm thinking, (he is) actually shooting to hit us."

Neither she nor Harley could hear anything because of the roar of Harley's snowmobile. Donna lurched when a bullet smashed into her shoulder. The motion caused Harley to look back. He saw Hastings, and goosed the throttle. Donna grabbed the sled frame as tightly as she could with her one undamaged arm while the Ski-Doo raced down the runway, Harley glancing back to make sure she hadn't fallen off. Donna thought they were far enough to be out of the gunman's range but Hastings fired a shower of bullets that impacted around them. One bullet slammed into Harley's back and another bounced off his Ski-Doo, which veered into a snowbank and overturned onto the runway, breaking one of Harley's legs.

Donna jumped free just before the Ski-Doo crashed, rolled and landed upright with Harley lying in the snow beside it. She ran to the still-running machine and tried to help Harley climb back on but she couldn't move him. "Come on, Harley, get up. I'll help you. We got to go."

Harley replied: "I can't get up, kid, my leg's busted. I can't move."

Hastings was walking slowly toward them. She couldn't see any sign of a gun but Hastings' gait was so purposeful she knew what he intended. "Harley," she said. "He's going to kill us."

"Yes he is, kid." Then Harley had a thought and grinned weakly. "Now look, both of us don't need to die. Go up and see if Les has a gun. I'll distract him."

Donna hesitated to leave but thought about her children and ran terrified through a nearby clump of trees toward the main trail, Hastings running after her. He stopped when Harley called, "Here I am, over this way." Hastings walked over to Harley, put two bullets into the back of his head and then headed off after Donna.

Donna was scrambling, frightened, up the trail. At the Heglands, she saw the door hanging open and papers spread around the floor. She thought, "My God, he's already been here." She walked past the cabin to a greenhouse in the back, then crouched down behind the greenhouse and listened while Hastings approached. She remembered that Harley once told her game animals often escape detection by remaining still. She froze and thought about lying down to hide but decided her family would consider dying that way cowardly. Donna went to the greenhouse doorway and sat down in the middle of it, tightly clutching her arm to stanch the flow of blood and stifling the sound of her breathing, thinking she was about to be killed. Hastings searched the house and peered toward the greenhouse, but Donna's position was out of sight from the house. She could hear his bootsteps on the porch, the wind whipping the greenhouse's Visqueen covering and her would-be murderer walking on the creaking boards of the house. She heard him yell: "There's one that ain't dead yet," as though he was calling to a second person, which added to her worry. Donna thought wistfully of the pistol she usually carried but had left home because she knew Harley would be with her for protection that day.

———

WHEN LYNN ELLIS' MAIL PLANE approached the McCarthy runway, he passed Gary Green's outgoing plane. Green warned Ellis against landing, saying that Louis Hastings had gone berserk and was killing people. Ellis called his office base and asked the radio operator to alert Alaska State Troopers. He then turned and flew back toward Glennallen, flying a beeline away from McCarthy.

The state troopers' office mobilized officers and called Alyeska Pipeline Service Company to ask for emergency assistance with a helicopter to fly a response team to McCarthy. Just minutes later a chopper and three armed troopers were getting ready to head for the bloody scene in McCarthy, but the village was a long hour and a half by helicopter from the Glennallen trooper base. Officers at the Glennallen post heard a radio message from someone in McCarthy: "This is an emergency. Any station in the McCarthy area please respond." Then the radio went dead.

Back in McCarthy, Hastings had run out of people to kill. He filled two duffel bags with weapons, ammunition and survival gear, tied them to the back of a snowmobile and headed into the wilderness. When troopers arrived they found the bodies of the two Nashes and Harley King at the airstrip, and the bodies of the Heglands and Maxine Edwards at the Hegland cabin. They poked through the charred ruins of Kennecott Lodge and searched the area for Hastings and any survivors. They found nobody alive and headed back to the helicopter. The troopers took off and circled the area until they spotted snowmobile tracks in the snow headed into the mountains.

About two p.m. they flew over a man driving a snowmobile who waved to them from a snow-covered trail 20 miles from McCarthy. The pilot landed nearby and the troopers approached the man cautiously, their weapons at the ready. The man on the snowmobile had bloody clothes and told the officers he was Chris Richards, one of the few survivors of the massacre in McCarthy. He said his neighbor Louis Hastings had gone crazy and was killing everybody in the village. He said he was lucky to escape and was racing to get help.

The troopers knew the real Chris Richards was then being treated for gunshot wounds at the hospital in Glennallen, where he told an interviewer Hastings had opened fire on him "out of the blue." When their conversation convinced Hastings they knew who he was and were about to arrest him, he said, "Well, I'm your man."

The officers confiscated his duffle bags, including the .223 rifle, a Ruger Mini-14 wrapped with black electrical tape. Its stock and front sight had been removed, giving it the appearance of a commando weapon. He had more than 2,000 rounds of ammunition in clips and boxes. They also found a police radio scanner, smokeless rifle powder, wire cutters, flares, a small flare gun, a large hunting knife and a knife sharpener. One bag contained a black homemade stocking cap, an outfit of all-black clothing and a coded computer printout containing the names of Hastings' larger hit list, 200 prominent Alaskans and police officers.

The troopers loaded Hastings into the borrowed helicopter, lifted off and flew back to McCarthy, leaving the duffel bags and snowmobile to be retrieved later. They loaded the wounded Donna Byram onto the helicopter with Hastings and headed for Faith Hospital in Glennallen. There Donna and Louis were treated for their wounds, then Hastings was driven to Anchorage for lockup and a magistrate's hearing. Bail was set at $300,000.

When Troopers arrived at the Heglands' cabin, they found Donna Byram still crouched in fear behind the greenhouse, nearly hysterical and weak from loss of blood leaking from her shoulder. At first Donna refused to believe they were police officers and thought the helicopter might be part of the murder plot. She balked at joining them.

Inside the Hegland cabin, troopers found Hastings' silencer on a nightstand, wrapped in a bloody beaver pelt. In Hastings' own cabin they found a pistol rigged so it could be concealed inside the sleeve of a jacket and fired by pulling a string. They dragged the cabin's three bodies 50 feet from the entrance and covered them with a bright orange tarpaulin. One trooper said they had been stacked in the bedroom "like cordwood."

When Bonnie Morris returned from the Heglands' house that morning she launched into her chores and listened for the sound of the mail plane. Maxine Edwards had never shown up for her cookies. Though Maxine was lying dead in the Hegland cabin, Bonnie assumed she had just gotten busy and decided to skip the visit. At noon she listened to Caribou Clatter, a radio show broadcast by KCAM in

Glennallen that featured personal messages for residents of the area's isolated communities. That day Caribou Clatter read a message from Ellis Air Taxi saying the mail plane would not be coming. The announcement was unusual but Bonnie headed for the woods to cut logs with her friend Malcolm Vance.

That evening she tuned to the news and heard that six people had been killed in McCarthy. "Six people," she thought. "That was just about everyone we could think of." Shortly afterward, a helicopter circled overhead and shined a searchlight down into the trees. Though the helicopter was looking for survivors of Hastings' killing spree, she said: "We thought there was somebody still out there in the woods. We huddled under the bed. Finally the troopers found us. We were the only light, the only surviving couple in town."

Hastings went to trial the following year for six murders and two attempted murders. He was convicted and sentenced to 634 years in prison, one of the longest prison terms in Alaska's history. Three McCarthy residents attended the sentencing but their names are unknown. They declined to be interviewed by a reporter. "It's over," said one man. "That's all. We will miss the people."

The judge called Hastings an environmental terrorist, a man who wanted to portray himself as the savior of Alaska, preserver of the wilderness, while murdering people to satisfy his anger. Hastings appealed the sentence claiming that he had been temporarily insane, his condition caused by inhaling heavy doses of organic copper while applying preservative log oil at his cabin. The appeal was denied. In a later interview the prosecutor in the Hastings case described Louis as "a very bright guy, a nerdy academic whose wig is probably a little too tight . . . There are a lot of parallels to . . . (Unabomber Ted Kaczynski)."

JO KING BURIED HER HUSBAND Harley beneath a tree at his favorite lake. Bonnie Morris was devastated by her own experience. While troopers were loading her friends' bodies into the helicopter, she told a newspaper reporter, "These are the people who inspired the rest of us when we came here to build a sane and healthy life. A nobody came in here and wiped out the pillars of one of the few self-sufficient communities in Alaska."

Chris Richards remained in Kennicott and, though emotionally scarred by the massacre, was known for caring deeply about his friends and neighbors, his dog and the fate of the little town in the Wrangell

Mountains. One winter when he was the only resident of the town, he proclaimed himself its mayor, a proclamation his neighbors in both villages enjoyed when they returned next year. In summer he gave tours of the area's historic sites and told tourists about incidents of visitor misbehavior while ranting about what he considered overzealous park managers. He still had bullet fragments in his skull and suffered from double vision and glaucoma. Visitors would look at his scars and ask what it's like to get shot in the face by your nearest neighbor in an isolated community.

Chris was considered a local hero for his actions during Louis Hastings murder binge, but he waived off the praise saying he didn't consider himself a hero. An Anchorage friend with ties to the McCarthy area said Chris was originally "generous and sweet, but Hastings injected this anger and poison in him that he never could work out." He carried a pistol in his pocket for the next eight years. "It wasn't like I was afraid for myself," he told an interviewer. "I can't lose any more of my friends and neighbors, even the ones that I don't like. They're my neighbors."

"This ain't Chicago," he told one writer in 1997. "It's not New York. We're not anonymous. Even the (neighbors) I don't necessarily get along with all the time, they're precious to me. Here, it was a major, devastating impact. If somebody killed 50 percent of New York or Chicago, Christ, they'd declare nuclear war over that. I mean it would be the end of the world."

Chris Richards died one December night in 2001 when his cabin went up in flames. He had been drinking heavily, a lingering effect of the harrowing massacre 18 years earlier, and didn't make it out. His dog Rudy waited outside the ruined cabin, so everybody knew Chris was gone. An Anchorage Daily News article about his death noted that more than one person said that when Chris died that night, Louis Hastings had finally claimed a seventh life.

After his conviction in 1984, Hastings asked that he be found guilty of murder and attempted murder but mentally ill. Such a finding would have called for him to be treated, perhaps in a mental hospital, instead of incarcerated in prison. Two psychiatrists hired by the state who examined him reported that Hastings had the mental ability to conform to the law and "did not suffer from any mental disease or defect which prevented him from forming the intent to kill." A third psychiatrist, hired by Hastings, testified that he did not believe the prisoner appreciated the wrongfulness of what he had done but probably had the ability to conform to the law. An appeals court ruling noted that "Hastings' actions were planned over a long period of time and were carried out according to that plan . . . . The nature of Hastings' plan and the number of victims are horrifying."

Alaska Superior Court Judge Ralph Moody denied Hastings' insanity plea and request to avoid imprisonment, saying "I don't think I have any choice but to ensure you never walk again as a free man." He sentenced Louis to six 99-year terms for the murders and two 20-year terms for the attempted murders resulting in wounds, all of the terms to be served consecutively.

In one of his earlier appeals, the court noted: "Clearly, whatever final sentence Hastings receives, his sentence is essentially one of life imprisonment without possibility of parole." Hastings subsequently took every avenue of appeal he could find, including claiming that he had ineffective legal counsel, which a judge found to be a claim without merit. Though he kept losing, he persisted.

Apparently because some of the murders took place on federal land, Hastings was initially confined by the Federal Bureau of Prisons pending resolution of legal issues by the State of Alaska court system. He was housed at Leavenworth, Kansas, and several other federal prisons over the years and finally, on September 15, 2003, was moved from a penitentiary in Pollock, Louisiana, to Spring Creek Correctional Center in Seward, Alaska. He was then 59 and had been held in the federal facility on a temporary basis for the best part of 20 years pending resolution of the murder charges by the Alaska Court System.

———————

THE CASE LANGUISHED and went through several stages but the appeal was ultimately resolved by the Alaska Court of Appeals in 2007. Hastings attempt to overturn his conviction was denied and he was ordered to remain at Spring Creek to serve out his endless sentence.

CHAPTER 7

The Problem Child - 1985

WINONA FLETCHER HAD a horrible childhood; she was a mess long before reaching her teens. Winona came from a long line of dysfunctional people. There was little hope from the beginning that she would turn out well—and she did not.

Her grandmother was molested by a family member and, when she complained, was sent to a home for wayward girls. When the future grandmother pleaded to stay with her family, her mother told her she was a bad little girl and nobody would ever love her. The grandmother raised her own children the same way and the young ones followed a similar pattern.

Winona's mother ran away at 15 and married shortly afterward. She soon became pregnant with Winona and gave birth before she was 16. The mother became an alcoholic and gave Winona her first drink at age six. Winona tried marijuana before she was seven and by age 12 was downing six to seven beers at a time and making money as a prostitute. By age 14 she was drinking a third of a fifth of rum a day and topped that off with LSD, cocaine, Valium and amphetamines.

Winona and her mother left Oregon for Alaska in 1983. The mother was following a boyfriend, an ex-convict who was kicked out of the Army for drug use and served time in a California prison. Winona and her mother first stayed at Anchorage's Clare house, a home for mothers and children in difficulty. In an interview years later the Clare House director remembered Winona as a troubled young woman with a foul mouth and a swaggering manner. She wore black leather pants and studs. And despite the swagger she had an overwhelming sense of worthlessness.

Winona occasionally ran away from home and, between bouts of rebelliousness, attended Clark Junior High School. She was held back for several years due to a learning disability, so she was slightly older than her classmates. Winona skipped school frequently, missing more than half her sixth and seventh grade classes, but she retained a rather positive attitude. Teachers noted she would disappear for days at a time then show up in school asking for the assignments she missed while absent. She would then dive into the homework, obviously trying hard to complete all of it, and struggled to please her teachers. "She just seemed to be one of those kids that needed a hug more than others," one teacher later told the Anchorage Daily News. "She had the demeanor of a tough little cookie, but this kid was a sponge for adult approval."

Winona was a religious child. She owned and often read a Bible, sometimes quoting it to her friends. Then she met Cordell Boyd, a 19-year-old black man and school dropout who would prove to be her downfall. In February, 1985, she moved in with Cordell, a drug user who raised money to support his habit by burglarizing houses. Winona's only criminal record to that point was an arrest for shoplifting but she adored her new boyfriend and her life was about to take a turn for the worse.

The pair began burglarizing homes together—and sometimes alone. On March 21 Cordell broke into a home on West 13th Avenue in Anchorage and was caught in the act. He was arrested and released the next day on 1,000 dollars bail, which he apparently posted from the money he made on drug buys. Four days later he spent the morning in court and pled not guilty to charges from the housebreak. In the afternoon he burglarized a house in another residential district. Occasionally Cordell and Winona found weapons during their burglaries. They sold most of them for drug money but kept two for personal protection.

On April 2 Cordell burglarized another house and was caught again. When he appeared in court next day, that charge was added to the first. A court hearing was scheduled for April 18 but Cordell failed to appear and a warrant was issued for his arrest.

The pair lived in an abandoned apartment just a few blocks from a large home on two acres bordering Russian Jack Springs Park, a popular city reserve named for an early Anchorage settler. The elegant and somewhat isolated home was owned by Tom Faccio, 69-year-old owner of Tom's Plumbing and Heating, who lived there with his wife Ann and Ann's sister, Emilia Elliott, both in their seventies. Emilia had retired as a nurse 10 years earlier and lived with the Faccios to keep Ann company during Tom's frequent travels.

TOM FACCIO WAS ONCE A COAL MINER in Wyoming, where he was born into a large Italian family during the Great Depression. The family was extremely poor and sent young Tom to live with a Mexican family, which put him to work in a coal mine. Tom learned to speak both Italian and Spanish, in addition to English, and often spiced up his conversations with expressions from all three languages. Tom worked hard, saved his money and invested it with some success. In 1949 he moved from California to Anchorage to help build military housing at the expanding Elmendorf Air Force Base. A few years later he opened his plumbing supply store, which succeeded both because of his business knowledge and an instinct that drove him to make sure every customer found the item desired and went away satisfied.

The Faccio home was plain from the exterior but Tom used his accumulating wealth to make the inside quite luxurious. It was a three-story house with an imported Italian crystal chandelier, one of the first in Alaska. It had a cascading waterfall, a sweeping grand staircase, a fully equipped workout room, a large barbecue pit and a glass-enclosed room where you could get a suntan or watch the rain fall outside. The house had a burglar alarm but the Faccios never used it when they were at home. Ann was afraid she might accidentally set it off by opening a window or door. Their view was a sweeping panorama of Mount McKinley and Cook Inlet.

The Faccios had three grown children, daughters Sharon Nahorney, an interior decorator and wife of an orthodontist, and Janet Lienhart, whose husband managed Tom's Plumbing and Heating. A son, Tom, had been born to a relative and adopted into the Faccio family.

ONE DAY CORDELL AND WINONA WERE WALKING by the Faccio home when they noticed how luxurious it seemed, how likely the owners were to have sizable amounts of cash on hand and how likely, because of its relative isolation, a burglary might go unnoticed by neighbors. Their normal approach to crime was to burglarize homes when they were empty. They decided to rob the Faccio place, but this time they would take a frontal approach and force the family to turn over cash the invaders might otherwise be unable to find. That would be risky since they would need to show Winona's cute young face to gain access to the Faccio home.

On April 22 they headed for the Faccio house and along the way talked about what to do with anyone they found inside. Boyd decided he would wear a ski mask. He didn't want to complicate his life by killing the occupants but since Winona would not be wearing a mask she argued that something would have to be done about them.

Earlier that day, Tom Faccio put in a full day at the store and received a telephone call advising him that an investment in oil stocks had paid off and he was getting a windfall. Tom called Ann, who began crying quietly.

"Why are you crying?" he asked. Ann said she was just happy because there were so many things she wanted to buy for her grandchildren.

While Tom finished work at the store, Ann attended church with her daughter Janice Lienhart to hear Janice's 15-year-old daughter sing in a choir competition. Then Janice dropped her mother off at home so Ann could prepare dinner. Emilia was working in her garden behind the house.

———

AROUND FIVE, YOUNG TOM FACCIO DROPPED BY. Ann gave him some chicken and shooed him away. The elder Tom and his adopted namesake didn't get along and Ann wanted to avoid problems by having her husband's dinner ready when he got home. Tom Senior had bought a new boat, a cruiser he named The Tomcatt, and had reservations to fly to Soldotna the next day to spend a few days fishing.

Tom was eating the remaining chicken while Ann and Emilia were watching the evening news when they heard a knock at the kitchen door. Tom put down his coffee, peered out a window and saw a pudgy-faced child standing on his porch. He opened the door cautiously to hear Winona say she and her friend were having car trouble and hoped they could use a telephone. Tom couldn't turn away anyone needing help so he opened the door.

Winona raised her pistol, pointing it at him. The .22 revolver looked like a toy cowboy weapon and Tom didn't think a young girl would really be carrying a gun. He grabbed the barrel and tried to wrest it away. The pistol went off, though the shot went wild and no one was hurt. Ann heard the noise and came running into the kitchen just as the masked

Cordell Boyd stepped into the room waving his own pistol. Cordell demanded money so Tom pulled $300 from his pocket and handed it to the boy.

The two invaders pushed the Faccios into their living room. Boyd stood watch while Winona searched the house, looking for Emilia. She found her trying to hide on the patio and ordered her back into the house to join Tom and Ann in the living room. Boyd handed his pistol to Winona, who then held a gun in each hand while Cordell went looking for materials to tie their prisoners up. He grabbed several neckties and bound the wrists of all three. While sitting and awaiting their fate, Emilia mentioned to Winona that she was unmasked and they could identify her. Emilia may have been hoping her comment would cause the pair to think about the possible consequences and break off their attack; instead it may have sealed the fates of all three victims.

Ann started to have physical distress and the two invaders assumed she might be having a heart attack so Winona gave Cordell his pistol and ordered Ann to go upstairs. Ann stumbled into the bedroom, fell to her knees and begged Winona to spare her life. Winona pointed the pistol at her head and fired, but Ann ducked and the bullet hit a wall. Boyd ran upstairs and stood behind Winona, who watched as Ann prayed furiously on her knees. Then Boyd looked down the stairs and saw that Tom was working his hands free. He ran down the stairs to finish tying up Tom. Winona put the pistol three inches from Ann's head, muttered "Shut up, bitch" and pulled the trigger. Ann fell over dead.

———————

DOWNSTAIRS, TOM HEARD THE SHOT and called out for Ann, asking what happened. Winona shouted that his wife had just been shot. Tom began to weep loudly. Winona returned to the living room and approached Emilia, who was lying on her back on the floor, her hands bound with a necktie and her head supported by a pillow that Cordell had thoughtfully placed there. Winona raised her pistol and shot Emilia in the head, killing her.

Tom had worked his hands free but was rendered helpless by shock. He pled for his own life and offered Boyd another $400. Boyd took the money, then Winona strode over to Tom and shot him in the chest, wounding him. Cordell took Winona's gun thinking it would make less noise than his own .38 and shot Tom in the head, killing him. He said later he was putting Tom, who was then spitting blood, out of his misery.

Unknown to the robbers, Tom still had $2,000 in cash in his pockets and a cache of weapons, valuable jewelry and other expensive and easy to carry items. All were left behind.

The two youngsters left the Faccio home and walked to the nearby home of Boyd's sister, dropping Cordell's unfired pistol in the woods through which they passed.

Next morning young Tom Faccio became concerned when he tried to call his mother and got no answer. He walked to their home from his own nearby cabin, stepped into the blood-spattered house and went into shock as he found the three dead bodies. Tom flew into a grief-stricken rage and kicked out a glass storm door, then called his girlfriend and the police. Neighbors could hear his anguished screams wafting across the quiet neighborhood.

Police found numerous fingerprints in the house but none matched anything in their files. Anchorage detectives and crime-scene experts spent a week bagging evidence and following the bloody trail through the house to re-enact the horrific murders. Outside, volunteers used metal detectors to sweep the grass and trees in the neighborhood in hopes of finding a murder weapon. Since young Tom had been the first on the scene, and since his ragged relationship with his father was public knowledge, he was initially considered a possible suspect but was quickly cleared. Young Tom had a record for drunken driving and malicious destruction of property, a reputation as a brawler and was on probation for a bar fight. He took two lie-detector tests and was ruled out as a suspect but the initial suspicions were emotionally devastating after the shock from the discovery of the murders. "God," he told his sister Janice. "Can you imagine how I felt after walking into that house and seeing my parents dead? It tore me apart, and now everybody thinks I did it."

The initial investigation turned up few useful clues. The Crimestoppers citizens group offered a $10,000 reward for information on the case. The two anguished Faccio daughters added $40,000, bringing the total reward to $50,000.

A street person came forward claiming he was a member of a group that killed the Faccios. The man told a credible story and led investigators to the Faccio home, but his claim soon fell apart. Police investigated his story for four days but there were too many things he didn't know. The man ultimately admitted that he was lying, that he had nothing to do with the crime and his knowledge of the case was entirely based on watching news coverage on a television at an Anchorage homeless shelter. He was hoping he might be eligible for the reward.

SIX WEEKS AFTER THE MURDERS, the case had gone nowhere. Calls and tips were flooding in because of the reward, but they all proved unfounded. None of the materials or fingerprints detectives found at the house led to any suspects. One of the 11 investigators working the case lamented that he wished the killers had left more of a mark on the crime scene, something like trashing the house or writing on the walls, something the police could work with. But the killers had not been smart, just lucky.

On May 30, Winona and Cordell broke into an apartment in South Anchorage. Police responded to a silent alarm and caught Winona but Cordell got away. At police headquarters Winona said she and 19-year-old Cordell had been doing burglaries together since February. While she was being questioned, Cordell called police headquarters inquiring about her. The call was traced to a Sears department store and squad cars convened on the place from around the city. Cordell heard them coming and hid in the store, darting from one department to another. He climbed to the roof, ran across it and jumped down into a trash bin. He hid there quietly for an hour, then ventured out to cross Northern Lights Boulevard. Police caught him nearby and took him to headquarters.

Boyd tried to bargain his way to freedom, offering to provide information on street cocaine dealers if police would be lenient with him on the burglary charges. He was arrogant, overplayed his hand and—when police declined to deal—boasted that he would "beat this rap" and be out on bail in a couple of days. His bail was set at $80,000, which he was unlikely to raise in any timeframe. At Winona's hearing on whether she should be tried in a juvenile court, he testified that he had been opposed to killing the family and Winona wanted them dead so they couldn't identify her.

Boyd's common sense was marginal and he bragged to a cellmate that he and his girlfriend had killed the Faccios and Emilia Elliott. After the cellmate was released he got a call from Cordell asking him to seek out Winona and lean on her to recant her confession about the burglaries. The cellmate had heard about the $50,000 reward for information and recorded the call, including Cordell's conversation about the murders. The cellmate called Crimestoppers, said he had the taped confession and wanted to claim the reward. Crimestoppers called police, who listened to the tape and got a court order authorizing them to listen to any phone conversations Boyd and Winona had for the next seven days, with each other or anyone else.

Boyd still sat in jail and worried constantly that Winona might confess to police about the burglaries and the murders, and name him as her accomplice and the prime motivator. He called the ex-cellmate numerous times, talked about the murders repeatedly and tried to enlist the cellmate's help in freeing Winona from the juvenile detention center where she was being held. Investigators checked Winona's fingerprint against prints found in the Faccio house and found they matched. With that evidence they charged both Winona and Cordell with murder.

When the arrests in the Faccio murders were announced in the press, a man went to police with a .22 revolver he said he had bought in a bar from Cordell Boyd, paying him $10. The gun proved to be the murder weapon in all three killings and had been reported stolen a few months earlier in a home burglary.

Though Winona was still only 14 years old she was tried as an adult because court officials decided she could not be rehabilitated by the time she reached 20. A judge determined she had low motivation for treatment, was rebellious toward authority figures, lacked remorse and had little insight into her problems. Her actions suggested she was "impulsive, manipulative and a chronic liar, and has no conscience, poor judgment and a low tolerance to frustration." Because of those failings Winona was considered unlikely to be amenable to successful treatment before the age of 20. If sent to the local juvenile facility she would be associating with experienced criminals until she was released—with little rehabilitation—at age 20. She and Cordell each received sentences of 297 years in jail.

———

WINONA'S INITIAL HEARINGS had been in Juvenile Court. The Faccio daughters, Sharon Nahorney and Janice Lienhart, wanted justice for their family and were determined to stay close to the criminal cases as they proceeded. But the rules of Juvenile Court barred victim family members from attending the hearings. Despite—or because of—their relationship to the defendants, the law prohibited them from playing any role in the process. The court system seemed more concerned with protecting the young murderers than in how it treated the injured family. This has to change, they thought. The system seemed only marginally better when Winona and Cordell reached adult court. Though victims' families could attend those hearings, their feelings were not to be considered. Sharon and Janice set aside their grief enough to pour their energies into a new nonprofit they formed to tackle the problem, an organization they named Victims for Justice.

Through the years, Victims for Justice has since counseled dozens of families that were impacted by crime, giving advice on how to deal with the courts and lobbying for important changes in how justice is administered in Alaska and in how victims' families are dealt with by the legal system.

The sisters wrote letters to editors and approached political leaders. Perhaps the most important change they won is that the Alaska court system expanded the concept of victims to include family members left emotionally distraught by crimes against their loved ones. Such secondary victims now have the right to be heard at sentencing hearings and their feelings considered, including hearings in otherwise private juvenile justice trials. Also, police may now fingerprint juvenile defendants just as they do adults.

Winona's sentence was later reduced to 135 years, three consecutive 45-year terms, making her eligible for parole in 2031 when she will be age 60. For a time she was imprisoned in North Dakota at a facility offering a special program for youthful offenders. In 1993 she was kicked out of that prison for having sex with an inmate and was returned to Alaska to serve out her sentence. Today she is housed at Hiland Mountain Correctional Center in Eagle River, Alaska, and holds the record as the youngest person ever to be convicted of murder in Alaska. Cordell Boyd is a prisoner at Spring Creek Correctional Center in Seward, Alaska, 140 miles south of Hiland Mountain.

While at Hiland Mountain, Winona has managed to get pregnant and have babies twice, though prison officials decline to speculate on how she might have become impregnated. The two infants were removed from the prison and given to Winona's mother to raise. That decision was puzzling since Winona's mother was known to be a troubled person and that Winona's childhood was adversely impacted by the mother's problematic behavior, which was almost certainly a factor in Winona's choice of a criminal career.

Prison seemed to bring out the better nature of both young people. Cordell was a manipulative person and his motivation might be questionable, but he voluntarily participated in a mediation program with the Faccio family, trying to help them understand what happened, and he tried to absolve Winona from guilt in the murders by taking claim for all three killings himself, saying he had told her to kill Ann Faccio and Emilia Elliot. He told them he had lied during the hearing on waiving juvenile jurisdiction for Winona, and still cared for her. Whatever his motive, the attempt went nowhere. Cordell's fellow prisoners at the Spring Creek Correctional Center include Alaska serial killer Robert Hansen (See Chapter 3) and Evan Ramsey, a bullied student who became a school shooter at Bethel Regional High School in 1997, killing a fellow student and the principal and wounding two students and a teacher.

Winona began training service dogs at the Hiland Mountain Facility, animals that are placed with handicapped people, and plays violin with the Hiland Mountain Correctional Center Orchestra, sometimes playing for concert audiences of 300 people. She doubles as the orchestra clerk.

In 2018, after 33 years in prison, both Winona and Cordell applied for release on parole. Winona tried to claim that she had wrongly been referred to adult court and should have been tried as a minor, in which case she would have been freed 27 years earlier. News of their moves to be freed prompted a small uproar from Faccio family members, their friends and members of the community, including retired police officials familiar with the case. In a piece she wrote for the Must Read Alaska on-line column, Tamera Lienhart, granddaughter of Tom and Ann Faccio, wrote that well-meaning people had told her: "Don't worry, you will get over it in time."

"This is not reality," she wrote. "While we have learned to live with what happened, we do not ever 'get over it.'" She described the day her brother pulled her out of her German class saying, "Something bad has happened." She and her brother raced across town "as he struggled to find the words or the place to tell me about the horrific news that no one should ever have to tell another person." Then followed their stunned cleaning of the house filled with bloodstains and bullet holes, and the fear they lived with until the unknown murderers were arrested.

Members of the family attended both parole hearings and presented victim impact statements, as was then their right.

More than 400 others wrote letters opposed to the release of the young killers, pointing to the callous nature of the murders, the years-long criminal records of the two before their capture and the need for the punishment to be long enough to be appropriate for the crime. Though the two had been behind bars for a third of a century, the release opponents felt they were still only in middle age and too young to be forgiven for their atrocious crimes. Boyd was then 52 and Winona was 48. He will be eligible for another parole hearing in 2028, when he is 62 and Winona in 2030, when she will be 60.

Chapter 8

A Beautiful Prisoner - 1996

Two utility workers drove Alaska's Kenai Peninsula on a sunny Thursday morning in early May of 1996. Chugach Electric's area foreman Mike Gephardt and assistant Morris Morgan were checking for winter storm damage on lines and equipment near Hope, a small town surrounded by spruce, birch and willow trees and close by the Turnagain Arm of Cook Inlet.

Gephardt and Morgan were performing a spring ritual, one that got them out of their offices at a beautiful time of year. When they reached Mile 11 of the 17-mile Hope Road, Gephardt pulled into a turnoff below the powerline right-of-way and peered through his windshield. The lines and support equipment all looked good but he saw a patch of red in the trail beneath the lines. Assuming it was equipment or clothing dropped by one of his crews, he climbed out and hiked up the trail, keeping to the frozen edge away from the thawing mud.

As he neared, he could see the bright red was clothing on a man lying in the trail. Gephardt hoped the man was a hiker napping in the sun. He yelled "Hello" but the man didn't answer. He walked closer, yelled again, and again, but the figure lay still. A few steps further and he could see that the man was lying mouth agape, one side of his face smashed open and bloody; he was dead.

Gephardt had police training and knew what to do. Several bullet casings were scattered on the ground; the spot was obviously a crime scene. Wondering if the killer might still be nearby he did a quick glance around before hiking down to the waiting Morris Morgan, stepping carefully into his own tracks as he went.

"Don't come up here!" he shouted. "We have a body." On the climb down he noted two sets of tracks in the thawing mud, one obviously those of the dead man and the other from a set of Vibram-soled boots, presumably worn by his killer. He climbed back into the truck and dialed 911.

Alaska State Troopers responded from offices all over the Kenai Peninsula and Girdwood, a ski town on the opposite shore of Turnagain Arm. Because of the distances involved, the first trooper didn't reach the scene for 50 minutes. The first to arrive was Rodney Pilch from the trooper office at Crown Point, 24 miles north of Seward and nearly 50 miles from the murder scene. Pilch climbed up the steep trail, keeping to the edge and stepping in Gephardt's tracks. He could see the victim's footprints but the Vibram-sole prints the utility worker mentioned had faded to the point they were barely visible.

Pilch circled the corpse and saw that the dead man had a chest wound, a massive hole in his face and blood dripping from his left ear. He wriggled a wallet and checkbook from the man's pocket and identified him as Kent Leppink, 36, with two addresses, one in South Anchorage and the other a house in Wasilla, 60 miles north of the city. The checks contained a second name, Mechele Hughes. Leppink's car keys were in his pocket; the keys were to a Dodge Omni. One pocket contained a life insurance form, the kind used to change beneficiaries.

The shell casings were from a .44 magnum, a powerful weapon often carried by Alaska outdoorsmen for protection against bears. Some rifles are chambered for .44 magnum shells but the bullets are more commonly used in pistols. Unlike automatics that flip out expended shells, the standard .44 pistol retains the expended shells in its cylinder until manually removed. The Trooper used yellow notepad sheets to mark the shell locations as he pondered what type of weapon might have been used.

When the first detectives arrived, Trooper Sergeant Steve DeHart and Investigator Ron Belden surveyed the location, noted the items flagged by Pilch, took photos and interviewed the two utility workers. First Sergeant Michael Stickler, deputy commander of the Soldotna Detachment and a firearms expert, saw the empty .44 magnum shells on the ground and concluded that the murderer was either inexperienced or in a big hurry, perhaps a younger person less inclined to reduce his own risk by picking up the empties. Stickler figured the weapon was probably a Desert Eagle, an Israeli-made semi-automatic pistol that flips the empty shells out as they are fired. It is also a firearm rarely seen in Alaska.

About 4:30 p.m. the dead hiker's body was zipped into a vinyl body bag and carried down to a van for transport to the coroner's office in Anchorage. Those loading the victim noted that the body was in full rigor mortis. It had been lying in the trail for quite a while.

In Anchorage Dr. Norman Thompson, forensic pathologist, did the initial exam and determined through bloodstains on the victim's clothing that he had been shot first in the back, then took a second bullet in the stomach and a third in the face. After the initial exam the body was placed on a gurney and wheeled into a refrigeration unit for autopsy the next day.

———————

ON FRIDAY MORNING, State Trooper Investigator Mike Sears borrowed a photo from the victim's wallet and drove the highway from Anchorage through Girdwood to the Kenai Peninsula and up the Hope Highway. He showed the photo to highway workers and store clerks. None recognized the victim. Then he drove three miles past the murder scene into the town of Hope and struck pay dirt at the Discovery Cafe. Cook Maria Motoyama said the bearded man had come in looking for his girlfriend. He thought she might be helping a friend repair a cabin roof in the area. The man showed Maria a photo of himself with a blond woman and asked if she'd seen her. Maria said no but she chatted with the man for a few minutes. After he left, the cafe's only customer joked about guys having girlfriend problems. Trooper Sears asked if Maria knew of anybody working on a cabin in the area. She did not.

Before leaving Hope, Sears called Trooper Dallas Massie at the Palmer Detachment and asked him to check out the address on checks in the victim's pocket, one in a residential neighborhood between Palmer and Wasilla. Massie and Trooper Mike Vandenberg went there and found Mechele Hughes, an attractive blond woman in her 20s who owned the house, plus John Carlin, a balding man in early middle age, and Carlin's son, 17-year-old John Carlin IV. The house was being remodeled and the three were working in a storage shed collecting items to be moved to a house in South Anchorage. They said they were taking back their own possessions which were left there by their housemate, Kent Leppink, who frequently stole from them. They said Kent lived with them when he wasn't sleeping on his boat or fishing in Prince William Sound.

Massie took the woman into the house for an interview while

Vandenberg talked to the Carlins in the shed. Mechele asked why the Troopers were there, saying she had just returned from a trip to Lake Tahoe with her boyfriend, Scott Hilke.

"Is Kent in any trouble?" she asked. "Has he done something?"

Massie said Kent had been found dead and his death appeared suspicious. Mechele broke into tears. She seemed shocked and confused.

"Did he have any enemies?" Massie asked. She shook her head. None that she knew of.

Massie asked her to tell him anything she could about Kent. Mechele said she didn't know of any outright enemies but he was sneaky and kept people's Social Security numbers, for what reason she didn't know. He might have angered someone that way.

Massie left the house feeling there was something disingenuous about Mechele's reactions. Her tears at news of her friend's death seemed like emotional release, as though she had just been waiting for the notification. When the Troopers finished their interviews they told Mechele and the Carlins to leave Kent's belongings where they were. They said investigators would want to look them over and needed them undisturbed. The detectives would also want to talk to them further back at Carlin's house in Anchorage, where they were all living.

That evening Mechele's boyfriend, Scott Hilke, called from California to check whether Mechele got home safely from Tahoe. Young John Carlin answered and told Hilke that Kent Leppink had been found shot to death near Hope. When Hilke expressed shock at the news, young Carlin added: "Yeah, he was gut shot."

———

MECHELE HUGHES WAS AN ATTRACTIVE and multi-talented young woman who moved to Alaska to make college money as an exotic dancer. She wasn't much of a dancer but had a delightful wiggle that went well with the music. Mechele looked great in skimpy costumes, could fascinate men with her conversational talents and had a knack for juggling relationships. Men often fell in love with her. Because she was disinclined to say "no," she said "yes" to three of them and was engaged to all three at the same time. She juggled the engagements skillfully, at one time living in the same house with three of her fiancés.

Mechele came to Anchorage from New Orleans in 1994 at a time when the North Slope oilfields were booming. Men returning from work in the Arctic had big paychecks and often spent them on women at their favorite strip clubs. Mechele accomplished her financial goal and left Alaska with a hefty bank account in 1996 to study veterinary science at Loyola University in her hometown, New Orleans. She loved animals and had five parrots, three dogs and a cat. Veterinary science was a natural fit for her. She volunteered at a local zoo, habitually picked up stray dogs and posted pictures of them on telephone poles until she found their owners.

At Loyola she met a handsome young medical student, Colin Linehan, who attended the much larger Tulane University. Colin planned to become a family doctor at a military base and was a member of the Army Reserve Officers Training Corps. His plans included a hitch on active duty when he completed medical training. The two moved in together and lived off Mechele's earnings as a dancer until Colin was deployed to Iraq.

By 2006 they were married, had a daughter and were living the good life in Washington state's capital city of Olympia, 60 miles from Seattle. Colin had a family practice at Madigan Army Medical Center at Joint Base Lewis-McChord. Mechele worked for several years as a compliance analyst for the Washington State Executive Ethics Board, the agency enforcing the ethics code for state employees. She was then 33, very attractive and highly regarded by her neighbors, co-workers and fellow volunteers.

The Linehans' neighbors were shocked when two Olympia police officers showed up at the family's doorstep to arrest her for a murder in Alaska 10 years earlier, the murder of one of her three fiancés, Kent Leppink. Colin answered the door and told the officers she was not at home. The officers told Colin he had one hour to surrender her. Within the hour Colin, Mechele and a lawyer showed up at Olympia police headquarters. She was arrested and placed aboard an Anchorage-bound airliner.

———————

WHEN SHE LIVED IN ANCHORAGE, Mechele worked as a dancer at The Great Alaska Bush Company, Alaska's best-known strip club. Her lack of dancing skills were more than made up by her knack for conversation. Men were drawn to an attractive woman who seemed genuinely interested in talking to them. The fact that she was good looking and half-naked motivated them to tip her lavishly, sometimes spending $1,000 for an hour or two of her time.

The Bush Company drew its clientele from the hordes of oil and construction workers and commercial fishermen who came to Anchorage,
often without their wives or girlfriends. Its name is a double entendre,
"bush" being a word that referred both to Alaska's wild back country and
to a woman's tender parts.

Mechele's mother was married twice, both marriages ending in divorce. The year her father died, Mechele developed scoliosis, a curva-
ture of the spine that required frequent hospitalization. She wore a body
brace for nearly two years and the condition left her with a stainless steel
rod fixed in her back, a device that gave her an artificially induced perfect
posture. Mechele was a good student; her grades were mostly A's and B's,
with the exception of a few C's in conduct, which her mother attributed
to talking too much.

Mechele left her New Orleans home at age 14 to try her luck at a
modeling career in New York. Police say she ran away and took her sister Melissa's identification card, which showed her age as 18. Mechele
says police are wrong and that she left New Orleans with her mother's
approval. Mechele's mother, Sandy McWilliams, says Mechele's version
is correct and that she gave reluctant approval to the New York move because she knew the headstrong young woman would go anyway, with or
without her permission. Sandy felt it would be better to give a mother's
tepid blessing in hopes of maintaining a relationship with her daughter.

Mechele had the face and figure for modeling jobs but assignments
were then hard to come by in New York. Pat Gigante, a New Jersey construction company owner, met her at the Iguana Club on Park Avenue
around 1990. He was then in his late 30s, she about 20. Gigante was
very impressed by the New Orleans beauty. "I'm from New York," he
told Megan Holland, an Anchorage newspaper reporter. "I come from
a pretty fast place. And let me tell you, she made me feel like I was
standing still."

Gigante and Mechele were a pair for about three years, living together and working in a deli he owned in Bricktown, New Jersey. Gigante told
reporter Holland that Mechele seemed to have a split personality. He said
she was fun to be with and often charming but "she's like a thoroughbred
racehorse bred for being cruel."

Mechele broke off the relationship and returned to New Orleans
in 1993. There she worked in restaurants while studying for tests that
would get her the equivalent of a high school diploma. Gigante said she
left New Jersey in a Volvo sedan she got by signing his name, leaving
him to make the payments. Her friends deny the allegation and say

Gigante was just bitter about the breakup. Mechele still wanted to become a veterinarian, but needed money for the expensive education, so she took a job stripping at a New Orleans club. Within a year she decided she could make even more money by moving to Alaska, where the North Slope oilfields were generating huge amounts of cash. She and a fellow dancer took off for Anchorage in the Volvo and got jobs at The Great Alaska Bush Company.

Mechele danced and did close-up lap-dances, then would sit and talk with her customers, known in the trade as "marks." She found she could often generate $1,000 to $2,000 in a single night. While working she stuffed her earnings into one of the felt bags that come with bottles of Crown Royal whisky. When she reached home at the end of a shift she would shake out the bag onto a kitchen table to count her earnings, dazzling her roommate with the sight of so many large bills.

MECHELE'S FAVORITE CUSTOMERS—those who gave the biggest tips and those she took a liking to—were granted special privileges outside work hours. They included former bridge painter John Carlin, fisherman Kent Leppink, traveling salesman Scott Hilke, North Slope oil worker Brett Reddell and several others. One special customer she referred to as "Elvis" was never identified.

Scott Hilke entered Mechele's life after he arrived in Anchorage in 1994 to train workmen for jobs in a new city power plant. Hilke was then getting a divorce from his wife in California and, like many unattached males in Anchorage, was drawn to The Bush Company. There he met Mechele and soon became one of her more intimate admirers. He asked her to marry him, spent $3,000 on an engagement ring and gave it to her on Thanksgiving Day 1995. Scott and Mechele had matching tattoos, a small purple dinosaur on one ankle. Scott got his tattoo after seeing and admiring Mechele's.

Scott also shared one of Mechele's dreams of opening a bird sanctuary in Costa Rica. Mechele was enchanted by the idea of making birds an intimate part of her life, even doing extensive research into the cost of building such a sanctuary and the feasibility of moving to and living in Costa Rica.

In March, Hilke had a falling out with the president of his company. He quit the job and began living on money in a 401k account he had been building for years. Hilke moved into the house Mechele owned in Wasilla.

Also living there was Kent Leppink, who seemed to be couch-surfing in houses where Mechele was living when he wasn't camping on his fishing boat. Hilke wasn't comfortable about having Leppink around but Mechele didn't seem to be involved with him so he went along with the odd arrangement.

One day Hilke was working around the Wasilla house when he drove a nail into a siding and saw the nail fly through the wood. There was virtually no resistance. He went to the cellar and pulled back wallboard to find that the house had extensive dry-rot. He was amazed it was still standing. Mechele hired a building inspector who said the house would need extensive remodeling before it could be made livable.

John Carlin had given Mechele the down payment for the house so she mentioned the dry-rot problem when she saw him at The Bush Company. Carlin jumped at the chance to have her near him and invited all three people—Mechele, Scott Hilke and Kent Leppink—to move in with him in South Anchorage until her place could be made fit for habitation. Hilke soon went back to work with a company in his field and traveled to jobs in the western states, returning to Anchorage when his schedule allowed. Leppink stayed at the Wasilla house until construction drove him out and then moved to Carlin's place, joining Carlin, his son John and Mechele.

Carlin had moved to Alaska after coming into a small fortune in his 30s. He had been a bridge-painter in Pennsylvania and received part of a settlement in a lawsuit over the lead-based paint he and his colleagues used. Carlin primarily worked on the Benjamin Franklin Bridge which carries traffic between Philadelphia and Camden, New Jersey over the Delaware River. His crew would paint the bridge from Philadelphia to Camden; by the time they finished it would be time to repaint so they would do it all over again. It's questionable whether Carlin suffered ill-consequences from the paint but when the suit settled a lawyer gave him a check for $1.2 million.

Carlin's wife was in poor health and Carlin claimed she wanted to see Alaska before she died, though most people believe it was John himself who wanted to visit the Far North and that the trip probably hastened Nancy's death. In late 1994 he loaded her and teenage son John into a car and headed for Alaska. The younger John Carlin told his friends that it was supposed to be a two-week vacation but his mother liked a doctor she saw in Anchorage and they decided to stay. Nancy died a few weeks later.

Carlin decided to buy a house in a South Anchorage subdivision and engaged real estate lawyer Kirk Wickersham for help in closing the deal.

Wickersham said he would help with the purchase and take the commission if Carlin insisted, but he felt most of the work in buying a house was straightforward and didn't require a lawyer. Wickersham was then developing a marketing and sales program called "For Sale By Owner." He said most of the work could be done by the seller without paying legal or realtor commissions.

The two men hit it off. Carlin was intrigued by Wickersham's real estate idea and offered $200,000 as an investment in the new business. Then Carlin mentioned one day that his wife had recently died and he missed their sex life. Wickersham said he was going through a divorce and in a similar situation so he invited Carlin to join him on a visit to The Bush Company. At least they could be in the company of attractive women, if nothing else. As they sat at the bar, Carlin watched mesmerized when a dancer named Bobby Joe paraded down a flight of stairs from the floor above. Wickersham said she was the club's star attraction.

Carlin made frequent visits to The Bush Company, buying personal "lap" dances whenever possible with Bobby Joe, whose real name was Mechele Hughes. He became a major contributor to the thousands of dollars Mechele was taking home each night.

When she wasn't available, he focused his attentions on other dancers. Carlin was not a handsome man but found he could win a dancer's admiration by sending her to the ATM machine to get him some cash. He would hand them his ATM card and PIN number; if his looks didn't impress them, surely his bank balance would. Mechele began spending time with Carlin outside work hours. He bought her expensive gifts—furs and jewelry—and gave her the down payment on the house in Wasilla.

———

CARLIN WAS A VOLATILE MAN, an aspect of his personality that Kirk Wickersham saw up close one night as they were leaving Sorento's Restaurant in Midtown Anchorage. Carlin had left his car in a no-parking area and walked out to see a tow truck driver about to hook it up and haul it away. Carlin flew into a rage, grabbed a tire iron from his trunk and threatened to clobber the tow driver. The man unhooked Carlin's car, climbed into his truck and drove off, happy just to get away from the madman. Carlin's display of rage shocked Wickersham; when the conflict erupted he ducked back into the restaurant wondering if he should call police before his friend committed mayhem. When the man left, Wickersham returned and climbed reluctantly into Carlin's vehicle. He was then amazed on the drive back to the office when Carlin chatted amiably as though nothing had happened.

Wickersham also witnessed Carlin's fury in phone calls the former bridge painter made from Wickersham's office to a lawyer in New York. Carlin was convinced the contractor on his old painting job should pay him punitive damages as well as compensatory damages. The compensatory payments were for prospective medical costs and lost wages. The punitive damages would have been punishment for letting the problem develop. The lawyer was reluctant and Carlin would grow furious, virtually screaming into the phone. After seeing Carlin's volatility, Wickersham decided he didn't want the man as a business partner. Without giving his reasons, Wickersham said he would consider the $200,000 a loan and pay it back, which he did as soon as he was able.

Carlin tried working in Wickersham's office but he didn't have a realtor's license and could provide little in the way of assistance. And then Carlin's son John started having emotional problems because he missed both his dead mother and his friends in New Jersey. The boy dropped out of school and frightened his girlfriend, Adella Perez, by taking a pistol out of a closet, waving it around and pointing it at his own head, telling the girl how easy it would be to pull the trigger. He also used marijuana and LSD, punched a hole in a wall of the house, smashed a fist against his car and was involved in a car wreck.

Mechele grew concerned about the boy, worried that he might commit suicide, and insisted that he be treated for mental illness. Carlin took his son to Anchorage's North Star Hospital, where he spent several weeks. The cost of young John's treatment caused Wickersham's insurance carrier to cancel the policy and sent Kirk scrambling to get new health coverage for his employees.

Mechele later learned that Carlin had spent money on at least one fling with a male prostitute. She apparently came by that information when she found evidence on a computer that Carlin was frequenting an online website called Gaymall. Scott Hilke considered Carlin a friend and wanted to give him fair warning. He sent Carlin a message advising him that Mechele had come across the website and knew about his night with the male prostitute.

Carlin had tickets for a multi-week trip to Amsterdam, a trip he originally planned to take with his wife. He decided to make use of the tickets and invited Mechele to go with him in August 1995. They had sex once along the way even though she was still engaged to Scott Hilke and, as Carlin soon learned, to Kent Leppink as well. Despite those romantic entanglements, at Christmas 1995 Carlin and Mechele called young John into his father's bedroom and told him they were engaged and planned to marry. Carlin gave Mechele a $3,200 fur coat and an $11,000 diamond ring.

All three engagements were still in effect though Hilke had lost all certainty that his wedding would ever take place. Kent very much considered her his bride-to-be. She encouraged that thinking and talked with him often about buying a wedding dress.

KENT HAD FAILED IN AN ATTEMPT TO SURVIVE in his father's business. He was caught embezzling $100,000 and got pushed out of his job. Kent decided to become a taxidermist and found a school for that in Tennessee. While there he attended a meeting of the Safari Club, a popular gathering of big-game hunters. There he met Russ Williams, a commercial fisherman from Alaska who hunted in his free time.

Williams befriended Kent and gave him the nickname "TT" which stood for Tennessee Taxidermist; the name stuck with him. Williams invited Kent to become a member of his boat crew if he came to Alaska. Russ owned a tender in Prince William Sound, a boat that picked up fish netted by catcher boats. The tender carried tons of the fish to canneries so the netting boats could continue fishing while the tender got their catch to the plant for processing.

Kent found the offer irresistible and moved to Anchorage in the spring of 1993. He spent that summer working on Russ Williams' tender, fell in love with the work and decided to make it his career. Kent's father still felt bad about the son's disastrous experience in the family business and flew to Anchorage with his wife and son Ransom to see Kent working on a tender. Happy that his son had found work he liked away from the family business; Kent's father decided to finance him in a fishing venture. Kent went shopping for a tender he could manage by himself or with a small crew and soon found one. His father put up the down payment and Kent began preparing for his first season on the water.

One night in Anchorage, Kent went to The Great Alaska Bush Company and met the dancer who went by the name Bobby Joe. Despite having rather confused sexuality he was enchanted and immediately fell in love. Within months during which he spent many evenings at The Bush Company, Kent was obsessed with her.

North Slope worker Brett Reddell was another man drawn into Mechele Hughes' orbit and began paying her homage. Reddell was project superintendent for an Alaska Native corporation providing support to oil companies operating on the North Slope. Brett was contacted by state trooper investigators in 1996 a few months after Kent's murder. Reddell told the detectives that Mechele was his girlfriend and he expected her to move to Barrow on the Arctic coast to live with him. He kept a red pickup truck in Anchorage for use when he was in town. He said he gave Mechele a set of keys and invited her to use his pickup anytime. When she needed money, as she often said she did, Mechele would call Reddell in Barrow and he would send it. Like the other men in her life, Reddell functioned as an ATM, dispensing money whenever she wanted it.

Reddell met Mechele on a visit to Anchorage to conduct business at his company headquarters and enjoy some time off. He spent an evening at The Bush Company and saw her there. His reaction was the same as those of the other men in Mechele's life. He was hers. The two began dating and she promised to move north to Barrow, though that was more a sales pitch than her true intent. When Reddell ran into Scott Hilke at Mechele's house, Mechele told him that Hilke was dating her female roommate, though Mechele had no roommate.

Reddell told Alaska State Troopers in his interview that he expected Mechele to quit The Bush Company, buy a trailer in Arizona and move it to Talkeetna, a village north of Anchorage, where they would live when he was off work. He said he was still supporting her after Kent's death when she was in college in New Orleans. He also gave her his bank debit card and its PIN number, so she had constant access to his bank account. Mechele occasionally visited him in Barrow. Despite their frequent opportunities, they had sex only once.

Mechele used her occasional visits to Barrow as part of her scheme to avoid Kent's tracking system, which was designed to learn when she was with Hilke. She told John Carlin that if Kent found her car in the airport parking lot—which Kent routinely checked when he didn't know where she was—Carlin should say she was visiting Barrow.

After Kent's murder, Reddell was amazed to learn that Mechele had driven his pickup to New Orleans and that Carlin had then taken it to his family home in New Jersey. Reddell tracked Carlin down and was told he could come and get the truck if he wanted it. One of Reddell's co-workers had a friend who was visiting near Carlin's New Jersey home; the friend agreed to retrieve the pickup and sell it for Reddell.

Kent proposed to Mechele in November of 1994, a month after they met. She accepted and he gave her a pendant and a diamond ring. He notified his parents and the family began planning for a wedding. Kent told Mechele they should celebrate their love by postponing sex until after the wedding. No firm date was set for the ceremony. A week after her engagement to Kent, Mechele also accepted a wedding proposal from Scott Hilke bringing her total list of fiancés to three. Her skill at juggling simultaneous relationships was nothing short of miraculous, especially given that at times they were all living together in Carlin's home in South Anchorage. Also living in the home was Carlin's teenage son, John Carlin IV, whose youthful libido intensified the corrosive atmosphere surrounding her.

Though four males and one attractive woman in the same household was bound to cause friction, Kent made the problem infinitely worse with his intrusive behavior. He spied on everyone, with the possible exception of young John. On one occasion while they were staying at Mechele's house in Wasilla, Kent spied on Mechele and Hilke when they were having sex.

Hilke gave Mechele a small pistol for her protection. The weapon disappeared and Hilke suspected that Kent had stolen it. Kent was upset about Scott's suspicions and tried to contact Scott's parents to discuss the matter, apparently hoping that Hilke's family would talk him out of his concerns. Kent's reaching out to his parents infuriated Hilke.

When Hilke was traveling on business, Mechele would often fly to meet him and the two would enjoy a few days together away from the Anchorage house. Her absences fanned Kent's ardor and his spying grew more intense. On one occasion when Mechele met Scott at a resort in Metairie, Louisiana, Kent tracked them down, showed up at the resort and served them breakfast in bed, his way of saying "gotcha."

Mechele had driven Pat Gigante's Volvo to Metairie so she decided to make use of Kent's unexpected appearance and prevailed on him to drive it back to Anchorage while she and Scott flew home. Kent did so and stopped to visit his family in Michigan along the way. When Hilke's business activities began to hinder his travel and opportunities to tryst with her, Mechele began spending more time with Carlin and accepted his offer of a trip to Europe. She told Kent she was just traveling with a friend and when Hilke raised questions about the trip she told him not to worry, that Carlin was impotent.

In February of 1996 Mechele and Kent approached insurance agent Steven Leirer and said they wanted to buy policies of $1 million on each of them. They said the insurance amounts were based on the value of Kent's fishing business and they were going into business together. Leirer said his company, New York Life, could write a policy for $1 million on Kent's life since he was essential to the fishing venture, but it would only write a policy for $150,000 on Mechele's life because she was not a central element of the business. Kent asked that Mechele be listed as beneficiary for 80 percent of his million-dollar policy and that his parents be designees for the rest. He was to be the beneficiary on her policy.

On April 18, Mechele and Kent met with lawyer Brian Brundin and asked that Kent's will be changed and that Mechele be listed as heir to everything he owned rather than his parents. While still in Brundin's office the couple got into an argument and he heard Mechele say: "I can compete if it was a girl." She was obviously angry at Kent's relationships. The next day Kent returned to Brundin's office and complained that Mechele had visited North Star Hospital, where young John Carlin was being treated, and asked an official if Kent had sought counseling there. A North Star worker told her that Kent had inquired about treatment but was referred to another facility. Kent was outraged that the hospital told her that much and wanted to know if he could sue North Star. Brundin told him he probably could not.

Kent was also furious because Mechele was stealing things from him, items including a $4,000 statue, a $6,700 laptop and some antiques. She had also gone shopping at Eagle Hardware and charged $4,600 in kitchen cabinets to his account. Brundin warned Kent that he had seen a lot of marriages come and go and that his match with Mechele did not seem promising. Brundin said he didn't see much chance that she would change.

Kent left Brundin's office worried. Then his worries took a worse turn. His spying convinced him that his housemates were planning to murder him. Kent had met lawyer Kirk Wickersham through Carlin so he went to Wickersham and said: "I'm going to get killed." Kirk urged Kent to contact police about whatever he had uncovered—and to leave that house. But he did neither. The next day Kent returned to Steven Leirer's insurance office and changed the beneficiary form he had filled out earlier. He designated his parents as his sole beneficiaries. Kent stuffed the form into a pocket of his jeans, planning to give it to his father, and walked out with his back stiff.

In late April, Kent's father Ken Leppink flew to Anchorage to help Kent get ready for the fishing season and to get a better understanding of the young woman his son was planning to marry. When Ken and his wife met Mechele on an earlier trip he got the feeling that Mechele was not as serious about the relationship as his son was. Though both his parents were skeptical about Mechele's intentions, Kent told his father that she would be flying with him to the Leppink family home in Lakeview, Michigan, near Grand Rapids, to look for places to have the wedding and reception.

Dad arrived in Anchorage on a Northwest Airlines flight from Minneapolis and was met at the airport by Kent and John Carlin, but Mechele was notably absent. Kent said she was on a road trip and would be along in a day or two. Carlin invited the elder Leppink to stay at his house with the others but Ken declined saying he would stay at the Golden Lion Motel.

Kent planned to spend the next few days scraping and cleaning the boat in preparation for its spring launch and his father expected to help with the work. But Kent worried about his father being fit enough for such strenuous work and said, since the elder Leppink ran a successful business and knew his numbers, his time might be better spent working on Kent's federal income tax. Ken was astounded; it was almost two weeks past the April 15 tax deadline. He said he would fill out the forms but warned Kent he might face a penalty for late filing.

They stopped briefly at Carlin's house before driving Ken to the Golden Lion. As they were parting in the hotel lobby Kent handed his father a sealed envelope. "Here," he said. "This is for you."

Ken opened the envelope and found a form designating him and his wife as the beneficiaries for a million-dollar life insurance policy. "Kent, I don't like the smell of this," he said. "This is not good."

"It's OK," Kent replied. "It's alright." Kent said the policy was a gift paid for by Mechele's grandfather. The two talked about the policy briefly then dropped the subject. The Leppink family business had been successful and his parents lived comfortably; they didn't need the money. If his son was getting married, why wouldn't he designate his bride as the beneficiary? And why would his bride's grandfather pay for such a policy. It didn't make sense.

Ken worked on Kent's tax return for the next several days and went with him to an Anchorage accountant who agreed to file the return and ride herd on Kent to make sure such paperwork was done on a timely basis in the future. On Monday, Kent drove his father to the airport with Mechele still nowhere to be found. Kent told Ken he thought she was visiting a girlfriend at a cabin under construction near Hope. All he knew was that the cabin belonged to Carlin. He had no idea why she hadn't been in Anchorage to meet Ken, who flew home to Michigan deeply troubled by his son's unpromising romantic entanglement.

––––––––––

ON MAY 4, TWO DAYS AFTER KENT'S BODY WAS FOUND on the trail near Hope, Ken called Alaska State Troopers and reported that he and his wife received a letter from their dead son. Inside the envelope was a handwritten note and another sealed envelope. The note said: "Please put the enclosed envelope in your safe deposit box. Do not open it. I talked to you about 'insurance policies.' This is mine. If I didn't think that things could get a little 'rough' up here, I wouldn't have sent you this. It'll be safer there. It's not funny to talk about getting killed, but in today's world you have to expect anything .... If you think anything fishy has happened to me, then you can open up the other envelope I've sent."

Ken and Betsy were already in shock from being notified of Kent's death and opened the second envelope fearfully. Inside was an angry but coherent note.

"Since you're reading this you assume that I'm dead .... It was my time, and there's nothing that can change that. There are some things I'd like you to do for me, though. I hate to be vindictive in my death, but paybacks are hell. Use the information enclosed to take Mechele DOWN. Make sure she is prosecuted:

Fraud—She took me for a lot of money on the impression we were getting married. This may be hard to prove without me present but give it a shot. It is a Class B felony in Alaska. $15,000 can be proved because you sent it to us.

Insurance fraud ... have the IRS audit her. Turn her in!"

––––––––––

THE NOTE SAID MECHELE HAD FRAUDULENTLY used Carlin's medical insurance and was probably not reporting her dancing income to the Internal Revenue Service. He listed Mechele's Social Security number and her mother's address for use in the investigation. He accused

Mechele, John Carlin and Scott Hilke of his murder.

"Make sure they get burned," he said. "Make sure Mechele goes to jail for a long time, but visit her there. Tell her how much I did (do) love her. Tell her you love her and help her.

He told his parents to sell his boat and keep the money, then use part of the million-dollar life insurance payment to pay off his debts and take a nice beach vacation. "Act like I'm still there with you," the letter said. "and do the things I would like to do."

The "letter from the grave," as the media would call it, devastated Kent's parents and was almost too much for them to bear. Their son had gone to Alaska because he went astray while working in the family business but they regained hope for him when he found work that suited him and seemed to find the woman of his dreams, but it had all gone up in smoke and he was dead. Kent knew who was going to kill him and his parents vowed to make sure his killers were found and brought to justice.

State trooper investigators were already hard at work and Kent's letter reinforced their suspicions about the people he lived with and the role they might have played in his death. The officers wanted to interview young John Carlin since he would have a unique perspective on what went on in the house and—based on the suspicions in Kent's letter—might not be involved.

His father insisted on being present, as was his legal right as a parent. They decided to hold off on the interview since young John would be reluctant to discuss anything his father might disapprove of if the father were present for the interview.

The detectives knew from the records they could find that Kent had purchased a Gateway computer. On May 1 they went to the house and asked Carlin where it was. At that point Mechele entered the room, overheard the question and told the officers that the computer had been malfunctioning. She said she sent it to be looked at by her sister, a computer expert in Moab, Utah.

Mechele asked why the troopers wanted the Gateway and assured them there was nothing on it. When they checked with Mailboxes, Etc., the company Mechele used to ship the computer to Moab, they found that she had actually mailed it the day after their visit to the house, when she said it was already on its way to Utah.

Trooper Sergeant Steve Dehart and Investigator Ron Belden asked to see Kent's possessions so Mechele and Carlin agreed to meet them at the Wasilla house. Dehart walked with Carlin to the storage shed while Belden interviewed Mechele in the house. Belden asked Mechele if she knew of a .44 magnum that might be in the house. She said she did and when Carlin rejoined them she asked: "Have you seen Kent's big black gun?" Carlin seemed unhappy about the question but hung his head and said he hadn't seen it.

Further investigation determined that Mechele had once participated in a gun handling class taken by Bush Company female employees interested in concealed carry permits. She showed up at the firing range with a borrowed Desert Eagle .44 semiautomatic pistol. The instructor knew the weapon would be too large and its recoil too strong for the relatively slight woman so he loaned her a lighter pistol for the class.

In early June, Carlin made a down payment of $18,000 on a $72,000 recreational vehicle and gave it to Mechele with the understanding she would be responsible for the payments. He also made Mechele the official guardian for his son John and set up a $200,000 trust fund for her use in supporting the boy in the years ahead. A few days later she and young John headed down the long Alaska Highway for California. She told Carlin she intended to take the boy to New Orleans and put him in a Catholic school there.

———————

MECHELE AND JOHN DROVE TO SACRAMENTO and visited Scott Hilke for a few days, then headed north to her sister Melissa's home in Moab, Utah. Melissa still had the computer Mechele sent from Anchorage but was uneasy about her request to wipe the drive clean. She had done nothing with the laptop and wanted to talk to Mechele before working on it. Mechele had told her that the laptop was entirely hers and she wanted to wipe it clean as a fresh start on her new life. When Mechele reached Moab and learned that Melissa hadn't wiped the computer, she was furious.

While they sat at a picnic table in Melissa's yard, the discussion got around to Kent Leppink and Mechele mentioned that Kent loved hunting, the killing of wild animals. Melissa told investigators that Mechele had said something that alarmed her. "She told me that he got what he deserved, that people didn't like him, that he hunted and stuffed animals and that . . . she felt he got exactly what he deserved." Melissa said Mechele slammed her hands on the picnic table and angrily stood up. "She said it was too bad that someone didn't torture him first."

Melissa said Mechele also mentioned that Kent had written a letter blaming her if anything happened to him. Young John Carlin had added his opinion that nobody liked Kent.

Young John wanted no part of Mechele's plan to put him into a Catholic school in New Orleans. When they reached the city he left immediately to visit his family in New Jersey and never returned. By then Carlin had gone through most of the million dollars from the insurance settlement and decided he needed to go back to work painting bridges in New Jersey. He sold his Anchorage house and headed down the highway. When he arrived at his old East Coast stomping grounds young John left his grandfather's home and moved in with his father.

Mechele went to Loyola to pursue her long-planned veterinary studies. There she met Colin Linehan and the two married in the spring of 1998. They had a baby daughter the following year. Colin planned to become a family physician and was a member of the Reserve Officers Training Corps. They moved to Maryland while he did his residency and later to Olympia, Washington when he was assigned to Madigan Army Medical Center at Joint Base Lewis-McCord near Tacoma. Later he was deployed to Iraq.

The two were having marital problems while he was in Iraq. She had several affairs including one with a doctor friend of the family and she reconnected for a time with Scott Hilke. But Mechele and Colin reconciled when he returned from Iraq. In Olympia, Mechele became a suburban housewife, earned a master's degree at Evergreen State College and became an intern at the Washington State Executive Ethics Board. She volunteered at her daughter's school and at a suicide crisis center and offered to assist with social programs at a local Catholic Church. She became an outdoor enthusiast active in kayaking, biking, hiking and rock-climbing, and filled her house with books, worked in her garden and threw parties in her back yard.

———

BACK IN ALASKA THE SHOOTING DEATH of Kent Leppink went unsolved despite Kent's damning letter pointing at Mechele and her lovers as his likely killers. Eventually the state trooper investigation was suspended for lack of progress and lay dormant until 2005, nine years after Kent's body was found. Then the file was assigned to a new Cold Case Unit financed by a federal grant and authorized to look into older cases with promising possibilities.

The case landed in the hands of Jim Stogsdill, a retired Alaska State Troopers investigator and summertime fishing guide. Stogsdill spent the warmer months on Alaska's famed Kenai River and the rest of the year looking into unsolved crimes. Stogsdill and his colleagues had access to computer equipment and investigative techniques that were unavailable when many cases were originally tackled. They were also able to take advantage of sometimes greater willingness on the part of witnesses to speak frankly about cases after multiple years had passed.

Stogsdill was first assigned to the case in 2003. One of the witnesses he became interested in was young John Carlin IV who had earlier been too young to interview without having his father present. John IV was then 27 and, as Stogsdill told this author in a 2009 interview: "The kid was a loose end. Nobody had talked to him."

Anchorage Police Detective Linda Branchflower was retired and working on contract with Stogsdill. Branchflower found young Carlin through one of his old girlfriends, a young woman he was still in touch with. He was then doing electronic drafting work for an engineering company near Seattle-Tacoma International Airport.

Branchflower, Stogsdill and a Washington State Trooper went to young Carlin's workplace in early May 2005. They interviewed him under a tree in the company's parking lot. Stogsdill said the youth seemed very nervous, smoked incessantly and his words came tumbling out. He told them, among other things, that his father had purchased a Desert Eagle .44 magnum pistol from a newspaper ad shortly after they arrived in Anchorage and that shortly after the shooting of Kent Leppink his father had washed the pistol with bleach in a sink, saying it was a good way to get rid of evidence.

When they returned to Anchorage, Branchflower went to the Anchorage Daily News and worked with the newspaper librarian to find the ad the senior John Carlin had used to buy the Desert Eagle. The man who placed the ad and came to the Carlin house proved to be an Army enlisted man then assigned to a post in Arizona. He had been based at the Army's Fort Richardson near Anchorage from 1991 to 1998. The soldier said he sold the pistol to a man in South Anchorage in 1995. Investigators showed him a photo of John Carlin III but he said that didn't look like the man. He said the room in the background and a bookcase looked familiar, but not the man. He described a burly man in his early 30s that sounded a lot like Kent Leppink, though it could also have been Carlin.

Alaska State Troopers were still holding the computer sent by Mechele to her sister in Moab, though it had not been examined because of ongoing disputes about its ownership. Mechele said she would stop cooperating with them unless she was given custody of it. The computer stayed in trooper evidence storage but was still unexamined. Detective Branchflower had it turned over to a computer forensics specialist working with the Cold Case Unit.

Stogsdill and his team took their evidence to a grand jury in early fall of 2006. Though the evidence was all circumstantial, the statement by young John Carlin about his father's handling of the missing pistol convinced the jury that the case should go to trial. John Carlin III and Mechele Linehan were indicted on charges of conspiracy and first-degree murder.

When Carlin learned of the indictment he flew back to Anchorage and turned himself in at the courthouse. His wife, a Russian medical worker he met online, found his briefcase and turned it over to New Jersey police. In it was a list made long ago of people to be notified if he was arrested. On the house mantelpiece was a statue of two deer that she had always disliked. She put it up for sale on eBay. Police spotted the ad and picked up the statue at the house. Engraved on its bottom was Kent Leppink's name.

The case drew national media interest, largely because the prosecutor claimed that Mechele and Carlin borrowed their murder plot from the movie *The Last Seduction*. In the film an attractive woman lures her lover into killing her husband on the promise they would split the insurance money. Even more sensational was the "letter from the grave" written by the victim and naming the people who would be killing him.

CARLIN WENT TO TRIAL IN MARCH 2007 in a jammed courtroom filled with media and onlookers drawn by the sex and intrigue-filled plot. The testimony recounted the lives of those in the Carlin household and included a suggestion by defense lawyer Marcy McDannel that one overlooked but likely suspect in the killings was young John Carlin IV. Young Carlin was a witness in the case so McDannel called John's old girlfriend Adella Perez, who testified that he was a volatile youth, sometimes violent and a compulsive liar. She said John was homophobic, hung around with a crowd that used drugs and was jealous of any man who got close to her.

Key testimony was provided by an Alaska State Troopers expert who examined the computer jointly owned by Kent and Mechele. He said an attempt had been made to delete files from the computer, but the attempt failed. Deleting the files simply eliminates markers that prevent the computer from overwriting anything saved in that space. Only over-writing everything on a computer can wipe out its original contents. The recovered files gave a detailed account of life in the household for the last few months of Kent's life.

At one point when legal motions were being offered, Judge Philip Volland noted that he would allow closing arguments suggesting that young John Carlin was the actual killer. He said considering the testimony given during the trial that the jury would probably be wondering about that anyway. On April 3, 2007 the jury found the elder Carlin guilty of first degree murder. Sentencing was delayed until after Mechele's trial that fall.

Mechele walked into Judge Volland's courtroom for trial in September. The jury selection was notable in several aspects, including the fact that lead defense attorney Kevin Fitzgerald assumed men would be more sympathetic than women in the trial of a former stripper. But the men almost invariably answered a question about strippers with a version of "You can't trust those dancers." Fitzgerald was amazed since he had grown up in old Anchorage, a town where the whorehouse madam was likely to be the justice of the peace. Even a prospective juror who sometimes danced during amateur night at The Bush Company gave the "you can't trust those dancers" answer. Young John Carlin was called as a witness and gave a new version of his father's washing of the missing pistol. He said Mechele was standing in the bathroom door while his father was washing the pistol in bleach; earlier he had said she was not present for the gun-washing and may have been elsewhere in the house.

Scott Hilke also testified and recounted his earlier statement that when he called after Mechele's return to Anchorage from Tahoe young John Carlin had told him about Kent's body being found and the fact that he had been "gut-shot." One police report indicated Mechele said she and Kent only pretended to be engaged; the pretense was to keep his parents from knowing that he was gay.

The jury returned on October 22 with a verdict of guilty. Mechele collapsed into the arms of her husband. Defense lawyer Kevin Fitzgerald and many observers were stunned since they didn't think the prosecution had proved its case.

Both Carlin and Mechele were sentenced to 99-year terms. Mechele was sent to Hiland Mountain Correctional Facility in Eagle River, the state's women's prison. Carlin was sent to Spring Creek Correctional Center, Alaska's maximum-security prison in Seward. Carlin was a troublesome prisoner disliked by many of his fellow inmates. He was visited by a film crew from a national network, which gave him an unwelcome notoriety in the prison. He was also given to walking into a recreation room and changing the television channel when other prisoners were watching a favorite program. He was beaten up by fellow prisoners three times, the third time fatally. His son sued the state for a half-million-dollars for his father's death and the estate, presumably controlled by young John, was awarded $160,000. Carlin's four attackers were charged and convicted, and time was added to their sentences.

At Hiland Mountain, Mechele trained service dogs and played cello in the string orchestra. She got in occasional trouble with the guards, once when she modified a prison uniform into a tank top for herself. She was also placed on a night shift because she was unpopular with many guards. One guard said some people thought she was too bossy.

When her appeal was heard in December 2009 her lawyers argued that inappropriate testimony had been allowed about the movie *The Last Seduction* and its similarity to her case. Also, Kent Leppink's letter from the grave had been inappropriately allowed because it was effectively testimony and, being dead, he couldn't be cross-examined. The conviction was overturned and Mechele was released on bail pending retrial. She got a job as a receptionist at a hair salon and was awaiting retrial when Judge Volland ruled in April that the inappropriate testimony and evidence had been used in her indictment, so that should be thrown out as well.

Free for the first time in five years, Mechele and her husband returned to Olympia and tried to rebuild their lives. When the time came for the prosecutor to decide whether to move forward on a new indictment, he told the court that a key witness would not be available.

Assistant Attorney General Paul Miovas told Superior Court Judge Larry Card that the lawyer for John Carlin IV, then 33, had informed him that if called to testify young Carlin would invoke his Fifth Amendment rights. The amendment mandates that a person cannot be forced to testify against himself.

Miovas later decided that the case would not be revived. Mechele and her husband were free to go on with their lives.

CHAPTER 9

Death of a Secessionist - 1993

JOE VOGLER WAS A CANTANKEROUS MAN—and most Alaskans loved him for it.

He was one of the most uniquely Alaskan characters of the 20th Century, an Alaska booster who wanted the 49th state to secede from the union.

One writer, Lucas Silver-Merrill, called him a charismatic front man for the secessionist movement. He ran for governor three times—in 1974, 1982 and 1986, losing every race but always collecting a respectable portion of the vote. Vogler was the nominee for the Alaskan Independence Party, the continuing political organization he founded and led for the rest of his life.

The notion of secession is rather weird to most people in the modern age and many Alaskans winked at Vogler's insistence that the state should actually leave the union. While they liked the idea of telling Washington where to go, relatively few people ever took the idea seriously. He was, however, welcomed into the state's councils of power, both for the size of his following and his innate entertainment value.

When Joe first ran for governor in 1974 he finished far behind winner Jay Hammond and the incumbent whom Hammond unseated, William A. Egan. In 1978 Vogler ran for lieutenant governor on an Independence Party ticket with Alaska Native leader Don Wright in the governor's slot. But Republican Hammond and write-in candidate Walter J. Hickel garnered the bulk of the votes and Hammond won the governorship. Hickel had been elected governor as a Republican in 1966 but resigned in 1969 to become secretary of the interior under President Richard Nixon.

Vogler ran for governor again in 1982 and 1986. The media and political pundits made much of a statement he uttered in 1986 that Alaska should "nuke the glaciers" in Southeast Alaska to make way for a highway to Juneau. Vogler later claimed his comments were misinterpreted and they were accepted as political hyperbole by most people but the media had its way with him anyway. And nuking the glaciers became part of the Vogler legend. The AIP took 5.5 percent of the vote in 1986, about 10,000 votes, and that led to its official recognition as one of the state's political parties. Most people thought Vogler didn't actually want to become governor and take on the duties involved, but running for the office gave him access to high-visibility forums where he could express his views. And expressing them was his joy. His trademark clothing items were a fedora hat and a bolo tie.

In 1990 Walter Hickel decided to make another try at the governorship. He was a long-time Republican but had philosophical differences with the party's nominee, Arliss Sturgulewski. Hickel and Fairbanks politician Jack Coghill, a longtime Vogler friend, met with Joe and convinced him to let the two of them run under his Independence Party's banner. Hickel had no serious interest in secession but let Vogler think he would entertain the notion if elected. The AIP nominated Hickel for governor and Coghill for lieutenant governor—and they won. The pair assumed the two offices but during their terms did little to advance Vogler's hope for secession.

———

VOGLER WAS A GOLD MINER, a line of work that involved frequent clashes with federal regulators who hassled him about the bulldozers and other heavy equipment he drove across government land. That occupation also put him in an adversarial relationship with environmentalists who fought him over protection of public lands. Vogler called them "posey sniffers" among other things.

———

HE WAS BORN IN KANSAS IN 1913, attended school there and won a scholarship to the University of Kansas, where he earned a law degree in five years to satisfy his father. He was admitted to the Kansas State Bar but never practiced law. Vogler had strong opinions about President Franklin D. Roosevelt and that got him crosswise with many of his contemporaries in Kansas and later in Texas, where he worked for a time. His patriotic Texas employer fired him in early 1942 for calling Roosevelt "a communist traitor." That March he moved to Kodiak, Alaska, where Joe hoped a man could voice his opinions without fear or favor. After a year there he moved to Fairbanks to take a job at Ladd Field with the Army Corps of Engineers. In 1951 he settled on a new career as a miner working on Gold Creek in search of the metal that made the creek famous. Over time he also developed a sideline as a real estate developer and bought 320 acres of land along Farmers Loop Road near Fairbanks.

Joe became known in Interior Alaska as a passionate writer of letters to the editor. His letters voiced fury at events transpiring in Washington, especially decisions he considered adversarial to Alaska, which was still a territory. Many residents feuded with bureaucrats in the nation's capital on a regular basis. Vogler's anger was also directed quite often to regional and local government officials. Author John McPhee wrote in his book "*Coming Into the Country*" that Vogler once said to the mayor of Fairbanks, "Get ready to look at this town for the last time, because I'm going to close your left eye with one fist and your right eye with the other." Joe referred to federal bureaucrats as "interfering government swine. If I ever get a revolution going," he said, "I'm going to import a bunch of guillotines and lop off their lying heads."

Vogler's fame spread far and wide in the 1950s when he feuded with University Bus Lines over a narrow bridge on which space limitations required buses to straddle both lanes. The Fairbanks Daily News-Miner referred to it as the "Battle of the Bridge," a struggle that continued even after a new and wider bridge opened. Because of its preferred route, the bus company elected to use the old bridge instead of the new one rather than drive out of its way. Vogler was furious.

Alaska gained statehood in 1959 and Joe was soon convinced it should be going in a much-different direction. He jumped into Alaska politics when major oil companies proposed to build the Trans-Alaska Pipeline from the newly discovered oil field at Prudhoe Bay on the Arctic Coast 800 miles south to Valdez, crossing broad expanses of wild country. Vogler was outraged by federal interference in the project and the long delay that caused before construction could begin. He felt Washington was treating Alaska like a colony and in 1973 circulated a petition calling for the state to secede. It garnered 15,000 signatures in just three weeks.

Author John McPhee told about Vogler canoeing to remote cabins to collect signatures one by one. Congress never responded even though the signees represented almost five percent of the state's 340,000 population. Joe said the response to the petition drive was "beyond my wildest expectations." He dubbed his petition group "Alaskans for Independence" which morphed into the Alaskan Independence Party.

One notable member of the Alaskan Independence Party was Todd Palin, wife of vice-presidential candidate and former Alaska Governor Sarah Palin. Todd was a member for seven years and only dropped out in 2002 when U.S. Senator John McCain asked the popular Sarah to join him in his race for the White House.

———————

PARTY OFFICIALS REPORT THAT VOGLER once stated "I'm an Alaskan, not an American. I've got no use for America or her damned institutions." In a 1991 interview for the Oral History Program at the University of Alaska Fairbanks, Vogler said "The fires of hell are frozen glaciers compared to my hatred for the American government. And I won't be buried under their damn flag. I'll be buried in Dawson (Yukon Territory, Canada). And when Alaska is an independent nation they can bring my bones home." As one writer put it, "More than anyone else, Joe was responsible for uncovering and publicizing the broken promises." The reference was to the promises of statehood and major federal legislation like the Alaska Native Claims Settlement Act and the Alaska National Interest Lands Conservation Act.

Vogler's mine on Woodchopper Creek was within the Yukon-Charley Rivers National Preserve managed by the National Park Service and that led to direct clashes. He got into endless battles with NPS officials over his operations plans, especially when he began driving his D-8 Cat and other heavy vehicles on the Bielenberg Trail in July, 1984. The 40-mile trail was established by miners during the Gold Rush and the state laid claim to it before the preserve was created, but federal agencies refused to acknowledge the state's claim. One day National Park rangers carrying semi-automatic weapons and sidearms used a helicopter to land near Joe's Cat and surrounded him, an unusual show of force. They charged Vogler with traveling through the park without a permit, not filing a plan of operations for mining, being off the trail and damaging the tundra. The trail was one used by most miners for access to their nearby claims. When Vogler got to federal court, government witnesses claimed Joe had uprooted trees and scraped away vegetation on a long strip of the trail six feet wide. One said the damage would require 100 years to repair itself.

The judge issued a permanent injunction limiting such operations and requiring Vogler to submit detailed plans before using heavy equipment on the trail. That got Joe even angrier and his arguments for secession grew more fervid. By 1992 he and his supporters were buying full-page ads in the Anchorage and Fairbanks newspapers comparing Alaska to Lithuania and the United States to the Soviet Union. Joe looked for a national delegation to sponsor him in a speech about Alaskan independence before the United Nations General Assembly in New York. The Middle-East nation of Iran offered to sponsor his appearance at the U.N., an Iranian attempt to goad Washington.

Joe was scheduled to give his speech in the spring of 1993 but he never made the trip. When friends went to visit him on Memorial Day they found his cabin empty. The night before, Joe had dinner with another old friend and was reported in good spirits and relatively good health for an 80-year-old man. His car was in the driveway, his five dogs had not been fed or let outside, his pet goose's cage was covered with a drape he usually put in place when going to bed, his wallet and heart medication were on the kitchen table and a .44 caliber pistol lay on the bed. His .32 caliber pistol was missing, as was his gray fedora hat. Alaska State Troopers said there was no sign of a scuffle or forced entry.

Investigators were initially baffled by the disappearance and speculated that Joe might have committed suicide. They learned that he had been very morose since his wife died the previous year and he buried her in Dawson. Friends said after Doris' death Joe had slowed down. He missed her terribly and was occasionally forgetful. He talked occasionally about ending his life if he ever became terminally ill, but no such illness was known.

Vogler's friends refused to accept the suicide theory and were convinced he was murdered, perhaps by political opponents or even by some clandestine agency of the federal government. His friend and political ally Al Rowe, a former Alaska State Trooper, said Joe was dating a widow and seemed about to ask her to marry him. Rowe said Joe was thinking of building a new house on his 50-year-old homestead. He said he visited Vogler the day before his disappearance to talk about clearing some land for the new house overlooking the Tanana Valley, one more chance for Joe to drive his beloved bulldozer.

Rowe's report that Vogler was missing touched off an intensive search by large numbers of his friends and a variety of government agencies.

They covered the surrounding fields, wooded acreage and the wilderness areas nearby. Search dogs, riders on horseback, a National Guard helicopter and even dousers who ordinarily swung their pendulums and wires to find submerged water; all were looking for Joe's body.

U.S. Senator Frank Murkowski asked the Federal Bureau of Investigation to get active in the case but the agency declined since Vogler's disappearance was not a federal matter and even his murder would not have been a federal crime. Because Vogler had been such a vocal critic of all federal agencies, many speculated that his enemies in the national government had silenced him. The thought that a local Alaskan might have killed Joe for his political views was rejected since he was well-regarded even by those who disagreed with him. Asked if the FBI or the National Park Service might have assassinated Vogler, one FBI agent said defensively, "If we don't go kidnap someone like Saddam Hussein, we're certainly not going to go after Joe Vogler." (The U.S.-led coalition that invaded Iraq to depose Saddam Hussein occurred five years later.)

Vogler's friends pooled their cash to hire a private detective and placed jars in stores and offices to collect contributions to pay a reward for identification of his killer. Lynette Clark, a Fairbanks miner and secretary of the Alaskan Independence Party, said "I think it could have been somebody he knew who had a bone to pick with him." Joe's nephew Lynn Vogler, a Kansas geologist, moved to Alaska to assist in the search. "It's one of the biggest mysteries in Alaska today," Lynn told an Associated Press reporter. Young Vogler moved into his uncle's house to be close to the investigation and to care for Joe's dogs and parrot.

———————

IN OCTOBER, JUST BEFORE WINTER reached Fairbanks, an Independence Party official asked area residents to search their property one more time before snow covered the ground and brought the hunt for Vogler's body to a close. Within weeks a heavy snowfall covered the ground. That February, 100 party members attended the AIP convention in a Wasilla hotel. One table was covered with bumper stickers, T-shirts and buttons, all asking "Where's Joe?" Pictures of Vogler in his fedora were everywhere. A television played and replayed video of his many speeches. It was the first AIP party convention held without its founder.

When the snow melted in the spring, searchers took to the field again. State troopers, search dogs and a search and rescue group combed and re-combed areas where they thought Joe's body might lie. By that time they assumed his body had been buried so special attention was given to surface areas that might have been disturbed the year before. Much of the search was focused on an area known as Skoogy Gulch off the Steese Highway north of Fairbanks, so observers assumed the searchers were working from specific information about Joe's general whereabouts. Lynn Vogler told a reporter that the search area was an old mining property and contained many shafts and passageways. River searches were planned in late spring after water levels dropped.

The initial investigation was complicated by the fact that the state's top police detective, Alaska State Trooper Sergeant Jim McCann, was tied up in an intensive search in another part of Fairbanks for the unknown person who murdered 20-year-old college student Sophie Sergie in a dormitory bathroom at the University of Alaska a month earlier.

McCann's commitment to solving the Sophie Sergei murder made it difficult for him to drop that case and dig into the disappearance of Joe Vogler. McCann wanted to stick with the Sergei investigation but his superiors were worried about the publicity being given to Vogler's disappearance and wanted a man with McCann's capabilities to tackle it. McCann argued briefly with his supervisor about switching assignments but eventually gave in and dove whole-heartedly into solving the Vogler mystery.

Within weeks McCann and his team developed numerous leads about the Vogler case. In public appearances, it became obvious that McCann knew something. He told reporters that the search would continue until Joe Vogler was found, alive or dead.

He said his team was working new angles and hunches in the case. Though he gave no specifics, it was obvious his investigators were working from clues they'd developed about what happened to the fiery secessionist. Once Vogler's remains are discovered, he told a reporter, the arrest of his abductor or killer was sure to follow.

One strong hint that investigators were making progress came when Lieutenant Governor Jack Coghill announced in a Fairbanks radio talk show that Alaska State Troopers had three suspects, two from Alaska and one man in Oklahoma. Coghill said the state investigators mentioned the suspects in a progress briefing they gave to Independence Party officials.

MANFRIED WEST WAS A LONGTIME VOGLER NEIGHBOR and an artist known for his cartoons. When McCann learned that West left Alaska with an airline ticket to Oklahoma City, he knew how to find him. A year before Vogler disappeared, the Federal Bureau of Investigation organized the Safe Streets Violent Crimes Initiative, a coalition of federal, state and local investigative organizations and prosecutors. The initiative enabled the agencies to work together and bring their various specialties to bear in tracking down fugitives. McCann knew West was a biker wannabe with a flair for art. A team from the task force went to a biker bar in Oklahoma City, ordered beers and had a look around. There on the wall was a large mural of Alaska being painted by Manfried West himself.

West was then only a suspect in the Alaska murder case and couldn't be arrested so McCann and Fairbanks District Attorney Harry West developed a plan to bring him back to Alaska on still-pending forgery charges from his time there. The fugitive artist was soon captured and brought back to Alaska, but then things started to go wrong. When he reached Alaska, West was promptly sent to a rehabilitation center for various addictions. McCann heard from an informant that West had run away from the rehab center and was hiding in his stepbrother's cabin off Farmers Loop Road in Fairbanks.

McCann obtained a warrant to arrest West for escaping from the halfway house. Then he and a tactical team of six Alaska State Troopers drove to the cabin and parked a motorhome outside. Investigator Lantz Dahlke lay inside the motorhome and watched the cabin waiting for West to show himself. West started to leave by his back door, saw the approaching trooper team and ran back inside. He shouted at the officers and warned them not to come near him because he was carrying a loaded rifle and said he had explosives taped to his chest. The troopers surrounded the cabin.

When McCann saw West running back into the cabin he returned to his patrol car and used a cell phone to call West's cabin. West answered and began an extended dialogue with McCann, one that was overheard by reporters and editors listening in on a radio scanner set up in the newsroom of the Fairbanks Daily News-Miner. The reporters frantically wrote down West's comments for their next edition.

McCann's tactical team waited outside West's cabin with their guns drawn while a helicopter hovered nearby. McCann was a masterful interviewer and listened attentively as West told him about his fateful confrontation with Joe Vogler the previous year. It was a robbery that went badly.

West said he had threatened Vogler with his .22 pistol but Vogler refused to give up either his gold or his currency and ordered West to get off his property. Joe pulled his own pistol, fired a shot in the air and shouted: "I told you to get the fuck out of here, and the next one I'm blowing your head off."

Vogler then took a shot at West's truck and West fired back twice. The first shot missed and the second one hit Joe, but the light .22 bullet didn't bring him down. Vogler turned and ran but West fired again and Joe fell dying.

West told McCann he thought the sound of the shooting would bring police or Vogler's neighbors. Manfried had waited quietly, worrying, but when nobody came he loaded Joe's body into his truck and drove to Nenana. There he wrapped the body in a blue tarpaulin, sealed it with duct tape and buried it in a three-foot-deep hole.

McCann's lengthy interview with West was taking a toll on the suspect, who grew increasingly distraught. McCann tried to get him to calm down, come out of the cabin and surrender, with no luck. In mid-evening the waiting officers saw smoke and flames coming from the cabin. Twice, while it burned, West ran outside and the officers called for him to surrender. Both times he turned and ran back inside. The troopers heard several small explosions but West never emerged. Eventually firemen arrived but they remained outside because the possibility of an even larger explosion was substantial.

When the cabin's roof caved in, the firefighters went inside. They found West hiding in a small tunnel beneath a cinderblock wall, covered with soot. "It was unbelievable," McCann said. "He looked dead, but then he just started shaking."

McCann talked to West enroute to a Fairbanks hospital, hoping to learn where he had dumped Vogler's body, but he stopped talking about the case. Eventually he refused to talk at all until he met with a lawyer. Initially West said he killed Vogler when he broke into Joe's home, intending to steal some explosives Vogler was using for his mining operations, but it later came out that he was looking for drug money. As West was walking up the stairs from the basement in Vogler's home, he heard Vogler approaching with his dog. Joe had a shotgun and tried to shoot West but the gun misfired and West shot him with his pistol. West wrapped the body in a blue tarp and buried it in a gravel pit.

In mid-October, troopers went to a gravel pit east of Fairbanks where West's former cellmate said the killer had bragged about burying

Joe. A cadaver-sniffing dog pinpointed the gravesite and a little shoveling turned up a body still wrapped in its blue tarp. The body was sent to the Alaska State Crime Lab in Anchorage. Its fingerprints confirmed the corpse was Joe Vogler's.

———————

THOUGH JOE VOGLER HAD NEVER actually held public office, Governor Hickel ordered state flags lowered for three days of official mourning. Joe's friends and admirers filled a church for his funeral service. The casket was covered with a large Alaska flag and the sendoff ended with the crowd standing to sing "Alaska's Flag," the official state song.

The reason for Trooper Sergeant McCann's initial suspicions about Manfried West came out during a grand jury hearing in December, 1994. There the manager of a Fairbanks trucking company, Darlene Dokken, testified that she heard West comment two months before Joe's disappearance about a stash of gold he had seen in the basement of Vogler's house. "You should have seen the stuff he had down there," West had said to her.

"As he was talking to me," Dokken told the grand jury, "it just went through my mind: 'God, if anything ever happens to Joe Vogler, I'll call and turn (in) this guy.'"

The grand jury also learned that West had fled to Oklahoma before the Vogler murder when he was charged with forging his girlfriend's mother's checks. West stole the checks to pay a debt to a cocaine drug dealer. He returned to Alaska four days before killing Vogler. He flew back to Anchorage, borrowed a car from one friend and gas money from another. Manfried told the second friend "he had to go and do somebody" and would be erasing a debt in the process.

West showed up at the woman's house several days after Vogler disappeared, looking for several guns, some cash and a video camera he had left with her. "He was nervous," she said. "His face was real flush. He'd been sweating quite a bit."

When troopers came to her home, the woman had turned the items over. The investigators traced the camera's serial number and determined it belonged to Joe Vogler's late wife, Doris.

By that time, West had boarded a plane in Anchorage and left for Oklahoma. McCann's team tracked him down and Oklahoma police arrested him for return to Alaska. He was charged with first-degree murder, robbery and theft but his lawyer plea-bargained on his behalf and

West was convicted of second-degree murder and evidence-tampering. The judge sentenced him to 75 years in prison.

———————

JOE VOGLER WAS BURIED BESIDE HIS WIFE Doris in a Yukon Territory cemetery, carrying out their pledge never to be buried in American soil.

Manfried West has continued his artwork while in prison. The walls of the old Palmer Correctional Facility were festooned with Alaska scenes and inspirational slogans he painted on its walls. West has also tried to do some good while in prison. When he heard about an art studio in Louisville, Kentucky, near where he grew up, he sent it several paintings and suggested the owners sell them and use the money for themselves or their favorite causes. One of the paintings was of a Dall sheep and another an abandoned and snow-covered automobile.

In November, 2018 the Alaskan Independence Party still had more than 17,000 registered members though at least one columnist pointed out that the number represented less than three percent of the state's registered voters, the minimum number to be an official party.

When Joe Vogler's body was found, writer Tricia Brown spoke for many Alaskans when she told The Seattle Times: "He's important to Alaska. You could like the guy without going along with his politics."

Trooper Captain John Myers in Fairbanks said of him: "The guy is a folk hero up here. He's sort of Alaska's answer to Paul Bunyan or Pecos Bill or whatever. Everyone in town knows him or knows of him, and everyone has a Joe Vogler story." He had slicked-back gray hair and looked, as one writer put it, "like an elder Indiana Jones."

CHAPTER 10

Murder in Bartlett Hall - 1993

THE MURDER OF University of Alaska Fairbanks student Sophie Sergei, the case that Trooper Sergeant Jim McCann was forced to set aside in 1993 to work on the mysterious disappearance of Alaskan independence champion Joe Vogler, went unsolved until 2018. Late that year a team of Alaska cold case investigators matched the DNA material found in Sergei's vagina to that of a Maine man who was an 18-year-old student at UAF at that time. In February of 2019 Steven H. Downs, 44, of Auburn, Maine, was arrested and charged with sexual assault and murder in the death of the 20-year-old Fairbanks coed. The arrest came almost 26 years after Sophie's murder.

Alaska Public Safety Commissioner Amanda Price announced Downs' apprehension in an Anchorage press conference on February 15, 2019. "This arrest is the culmination of years of effort and tenacious attention by this department to solve a horrendous murder," she said. "The impact of that murder was felt statewide. The many investigators who have continued to work this case never let the loss of Sophie leave their minds." Standing near her as she spoke were members of Sophie's family.

Downs was employed as a nurse in Maine but lost his job after being disciplined for unprofessional behavior. A reprimand on his Maine nursing license notes that several female co-workers accused him of making them "uncomfortable" on the job by making inappropriate personal comments. He also made mistakes in administering medicine to patients. The Maine Board of Nursing records reported that Downs was fired from his job at a 12-bed intermediate care facility for "a totality of substandard performance." One co-worker said she saw Downs mistreat one resident in 2018, hurting the patient and making condescending comments while he was treating her wound. Another patient asked that a second professional person be present while Downs was treating her because she was "scared of him and felt he would hurt her or give her medicine she doesn't need." He was given a warning by the nursing board after completing a course called "Professional Boundaries in Nursing" and had been unemployed for about a year.

Cold Case Unit investigators for the Alaska State Troopers worked on the Sophie Sergei case sporadically over the years. They never quite got a break, even when the Alaska Scientific Crime Detection Laboratory in Anchorage ran the DNA found on Sophie against databases built with samples from known criminals. But in recent years detectives began to have some luck by running their samples against DNA databases established for people who wanted to find information about their family histories. The new data pools yielded success and people researching their predecessors sometimes provided information pointing to relatives who committed crimes and left their DNA at crime scenes over the years.

The Alaska State Troopers have cold case teams for a very good reason. Some crimes go unsolved for many years with no new leads showing up for long periods of time. But the dogged detectives of the cold case teams revisit old cases that have already been exhaustively investigated because technology changes, and so do available data pools. When a new look is taken at an old murder, and new technology and information sources are applied, in some very important cases the new look points the finger at a murderer who is living free despite committing a horrific crime.

———————

THE MURDER OF SOPHIE SERGEI was discovered at 2 p.m. on Monday, April 26, 1993 when a janitor ran screaming from a bathroom of the second- floor Bartlett Hall dormitory. The man found the young woman's body in a blood-streaked bathtub, two knife wounds in her right eye and a bullet in the back of her head, a fatal injury. Her pants and underpants had been pulled down around her ankles, her sweater and bra pushed up exposing one breast. Her cigarette lighter lay under her body. Sophie's hair and clothing were damp, indicating that the water had been run in the tub after she was placed there. An autopsy indicated she was sexually assaulted and was still alive when she suffered the stab wounds to her eye. Neither of the two weapons used in the assault, the instrument used to inflict the stab wounds and the gun, could be found.

The screaming janitor grabbed a passerby in the hallway and dragged him back to the bloody scene in the tub. The janitor then stood guard while the second person notified police, who raced to Bartlett Hall and were soon swarming over the dorm. The building was then half-empty due to the completion of many courses and departure of some students for their summer break. Those near the murder scene could tell from what the officers were saying to each other that someone had been found dead in the bathroom.

Students had been in and out of the bathroom all day without spotting Sophie's body in the adjoining tub room. She wasn't found until the janitor walked by the sinks and shower stalls and opened the door to the more private room equipped with a single bathtub. Word of the discovery and rumors about the frightening murder spread quickly among students still in the dorm, leaving them shocked and traumatized. Journalism student Jen Roy told the Fairbanks Daily News-Miner "I stood there for a long time. I was thinking this couldn't be happening." Student Tara Hotrum nervously played a Gameboy outside the dorm, her hands trembling. She told the reporter "I'm supposed to be studying, but I can't really put myself in the thinking mode."

———

SOPHIE WAS A VERY BRIGHT STUDENT majoring in marine biology. She attended college on a full-ride scholarship from the major oil company, British Petroleum, but had taken that spring semester off to work as a teacher's assistant near her home in the Yupik village of Pitkas Point, a community of about 150 people 525 miles southwest of Fairbanks. Sophie also took a second job as a clerk in the village of St. Mary's near Pitkas Point. She was an intelligent, hard-working, respectable young woman.

Sophie was in her third year of college and wore braces on her teeth. She took the work break to raise money for some orthodontic work, including having her braces adjusted and progress checked. Whenever she went to Fairbanks, she had to take a flight from Pitkas Point south to Bethel, then a hop east to Anchorage before the final northbound leg to

Fairbanks. It was a long and roundabout trip but not an unusual one for Alaska. Patients in rural Alaska must often travel great distances to see a dental or medical specialist. While in Fairbanks she stayed on campus with one of her best friends from Pitkas Point, Shirley Wasuli. Shirley lived in Bartlett Hall so Sophie often took the opportunity to visit her friends and classmates on campus.

The night of Sophie's death, she and three friends had watched a movie, then took a drive to the Murphy Dome Recreation Area. Afterward they returned to Bartlett Hall, where Sophie joined Shirley and her boyfriend, Noah Taylor. A little after midnight, Sophie said she was headed outside to smoke a cigarette. Shirley cautioned that the weather outside was cold and Sophie might prefer to smoke in the shower room. She could huddle near the exhaust fan to keep smoke out of the building. Shirley departed to spend the night with Noah in another dormitory.

Shirley returned to her dorm room the next morning and was irritated to find its door unlocked and Sophie gone. The bed was still made, suggesting that Sophie had not slept in the room and a note telling Sophie where she and Noah had gone was still attached to the door. Those discoveries worried Shirley and made her wonder if Sophie's seeming carelessness might be something more ominous. She looked around the dormitory and commons area but could find no sign of Sophie. Later she called the orthodontist and learned that Sophie had not showed up for her appointment, information that really made Shirley worry about what might have befallen her friend.

PEOPLE HAD BEEN GOING IN AND OUT of the bathroom all day but the tub in which Sophie's body lay was in a small room off the main area of the bathroom. Police later determined that the dead girl had been lying in the bathtub for approximately 13 hours. They estimated she was killed sometime between 1 and 5 a.m. that morning.

The crime scene was difficult to analyze for clues pointing to a suspect. In Bartlett Hall men and women were segregated by floors but students were generally free to move from one floor to another, as well as to other dorms, and often used whatever bathrooms were closest. When men used a women's bathroom it sometimes created conflicts, but the problems were tolerated.

One puzzling aspect of the case was that, despite the fact that Sophie was killed by a gunshot in the middle of the night, nobody in Bartlett or either of the other two dorms in the complex heard anything. When the initial investigation was ramped up, final exams were already under way or completed. Since many students had already left campus, some never to return, interviewing possible witnesses was problematic. The three dormitories in the complex housed a total of 670 students. And visiting non-students had free access to the three buildings as well.

Detectives worked at Bartlett Hall until 9 p.m. that evening, interviewing residents and carefully searching the tiled bathroom and the tub room where Sophie had met her fate. They swept and vacuumed up fibers, hairs and other physical evidence and took samples of semen from Sophie's body. One girl said she had been in the shower room that afternoon and heard some noise from the tub room, both thumping and muffled voices, but the sound was only loud enough to tell her that someone was in there.

In 1993 the science of DNA testing had not yet been perfected and there was no national DNA database. But crime scene analysts routinely preserved any DNA they found for future reference. Opportunity lay in the future.

The DNA sample was run on the newly developed database in the late 1990s and then again in May 2000, but it didn't match any in the national database nor any of the potential suspects in the case.

University Chancellor Joan Wadlow ordered flags flown at half-staff in Sophie's memory and more than 300 people attended a memorial service in the university's Constitution Park. An enlarged photo of Sophie's smiling face sat on a table covered by a white cloth and surrounded by roses, daisies and snapdragons. Professor James Nageak, an Alaska Native professor, led the service in his Inupiat language and Native drummers performed. University President Jerome Komisar noted in his remarks that death had no boundaries and violence no limits. "She brought with her the wisdom of 1,000 years and a vision for the future," he said.

———————

THE COLD-CASE UNIT OF THE ALASKA STATE TROOPERS was established in 2002 at a time when there were 101 unsolved murders on their books, killings that took place between 1961 and 2001. In 2007, retired Trooper Lieutenant Jim Stogsdill, a Soldotna resident and summertime fishing guide on the Kenai River, joined the investigation and picked up on a suggestion by an independent forensic investigator that re-energized the case. The forensics expert told Stogsdill that, since nobody in or near

Bartlett Hall had heard a shot in the second-floor bathroom, perhaps the girl had been killed somewhere else and her body dragged to the bathroom afterward. That raised many more possibilities for the location of the crime scene, new avenues to investigate and new people to interview. One of the more difficult aspects of that assignment was tracking down people who had been living in that dormitory 14 years earlier. The investigators had the names and old addresses but locating the individuals was a major undertaking.

Sophie was last seen smoking a cigarette with a group of people in front of Hess Commons, which adjoins the three dormitories on UAF's upper campus. Stogsdill noted that Sophie had not been drinking or hitting the bars. She had been doing nothing dangerous, nothing that might trigger violence.

"Sophie was truly a victim," he said. When a friend asked her to pose for a picture in her brightly striped sweater, Sophie threw her arms wide and flashed a wide grin, a notable last photo of a happy and friendly young woman.

By 2007 memorial services for Sophie and other victims of unsolved murders were being held annually on the campus. And that year Sophie's mother Elena and family friend Leslie Hunter attended. Leslie told a reporter that Elena Sergei very much needed emotional support in her daughter's murder.

"She needs closure," Hunter said in a tearful interview. "I live with her, and she's hard to live with sometimes."

"Because of it," Elena interjected.

"There's anger in her yet," Hunter added.

Cold case investigator Lindy Minnick said the case was complicated and interviews were difficult to obtain because the university's student rosters were inaccurate. She said students reported there had been a lot of shifting around and those listed as residing in a room might not be there at all and could be living elsewhere on or even off the campus entirely. The dorm had not been locked down after the body was discovered, so finding signs of a struggle was difficult and none were found. She said the killer was probably someone who lived in one of the dorms and would easily blend in with the other students.

THINGS CHANGED AT THE UNIVERSITY after Sophie Sergei's shocking murder. Father Jim Kolb, a priest at St. Mark's Church, observes that it had been a turning point for the worse. Before Sophie's murder, he said, "the campus had a much more open spirit. There was much more communal interchange. A sense of freshness. A sense of youthfulness. A lot of that came apart after the murder of Sophie Sergei."

Father Kolb said that the campus became "an armed camp," a problem that persisted for several years.

Sophie was buried in the Pitkas Point community cemetery next to her grandmother. When her mother Elena laid flowers on the grave she said her daughter's death seemed to be a dream from which she would someday awake. "For me," Elena said, "she's just away somewhere and she'll be coming home soon."

The Fairbanks Crime Stoppers organization offered a $20,000 reward for information leading to the arrest and conviction of Sophie's murderer. At the university, the campus security organization began offering round-the-clock escort services for students traveling between dormitories and classrooms. An attempt to name the university's new Student Recreation Facility after Sophie failed because people felt it would be inappropriate to tie such a sad event to a building intended to improve morale.

When cold-case funding ran out and Jim Stogsdill had to close out the unsolved Sophei Sergei murder case, his file consisted of 14 volumes of notebooks and three to four boxes of reference materials he and his colleagues had collected over the years. Stogsdill estimated it would take a new investigator six months to read through the entire file and study all of the reference materials. If somehow a new tip came in to one of the still-active state trooper investigators, the officer would have to do that onerous review just to be able to evaluate the importance of the tip.

"It's been one of the larger mysteries," said Alaska State Troopers spokeswoman Beth Ipsen. "This is a true whodunit."

Included in Jim Stogsdill's file was the report of a cold-case investigator who was re-interviewing residents of Bartlett Hall living there at the time of Sophie's murder. The officer talked to Nicholas Dazer, who shared a room on a third floor, one of the men-only floors in the eight-story building. It was one floor above the spot where Sophie's body was found. Dazer was re-interviewed after investigators learned that he had been working as a UAF security guard—and helped secure the murder scene—but was later fired for possessing a firearm in the dormitory.

The investigator asked Dazer if, when he was living in Bartlett, he had owned a gun that fired .22 caliber ammunition. Dazer said he had not but his roommate, Steven Downs, owned a .22 revolver and several other guns. Though interesting, that lead apparently wasn't followed up before cold-case funding ran out. Downs was a student at the University of Alaska Fairbanks from 1992 to 1996.

One of Stogsdill's most difficult chores came in 2015 when funding ended for the cold-case work and he had to tell Sophie's mother Elena that the search for Sophie's killer would have to end. And one of the questions that bothered Stogsdill most was how a woman could be shot in a dormitory with people on every floor without having anyone hear or see anything. Closure of the cold-case program put some top investigators out of their part-time retirement occupations, including Stogsdill of Soldotna, James Gallen and Randel McPherron in Anchorage, and Lantz Dahlke in Fairbanks. Together the retired detectives had 130 years of valuable experience and were working on more than 100 unsolved crimes. Their cases were assigned to active investigators but those officers were busy patrolling and working with fresh evidence in recent cases and had little time available to devote to the older crimes.

———

IN 1994 SOPHIE'S MOTHER FILED a $4 million lawsuit against the University of Alaska alleging that poor security had led to the girl's death. According to one online report, shortly before the murder the university had cut down on the use of front desk dormitory attendants as a cost-saving measure. The student rooms could be accessed by simply walking through the front door. Around the time of Sophie's murder a drunken and naked man was found in one of the women's bathrooms. And reports of violence toward women were rising.

The lawsuit failed in court but police were convinced it had gotten in the way of the investigation. Lieutenant Lantz Dahlke, a member of the cold-case team working the case, said "there was a lot of information released in the civil suit that never should have been released to the public." He said the information should have been sealed and made available only to officers working on the Sergei case. Dahlke said the killer "holds the key and if he knows what we hold, he is more likely to protect what we don't hold."

"Only those crucial witnesses who hold one piece of what happened and the actual player who holds all pieces should be the ones with this kind of information," he added. "It's our job to come together as puzzle-masters to put the pieces together. When we put the pieces together, we may not have a full picture of what happened, but the person who knows the missing details . . . is the bad guy."

Trooper Sergeant Jim McCann said Sophie's murderer was probably a UAF student who left the campus after killing her. He said she likely did not know her murderer and was a random choice for a victim. Sophie was what the homicide detectives considered a "low-risk" murder victim. She did not have a boyfriend, nobody was stalking her, she had no known enemies and she wasn't being stalked by anyone. No one had seen Sophie with a man or noticed anything unusual about her behavior. McCann said the victim "could have been any one of those girls. He told a reporter for the Fairbanks Daily News-Miner that Sophie "was just in the wrong place at the wrong time. Whoever did this is very, very angry at women . . . and is likely to have fantasized about committing similar acts. The killer thought enough ahead to bring a gun." McCann said several good leads were developed during the investigation. Based on that information, he said, there was a 50 percent chance that the killer had already left the Fairbanks area, either because of graduation or summer vacation. McCann said it was highly likely the murderer was a UAF student. He asked the public's help by reporting anyone who showed unusual or frightening changes in behavior after returning from the university.

Dave Sperbeck, a forensic psychologist and director of mental health at the Alaska Department of Corrections told the News-Miner that whoever committed the crime may have "psychological problems to convert frustration and rage into sexuality. That is an addiction that he can't control. My feeling is, whoever sexually assaulted Sophie had done it before and will do it again." He said some mentally warped attackers can go a long time before striking again, but they always have another in mind. They fantasize, he said, feeding on pornography and memories of past crimes.

Investigator Jim Stogsdill put out a request for information for anyone who might have been in front of Hess Commons outside Bartlett Hall when Sophie was there smoking with her friends.

The unsolved murder of Sophie Sergei reached a national stage when Alaska Senator Lisa Murkowski referred to it while responding to a 2018 report by the Urban Indian Health Institute. The report focused on the alarming number of missing and murdered indigenous women and the lack of adequate data to combat the violence.

When Steven Downs was arrested and placed in Maine's Androscoggin County Jail before being returned to Fairbanks in May, 1993, a string of bloggers wrote notes of joy, especially those who had gone to school with Sophie. "I knew Sophie," noted Christy Morris. "We were in the same dorm freshman year. She was killed a week before my birthday and her death still haunts me. My prayers and love to her family. One day justice will be served to whoever did this."

A woman named Ethel wrote: "I knew Sophie from Academic Decathlon in high school when we met in Anchorage for competition, even then she was a powerful albeit tiny young woman. She was a peer that was academically and socially stellar. We met again when we entered as freshmen at UAF when she lived in Wickersham (a dormitory). She would have been a shining star for UAF, Alaska and women. Her death has troubled me for 20 years (I was 1,000 miles away when she was taken and it was shocking then).

"I hope that Sophie's death can be solved. I don't think anyone really understands what a loss her death is to the world. It was a violent act not just against Sophie, perhaps targeted because she was that wonderful, but against us all."

Heath E. Hilyard wrote "I remember it like it was yesterday. It was odd to know I had been one floor down when she was murdered."

IN 2017 THE ALASKA STATE TROOPERS revived cold-case investigations and assigned retired Trooper Randy McPherron, a homicide detective, to delve into inactive crime files. The following April, McPherron heard about California investigators using genetic genealogy to find and arrest Joseph James DeAngelo, the serial murderer known as the Golden State Killer. DeAngelo is believed to have committed at least 13 murders, 50 rapes and 100 burglaries between 1974 and 1986. He was arrested after investigators ran his DNA on a family-research database.

Genetic genealogy is the program used by people researching their family trees with DNA databases assembled for the purpose of finding the names of noteworthy ancestors. The databases contain information on an estimated 1.4 million individuals. Using the genetic genealogy DNA files in criminal investigations has proven to be very fruitful, pointing the genetic finger at dozens of suspects in cold cases. The technique raised a host of privacy concerns that had not yet been addressed.

McPherron dug out the DNA data from the old Sophie Sergei case and asked a forensic genealogist at Parabon Nanolabs in Virginia to run it against a genealogy DNA database. Parabon had already worked on most of the cold cases cracked using genealogical databases, including the Golden State Killer case. The man ran his test of materials found on Sophie's body on December 18, 2018. The effort came up with a close match, that of a woman who proved to be Steven Downs' aunt, a woman who had voluntarily submitted her own DNA to gain information about her family tree. Downs, then 44, is the former UAF student whose roommate said he owned a .22 revolver in 1993 when they both were freshmen living in Bartlett Hall a floor above the tub room where Sophie's body was found. Eyewitnesses placed him in the dormitory on the night Bonnie was killed.

Downs was born in Maine and graduated from high school there in 1992, when he left to attend the University of Alaska in Fairbanks. When finally discovered in the search for Sophie's murder he was living in Auburn, Maine, and had never been arrested for anything. He also had never had his own DNA tested and likely knew nothing about his aunt's personal experiment in genealogical research.

Maine State Police visited Downs' home with a search warrant, took a cheek swab for a DNA sample and had it tested by the Maine State Crime Laboratory against the sample from Sophie's body. The Maine crime lab came back with its report in less than 24 hours. It showed Downs was an exact match to the man who killed her and strongly suggested that he was indeed the long-sought killer.

UAF Chancellor Dan White issued a statement about the arrest in Maine, saying "Sophie's tragic death was a heartbreaking loss for her family and friends. It sent shock waves throughout our university and local community, and challenged our sense of security. While today's news is a step toward justice for Sophie and her family, it is also a reminder of a traumatic chapter in our community's history. If you are struggling with this news, please reach out for help."

HIS LAWYER ARGUED THAT DOWNS couldn't have done the crime; he was a peaceable pet-loving, mild-mannered, caring man with a clean record. Maine Governor Janet Mills signed the warrant for his arrest.

The Fairbanks News-Miner reported that Downs was arrested outside the Auburn, Maine, inn where he was staying by officers of the Maine State Police Tactical Team accompanied by two members of the Alaska cold-case team and several members of the Auburn police force. He was held in Auburn's Androscoggin County Jail while the case worked its way through the Alaska and Maine legal systems and was transported back to

Alaska in May to await trial.

When interviewed about Sophie's murder, Downs told investigators "I remember the pictures; it's terrible, poor girl." He said he had been in his girlfriend's fourth-floor room on the night of the murder and said he thought soldiers from nearby Fort Wainwright might have killed her. He said soldiers from the base were often in the building. Downs added that if he knew anything about the murder he would have been "forthright from the jump," and added "I never knew or saw anything to begin with."

Downs lived in Alaska for several years after graduating from UAF. Afterward he moved to Arizona and lived there for several years before returning to Maine to work as a nurse. He was arrested and charged 26 years after Sophie Sergei was murdered.

Lewiston, Maine lawyer Jim Howaniec, Downs' attorney appointed by a Maine court, noted of Sophie's killing: "This is a rage crime, this is an allegation of violent sexual assault, followed by a stabbing and gunshot to the head. This is completely out of the character of this individual who is highly intelligent."

Elena Sergei attended the February, 2019, news conference where the arrest of Steven Downs was announced. She was obviously emotionally distraught, appeared unable to stand and sat exhausted in a wheeled office chair. Afterward, Colonel Barry Wilson, director of Alaska State Troopers, helped Elena's son Stephen wheel his weeping mother out of the room.

Wilson said at a press conference: "Through their dogged persistence, advances in technology and the spirit of co-operation exhibited by each agency that touched this case, justice for Sophie is finally within reach. While an arrest doesn't bring Sophie back, we are relieved to provide this closure. This case has haunted and frustrated Sophie's family and friends, the investigators and beyond. However, we did it. Investigators never gave up on Sophie. I am both honored and humbled to help bring some closure to Sophie's family."

The Washington Post noted in its report on the news conference that the arrest of Sophie Sergei's killer resolved what was then one of the state's most notorious cold cases.

Downs appeared in a Maine courtroom on February 19 and stood silently in handcuffs. His defense attorney, Richard Charest, contested the extradition request from Alaska and claimed that police had arrested the wrong guy. "This is a very old allegation, your honor. He thinks there must be some mistake." Charest said his client would not voluntarily return to Alaska. "He doesn't want to go back to Alaska. He feels like he shouldn't have to go back to Alaska and he feels like he's innocent of the allegations."

A Maine prosecutor countered that "We have received a DNA sample from those sperm cells (referring to the semen found on Sophie's body). "We've got a DNA sample from the defendant and the Maine state crime lab says those are a match." Downs was ruled a fugitive from justice and ordered held without bail.

Downs' arrest and the national attention it brought was a shock to his neighbors in Auburn, a town of about 20,000 people. "Auburn is a pretty quiet town usually," one man said, "so it's just surprising. I just looked in the paper and said, 'Oh gosh, he's from Auburn.'"

Another added: "In this day and age, nothing surprises me—anybody can be from anywhere and you never know what their past is." People living near Downs' home said they hoped his arrest would give some emotional relief for Sophie's family and achieve justice after so many years of unrelieved mourning. "It's unfortunate and I feel for the parents," one neighbor said.

CHAPTER 11

A Motivated Mother - 1994

WHEN AN UNKNOWN MAN killed Bonnie Craig, he unleashed a force that changed criminal justice systems across America, Bonnie's mother.

Karen Foster was sure her daughter had been murdered even before she spoke to the Alaska State Trooper who tracked her down in Florida. The trooper sergeant and others investigating Bonnie's death said it was a tragic accident, a fall from a cliff. But Karen knew Bonnie had been murdered. Nothing else made sense.

Bonnie was 18 years old when she left her Anchorage home at five a.m. on September 28, 1994 for the two-and-a-half mile walk to the bus station on Lake Otis Parkway, a 45-minute hike. There she would catch a ride to her seven a.m. class at the University of Alaska Anchorage. Bonnie was a freshman and started college studies a few weeks before. She intended to study psychology as her major and a possible career.

Shortly after two p.m. a young woman stopped at McHugh Creek for a short hike. When she reached the base of a cliff she looked in the water and did a double-take. A human body was floating face down in the creek. The shocked woman ran back to her car, raced to a weigh station phone and called Alaska State Troopers.

Bonnie was a conscientious young woman already dating the man she intended to marry. Cameron Mayasaki started his own classes at the University of California at Berkeley two months earlier and the two worried about maintaining a long-distance relationship. When they were last together at the ghost town of Portage in July, Bonnie gave Cameron a ring. "I guess it was sort of a promise ring," he said, "that we would be together."

On the way home from Portage they stopped at McHugh Creek, a popular hiking and picnic area 10 miles down a scenic byway south of Anchorage. "We sat on some rocks and watched the sun and talked," he said. "We were very serious about one another. We were very much in love, just talking about the future." The two young lovers kept in close contact for the rest of Bonnie's short life, using email and a computer chat program.

When Cameron talked about their relationship in a courtroom, he cried, something he'd been doing a lot since the day she died. He talked about sneaking Bonnie into his house the night before leaving for Berkeley. They cried a lot together and stayed awake all night. His drive to the airport next day was one of the saddest of his life.

―――――――

WHEN THE ALASKA STATE TROOPERS began looking for her, Bonnie's mother, Karen Foster, was on a chartered sailboat off southern Florida with her boyfriend Jim Foster. The two had flown from Anchorage to Jim's old stomping grounds just two days before. Bonnie was then living at the home of Karen's ex-husband, Gary Campbell, where the 18-year-old could have a room of her own while still in school. Space at Karen's home was limited and a teenager's privacy needs were more difficult to accommodate there. Gary had been a primary caregiver for Bonnie since she was about age three.

Karen and Jim's trip had temporarily stalled when the sailboat ran aground on an oyster bed near a popular Florida restaurant, Posey's Oyster Bar. They fell asleep waiting for the tide to come in. When the rising water lifted the boat, they restarted the engine and motored to a nearby marina where they were to meet Jim's younger brother Ken and Ken's bride-to-be, Valeri.

After a pleasant evening with Ken and Valeri, the visitors left while Karen and Jim bedded down on the boat. At three a.m. they awoke to a knock on the companionway door. It was Ken, his face anguished and eyes misting. "What is it?" Karen asked fearfully.

"It's Bonnie," Ken said. "She was in a hiking accident."

Karen didn't believe it. Bonnie would be in school, not hiking. "Who told you that?"

Ken held out a Post-It Note. "I'm so sorry," he said. "An Alaska State Trooper called me." Karen hesitated to take the note. She knew the information would be devastating. She reached for and unfolded the ominous yellow sheet. It contained only the trooper's name and phone number.

She and Ken got dressed and hurried to a pay station near the dockmaster's office. Karen tried to dial the trooper's number but her hands shook so much that Jim took over and made the call. He handed her the phone and rubbed her back while she waited for the trooper to answer.

"Hello, this is Sergeant Mike Marrs of the Alaska State Troopers," the voice said. "Is this Karen Campbell, Bonnie Craig's mom?"

"Yes."

"I'm sorry to have to tell you this, Mrs. Campbell. Bonnie's body was found out at McHugh Creek. She fell off a cliff, Mrs. Campbell. She's dead. I'm very sorry."

Karen was a volunteer reserve officer with the Anchorage Police Department. She was naturally suspicious so her detective training and instincts kicked in. "Who was she with?"

"No one, Mrs. Campbell. She was out there alone."

"How did she get there? She doesn't drive, so how?" Karen kept hoping the sergeant was wrong, that it wasn't Bonnie.

"We don't know, ma'am."

"What time did you find her?"

"About 2:30 this afternoon."

"No, she would have been in class. She'd never miss. How did you identify her?"

"Her name was on a class ring." Marrs said they had looked up her state ID. "We identified her from that picture."

"Could she have been raped?" Karen asked.

"No, Mrs. Campbell. All her clothes were on. Nothing was ripped or torn. All her buttons were done up, as was her zipper."

"That doesn't mean somebody wasn't raped."

Karen mentioned that she was a volunteer with the APD and her team had recently been involved in a major drug bust. She wondered if the narcotics gang might have been taking retribution. "Maybe they thought it was me," she said. "Bonnie looks just like me."

"No, Mrs. Campbell. She died from a fall off a cliff. It was over 30 feet, ma'am. I'm very sorry."

Karen's suspicions were influenced and compounded by the sometimes contentious relationship between the local police department and Alaska State Troopers. She was sure the state officers must be wrong. "If it's Bonnie, it's not a hiking accident," she said. "It's got to be murder."

"No ma'am," the sergeant insisted. "It was a hiking accident. If it were an act of retribution they would have used guns. Or there would have been duct tape, something binding her. This wasn't murder or rape, Mrs. Campbell. I'm afraid it was just a tragic accident. She fell from a great height."

Karen asked if the troopers collected evidence from the scene. Marrs said there was no evidence to collect. They had found her class ring but that was all. "There's nothing else to look for, I'm afraid." Though the trooper sergeant didn't tell Karen at the time, his investigators had been combing a 40-mile stretch of the highway between Anchorage and Girdwood, checking all turnouts, trash containers, culverts and road-sides along the way.

"I'm in Florida," Karen replied. "I'll be on the next plane back."

She hung up and Jim called to make return reservations while Karen struggled to comprehend how her beloved daughter could be dead, especially under such unlikely circumstances. Bonnie would never have done something so irresponsible. She would not have skipped her UAA classes, especially for a capricious outing at an unlikely place. Bonnie was young and sometimes made mistakes of the young, but this was very unlike her. It was not a diversion she would have chosen for herself.

Karen called her ex-husband, Gary, and learned that he and Bonnie's two siblings had been notified by a team of state troopers who knocked on the door at 10 p.m. accompanied by a police chaplain. They were already worried since it was long past time for Bonnie to be home—and she hadn't called. When Gary saw the look on the troopers' faces he knew the news would be bad and thought briefly about shooing the kids into another room. The officers took Gary out on the porch and told him that Bonnie was dead; Gary fell to his knees. The officers helped him up and then returned with him to tell the other children. Gary stood beside them as Adam and Samantha sat at the kitchen table and listened horrified to the officers' words.

Karen and Jim were met at the Anchorage International Airport terminal by Police Chaplain Bert McQueen and Trooper Sergeant Marrs. When her old friend Chaplain McQueen expressed his sorrow that Bonnie had died in such a tragic accident, Karen snapped: "It was not an accident."

Sergeant Marrs asked her to come to the funeral home to identify her daughter. When they reached Gary's house, Karen's two surviving children were waiting. They threw themselves into her arms, weeping.

Then the couple drove to the funeral home and watched in horror as an attendant pulled a sheet away from Bonnie's face. It was indeed her daughter. She could no longer refuse to believe.

As she stared at her daughter's pale visage, Karen Campbell immediately chose a new life role for herself. She was certain Bonnie was murdered and vowed to prove it, to expend whatever time, energy and resources it took to prove that Bonnie had been killed by another human being and somehow to bring that person to justice.

Karen rattled off questions for the troopers. She knew Bonnie would have been carrying her book bag and keys, with a pepper spray tube attached to the key chain. She wanted to know if the pepper spray had been used. If so a residue would be on her body and any items used by her killer. The spray was oily and even the cold waters of McHugh Creek would not have washed it off. Her book bag and keys had not been found, but detectives told Karen there was no evidence a pepper spray container had discharged. She asked for details on the discovery of Bonnie's body.

———

BACK AT GARY'S HOUSE she was deluged with calls from Anchorage news media. Karen had once worked as a television news reporter and understood how they worked, what they needed and how to generate interest in her opinion on how her daughter came to be found dead in a creek. They came to her home for interviews and she told all that she disagreed with the state troopers and was convinced her daughter's death was no accident.

The children wanted to see Bonnie, so the family returned to the funeral home the following day. Karen took Bonnie's hand and clasped it to her forehead. Then she noticed something very strange; Bonnie's knuckles were swollen and broken. She slid the sheet down her daughter's side and saw extensive bruising on her arms.

"Get the troopers back in here," Karen demanded. "These are defensive wounds."

The funeral director asked about arrangements but Karen refused to discuss them, insisting that first the troopers return and look at the injuries on her daughter's body. She called the troopers herself and told them about the injuries while her family checked Bonnie's body themselves and saw the marks she described. Karen called her co-workers at the Anchorage Police Department and asked them to intervene in the investigation; they declined because the troopers had jurisdiction. McHugh Creek was outside the boundaries of APD's patrol area.

When the family left the funeral home they were surrounded by television and newspaper reporters who had updated information on the case and wanted new interviews. The case was being widely accepted as a murder but that raised many new questions about who might have killed Bonnie, when and how.

———————

THE NEXT DAY, TROOPER SERGEANT MARRS met with Karen and told her that his detectives had indeed discovered the evidence of injury on Bonnie's body. The coroner had also found male semen in her body. But they were sticking to the accident story for public consumption in hopes that someone with evidence might come forward, someone who would be deterred by the knowledge that police were already investigating it as a homicide. At that point the public was still unaware that Bonnie's backpack, keys, calculator, wallet and pepper spray on a keyring were all missing. He wanted it to stay that way so the killer would not consider them evidence of what he or she had done and dispose of them. He asked Karen to back off from her publicity campaign. Marrs requested that Karen pretend to believe that Bonnie's death might have been an accident though that cat was already out of the bag.

Marrs asked Karen to trust that the troopers knew what they were doing and were doing the right thing.

"So you are investigating it as a murder?" She said.

"We're investigating all possibilities."

"Then you agree it wasn't an accident?"

"It's an investigation, Karen." Marrs said media involvement would only complicate the troopers' problems and hamper their work.

"We're concerned about you trying to take the investigation into your own hands. It isn't a good idea for you to be calling Bonnie's death murder when we have no evidence to support that statement."

"No evidence?" Karen countered. "What about broken knuckles and bruised arms? That's not evidence?"

"Look at it this way," Marrs said. "The more the media knows and talks about, the less likely it is that someone will give us what we need to solve this case. We didn't want the media to get wind of the fact that Bonnie's backpack and keys were missing, because once they get that bit of a story, obviously they're going to try to get the rest of it, and that may hinder our efforts."

The sergeant said they were investigating it as a possible murder but it was also possible that Bonnie's death was an accident. Though Karen complained about the department's slow-motion approach to the investigation, Marrs asked her to be patient and allow the investigators to do their job and for the process to play itself out.

Marrs said he wanted Karen, her ex-husband and Bonnie's stepfather Gary, their son Adam and daughter Samantha to come into police headquarters to be fingerprinted and DNA samples taken. He said Karen and her remaining two children were not suspects, but if he asked Gary alone—who was a potential suspect—to come in Gary might get suspicious and lawyer up.

Karen worried the experience at police headquarters might be traumatic for the kids, especially if they learned that the treatment they were given was for potential suspects. Marrs suggested that Karen deal with the kids. When she did they said they were fine with it. As they were leaving the station Marrs called Karen aside and told her Gary had been eliminated as a suspect because witnesses, including her children, had seen him in other places at critical times. The children saw him scraping ice off his car windshield at 7 a.m. and his co-workers saw him at the office throughout the morning.

Five undercover police officers attended Bonnie's funeral, mingling with the crowd in hopes they might spot her murderer, but the effort yielded no results. The next day Karen retraced the steps Bonnie took on her daily walk to the bus station and was appalled at its length, thinking Bonnie had kept that bit of information to herself for fear of having to move from Gary's house. One of Bonnie's close friends had been killed in a drunk driving accident, an emotional event that deterred Bonnie from learning to drive. Enroute to the bus station Karen had an encounter with an aggressive moose that chased her slowly around a light pole twice before retreating when a pickup truck drove up to help.

————————

KAREN'S FAMILY LIFE HAD ALWAYS BEEN COMPLICATED, with three marriages, divorces and a new life with boyfriend Jim Foster. Both Karen and ex-husband Gary were originally from Canada, she from Calgary and he from a small town on Prince Edward Island. When discussing funeral arrangements, Gary said he wanted to bury Bonnie in his hometown on PEI but Karen was adamant she be interred in Anchorage. They also argued over who got which of Bonnie's meager possessions.

Difficulty then arose with the funeral parlor, which wanted to be paid far more than Karen could put together in her diminished financial circumstances, and nobody offered to help.

Karen's persistence in demanding information about her daughter's murder was a constant irritation to the investigators so, in hopes of diverting her energies, Marrs suggested she reach out to Janice Lienhart at *Victims for Justice*, a non-profit advocacy group formed by Lienhart, whose parents and aunt were killed by a young couple who murdered them for thrills. *Victims for Justice* had won a place at the legal table for the relatives of crime victims, people whom the justice system came to understand as victims themselves. Lienhart's group promoted and won an amendment to the state constitution establishing victims' families as victims under the law.

When Karen called *Victims for Justice*, Janice Lienhart answered and said: "Why don't you come down for a chat? I'd really like to meet you. We have a lot in common." Karen met Janice and listened fascinated as she told her own story and about the voter-approved constitutional amendment her group won to give victims standing and a voice in the legal system. She was enthralled by the way Lienhart turned tragedy into a personal cause that brought important change to the way the families of crime victims were treated by the courts. Karen went away determined that she would use her own experience to work for changes that would benefit others.

With help from Lienhart and other volunteers, Karen launched a campaign involving signs, bumper stickers and posters demanding to know "Who killed Bonnie Craig?" The campaign materials were placed throughout Anchorage and supported by calls to news media, interviews, articles, and radio and television pieces asking the public for information on Bonnie's murder. The campaign was highly visible to anyone living in the Anchorage area at that time.

One volunteer and her husband offered to help with publicity and launched a drive asking for funds to pay a reward to anyone bringing information on the case. Sandy Cassidy had a degree in journalism and public communications, and was a frequent volunteer with Habitat for Humanity. Her husband Maurice was a skilled and helpful partner. With their help and Lienhart's, Karen was able to launch and sustain a high-visibility campaign that repeatedly asked the community "*Who Killed Bonnie?*" The volunteers kept the question on the public's mind for many months—few who lived there could go unaware of it—but nobody came forward. The reward total eventually reached $50,000 but went unclaimed.

In early January, more than three months after Bonnie's death, Janice Lienhart called Sergeant Marrs and got permission for Karen to review the autopsy report. Karen and Janice went to Marrs office and met Dr. Norman Thompson, the medical examiner who wrote the autopsy report. Near the top of the page were the words: "*Manner of Death - Homicide.*" It was the first time she had seen official acknowledgement that Bonnie had been murdered and that troopers were investigating it as such. She also realized that the investigators had considered it a homicide since virtually the beginning.

"There is only one piece of positive news that comes out of this," Thompson said. "Whoever did this to your daughter left behind his DNA." Thompson said the killer's semen, containing his unique genetic code, had been found in Bonnie's vagina and on her clothes.

The public relations campaign developed by Karen and her new friends continued unabated. Three years after it started the signs changed to the words: *Someone is getting away with murder*, a wistful reminder that the case needed to be reinvestigated and the killer identified.

———

BONNIE'S MURDER WENT UNSOLVED for 12 years but Karen's work never stopped. Then in January 2007 Karen was on vacation with a female friend in the Philippines when she checked her email and found a heart-pounding message with a subject line that just said: *Bonnie.* Her eyes swept downward.

Karen, my name is Tim Hunyor, and I am an investigator with the Alaska State Troopers, Cold Case Unit. I know that you are out of the country, but it is important that I talk to you, as we have new developments in Bonnie's case.

Can you please call me or send me a telephone number where I can reach you.

Karen ran to the front desk, borrowed a phone and tried to call Hunyor but the call failed to go through. She returned to her room and sent him an email. Karen and her friend went to the shore and were sitting in beach chairs when her laptop pinged. It was a note from Hunyor:

. . . we have some information about an individual that is in prison in New Hampshire and we are trying to do some background on him. I would like to talk with you and let you know what we have so far.

Despite the sporadic phone communications, Karen and Trooper Hunyor were able to email and she learned that the semen found in

Bonnie's body had been entered into a national database several years before and a match had finally been found with Kenneth Dion, a federal prisoner in New Hampshire. Dion had been in the military and assigned to Fort Richardson in Anchorage at the time of Bonnie's murder. He was in prison in New Hampshire after being arrested there for robbery.

Hunyor and State Trooper Merlin D. Ehlers had flown to New Hampshire and interviewed Dion. The suspect said he remembered publicity about the case but, when shown a photo of Bonnie, denied ever meeting her. He said his wife would have killed him if he fooled around. Dion admitted he was a martial arts buff and, while living in Anchorage, had owned a set of weapon-style nunchucks. Hunyor asked Karen and her family to keep everything secret, to give out no information about Dion to avoid affecting the court case.

Hunyor was then a retired trooper who had been a member of the troopers' original response team at McHugh Creek and returned to the force as a contractor investigating old cases that had gone cold but justified renewed investigation. Bonnie's murder case had been reopened and Hunyor was taking a second try at cracking it when the prisoner Dion's DNA was matched with the semen from Bonnie's body. During the new investigation Hunyor's efforts included, among other things, going to Anchorage television station KTVA and requesting archived footage of the scene at McHugh Creek with the dead Bonnie floating in the water.

On April 27, 2007 Kenneth Dion was indicted in Anchorage Superior Court for first-degree murder, second-degree murder with extreme indifference and first-degree sexual assault. The judge set the trial date for September, 2008. The indictment brought news coverage of Dion's involvement in the case and an article in The Anchorage Daily News mentioned that Dion had been in an Alaska prison for two months before Bonnie's murder; he was released on parole and went back to prison for a parole violation after the murder. News articles reported that Dion had a long rap sheet that included 18 convictions, 10 misdemeanors and eight felonies, including assaults against women. He had rarely gone more than a year without being arrested for an offense of some kind. At the time of Bonnie's death Dion's wife Tammy was in the hospital after giving birth to their child. Tammy later testified that her husband often disappeared for a week or more at a time.

It occurred to Karen that if Kenneth Dion's DNA had been taken when he was arrested and checked against the national database, Bonnie's murder would have been solved years earlier, perhaps weeks after her death. The thought preyed on her mind, so Karen launched what became a national campaign to take DNA samples from suspects when they are arrested. Her research showed there were 5,000 DNA samples waiting to be entered into the national database in Alaska alone. And thousands more prisoners had yet to have DNA samples taken because they hadn't yet been convicted. The entire national database contained only 1.8 million samples from the nation's 2.3 million prisoners, and most of those were taken only after convictions.

Karen learned that only six states routinely took DNA samples on felony arrests—Virginia, California, Maryland, Texas, Kansas and Minnesota. This was a huge defect in the national crime prevention and resolution system. A federal official in Washington told her that any person could propose such a law. She did that in Alaska, then met with Governor Sarah Palin and legislative leaders. They were easily convinced and Karen's law was passed in just 12 days. That September, Kenneth Dion was returned to Alaska to face trial.

A few weeks later, Karen received a call from the Alaska Scientific Crime Laboratory asking her to speak at a national convention of law enforcement workers on the legislation she got passed in Alaska. She accepted the invitation and spoke at the convention. One of the great failings of the legal system, she told the conventioneers, was that criminals generally had their DNA taken on conviction but it really needed to be done on arrest—and done routinely. If taken on arrest and uploaded to the national database, many crimes could be solved much faster than when posting of such critical evidence is deferred until the legal process plays out, usually over the course of years.

On her return to Alaska, Karen began campaigning for a new crime lab in Anchorage, a lab with state of the art investigatory technology.

———

PREPARATIONS FOR DION'S TRIAL dragged on. At indictment the judge initially gave the lawyers a year to prepare but then September, 2008 was changed to January, 2009, and later moved back to May of that year. At first Dion's public defender needed more time to prepare, then the court wanted more information on the DNA evidence, then the trial judge was scheduled to take a family vacation, then a defense lawyer was changed and then the assigned judge was arrested for drunken driving and withdrew from the case. A third defense attorney was assigned to the case. The new lawyer, Andrew Lambert, told the new judge that Dion's first two defenders did little that he could use and he would need a year to prepare for trial.

Karen was by then an emotional wreck. A hyperactive person by nature, one so highly motivated she could channel her energies into good works like legal reform, Karen found the repeated delays difficult to deal with. She and her friends went shopping together, dined out, went hiking, camping and whitewater rafting, and took frequent vacation trips, all to get their minds off the pending trial and the unsettled fate of Bonnie's killer.

Karen had been in the real estate business for years, a venture that enjoyed considerable success until her interest and energies were consumed almost completely by her legal system causes. She closed her Anchorage agency and moved to Boca Raton, Florida to work for an organization focused on tracking down and winning prosecution of users and traffickers of child pornography. The organization was called TLO, which stood for The Last One. The group's founder said it meant they wouldn't rest until the last pedophile was in jail. The founder, Hank Asher, had made a fortune in data mining and was using his wealth to support an organization focused on a critical national problem. Asher felt Karen's activities were a good fit for his group and he would provide funding and an operating base for her. From Boca, Karen could use phone, email, personal travel and public appearances to pursue legislation requiring DNA testing on felony arrest in all 50 states. With Florida as her base, Karen could generate publicity supporting her cause that would have been impossible in Anchorage because it might affect Kenneth Dion's pending trial. And Florida was one of the critical states that Karen hoped would adopt new DNA legislation.

Just three days after arriving in Boca, Karen received a phone call from her son Adam's wife Trina. Fear struck at her heart once again. Adam's car had been rear-ended in Anchorage, the car was accordioned and he was in the hospital with severe injuries. Trina, and later Adam himself, told her to stay in Florida where she had an important job to do. Then 18 months later a call came from a hospital near her father's home in Canada. He was in the hospital with a kidney condition and disorientation. She packed her bags and moved to Calgary to care for her dad and wait for Kenneth Dion to face justice.

THE TRIAL BEGAN in Anchorage Superior Court on May 10, 2011, almost 17 years after Bonnie's body was found floating in McHugh Creek.

Prosecutors were Assistant District Attorneys Paul Miovas and Jenna Gruenstein. The defense lawyers were Andrew Lambert and Leigh Ann Bauer. Presiding was Judge Jack Smith. Dion was led in wearing a suit and tie, his red hair neatly trimmed. The tattoos on his knuckles told a contrasting story. One hand bore the word *Lost* and the other said *Soul*, words that had people nodding to themselves in agreement. A bailiff removed the handcuffs as he took a seat with his defense attorneys.

Trooper Tim Hunyor sat at the prosecution's table. Before the trial, Miovas invited Karen Foster and her family to be active in the trial on an advisory basis, including selection of a jury. "I value your insights," he told her. The invitation was almost certainly a reflection of the new attitude held by those in the legal system toward the families of victims, a change brought about by Janice Lienhart and Victims for Justice, Karen's early advisors.

Miovas asked Karen to refrain from talking to the press while the trial was underway and when the television stations ran old footage of Karen vilifying the defendant, defense attorney Lambert complained and Miovas had to explain to the judge that the footage was indeed old and Mrs. Foster would be discreet during the trial itself. Judge Smith reminded the jurors that they were not to watch the news while the trial was ongoing. He also cautioned spectators to be cautious about anything they tweeted on their cellphones and avoid filming or talking about the jurors.

The prosecutors offered the defense a plea deal; if Dion pleaded guilty he would be sentenced to 75 years in prison. The family would have been spared a trial, but it wasn't much of a deal for Dion. If found guilty the maximum sentence on the murder charge would have been 99 years. Dion was then nearly 40 years old. Taking a plea would have reduced the time and expense requirements for the legal system. But even considering the time discount for potential parole on all of the charges, he would be an old man before seeing freedom again. Dion's prison time on the New Hampshire robbery charges was completed during the wait for his murder trial to begin, so if he were somehow found not guilty in the Bonnie Craig case, he would walk free.

The court spent the first day whittling the jury pool down from about 120 people to 15 who would hear the case. Before the decision, three jurors would be excused and the last 12 would decide guilt or innocence.In his opening statement, prosecutor Miovas described the conscientious young woman of whom her mother was so proud, working hard in her UAA classes and at her part-time job at Sam's Club, where she worked 30 hours a week, and frequent babysitting. Miovas told the jury of the young hiker who found Bonnie's body face-down in the creek 30 feet below the cliff and of investigators finding a drop of blood on a leaf at the top of the cliff, Bonnie's blood. Karen's heart leaped when she heard Miovas mention a drop of blood. That was news to her and suggested that Bonnie was indeed injured before she fell from the cliff. He also told jurors that when the investigators pulled Bonnie's body from the creek they found injuries to her head, knuckles and other parts of her body, the injuries Karen had noticed in the mortuary.

When lead defense attorney Andrew Lambert stood to make his comments, he told the jurors they would learn that Bonnie actually had consensual sex with Kenneth Dion sometime before her death and that she was apparently alone at McHugh Creek and had suffered her injuries when she tumbled down the cliff into the water. Lambert also told jurors that the investigators had made mistakes, that no photographs were taken of scuff marks at the top of the cliff or of the drop of blood found on a leaf. Video was taken of the entire crime scene but the video was lost. Lambert said the trooper sergeant in charge of the investigative unit was out of town that day and his substitute, a corporal, had minimal qualifications to direct such an effort. He had assigned an even younger officer to lead the on-scene probe. Lambert said the tapes of interviews with potential witnesses were made wrong and came out blank.

Most telling, Lambert said, would be the testimony of Dr. Arndt von Hippel, a physician who was hiking at McHugh Creek that day and saw a young woman who looked just like Bonnie "happy, joyful, having a good time with two guys and a girl that are not that guy over there." He was pointing to Kenneth Dion. Karen began to weep.

When the judge ordered a break, someone approached the prosecution table with the news that an Alaska State Trooper had read that the video tape of the witnesses and scene had been lost; the trooper conducted a new search and found the tape, which would be presented as evidence.

The first witness was Bonnie's sister and roommate Samantha, who told of Bonnie's home, school and work life, and described Bonnie as her best friend and role model. Samantha said Bonnie was planning to attend UAA for another year before moving to California, where her boyfriend, Cameron Miyasaki was attending Berkeley. Cameron, however, was trying to get Bonnie to continue her classes at UAA. On the day of her death, Samantha heard Bonnie running down the stairs around five a.m. and slamming the front door as she left, obviously in a hurry.

Samantha was followed to the stand by Bonnie's old boyfriend,

Cameron, who was by then married and told of his life and plans for the future with his lost love Bonnie. Cameron was a talented young man and was then working as a film illustrator at Pixar Animation Studios in California. He and Bonnie met when both were in the first grade in Concord, California, years before both moved to Alaska and renewed their friendship while attending Anchorage's Hanshew Middle School. Cameron moved to London for two and a half years before returning to Alaska. He and Bonnie began dating in their junior year of high school, eventually developing an active sex life, much of which took place in his car and occasionally at their homes when nobody was there. He told of one day when they were driving south of Anchorage and stopped at McHugh Creek, sat on a rock, watched the sun and talked.

———————

AS PROMISED BY THE PROSECUTION, one of the key defense witnesses was Dr. Arndt von Hippel, a physician who said he was hiking at McHugh Creek on September 28, 1994 and saw a group of four young people running along the trail, obviously happy and having a good time. Von Hippel said one of the four looked exactly like Bonnie Craig and, indeed, was Bonnie Craig. The doctor had come forward with his information on September 30, two days after Bonnie's body was found.

But the Alaska State Troopers who investigated the case were skeptical of von Hippel's account and felt he was probably influenced by publicity about the case and managed to convince himself that one of the young women he saw there that day was Bonnie. Trooper Curt Harris, lead investigator, testified that he was not convinced that Dr. von Hippel had actually seen Bonnie herself. Von Hippel's account placed him on the trail at 10 a.m. but the medical examiner reported the approximate time of her death was eight a.m. Though the physician had called police two days after Bonnie's murder, Harris didn't interview Dr. von Hippel until about five weeks later.

Gary Campbell, who was Karen's ex-husband and Bonnie's stepfather, testified after flying to Anchorage from the Sultanate of Oman, where he was on assignment for British Petroleum. Campbell said Bonnie would often take care of her two younger siblings, Adam and Samantha, when she got home from school or work. He said Bonnie usually worked at Sam's Club three days a week, starting in late morning after her classes, and took her blue backpack, a gift from him, wherever she went. She also habitually carried her purse, key ring with pepper spray device and a rubber band that fit over her wrist, her calculator, books and wallet. All were missing and never found despite a determined effort by investigators at McHugh Creek, her home and presumably her school. Campbell said Bonnie always wore clean clothes and that when he travelled for his job he would often return bearing gifts for the kids, including several of the treasured items that Bonnie habitually carried. When he was in Anchorage, Campbell coached hockey and soccer and took the children to their swim and cross country meets, and other extracurricular activities.

When asked by prosecutor Miovas whether he thought it unusual that Bonnie would be at McHugh Creek that morning, Campbell answered: "Yes, I couldn't believe that Bonnie would skip school and be somewhere other than school or on the Internet with Cameron."

During the trial Kenneth Dion's defense lawyer, Andrew Lambert, argued against bringing into the record information about Bonnie's mother Karen Foster and the publicity campaign she had been generating. Prosecutor Miovas countered that Dion claimed he didn't recognize Bonnie's photograph and didn't remember anything about her even though during Karen's campaign the community had been inundated with her image and it was the most highly publicized case at the time. Miovas noted that when investigators asked him, "Mr. Dion . . . said 'I read the newspaper and I was aware of the news, but I don't remember anything about Bonnie Craig and I don't recognize that girl.'"

Miovas noted that the campaign involved bumper stickers, fliers, signs and billboards - all with Bonnie's picture and asking for information. When the jury was out of the room, he mentioned to the judge that it would have been hard to miss the all-encompassing publicity, especially about a young woman whose body contained the defendant's semen, even if as he claimed the sex had been consensual.

Jennifer Larsen, the young woman who spotted Bonnie's body said the person she saw floating was wearing a jean jacket. She testified that when she saw the body she started to leave and then scrambled back to make sure her eyes had not been fooling her. The jacket was pumped up by air and looked bulky, making her think it was a male, but she could tell that the person was dead. She jumped into her car, drove to the weigh station at Potter and asked to use the phone to dial 911. She said that when she was at McHugh Creek there were four or five cars in the upper parking lot where she left her car. Larsen said an Alaska State Trooper met her at the weigh station and she went back to McHugh Creek with him, hiked up the trail and showed him the body below. The location was a considerable distance from the road and required a hike to get there.

She then helped the trooper mark off the area with yellow crime scene tape. Jennifer was taken aback when she learned that the body was that of a young woman.

Dr. Norman Thompson, the medical examiner who did Bonnie's autopsy and was then working at Bartlett Hospital in Juneau, testified that in any suspicious death involving a female his office routinely did a sex assault kit workup looking for any sign of rape.

"We tend to err on the side of suspicion, sometimes when none is warranted," he said. "I'm looking for evidence of semen . . . one uses a cotton swab, swabs the inside of the mouth, air dries those swabs, labels them and saves them. Mouth, the anus, or the colloquially and kind of vulgar terminology would be butt hole and also vagina, and sometimes we do scrapings of fingernails to look for foreign material, hairs and that sort of thing."

Thompson said he found a laceration, bleeding and bruising inside Bonnie's vagina, injuries that occurred when she was still alive. The injuries occurred within a few hours before her death. She also had broken fingernails and many of the wounds to her hands and body were defensive ones. Some injuries on her hands appeared to have been suffered when she was trying to ward off blows to the head, which also showed up in places where one would expect: "If somebody was covering the back of their head with their hand, then the injuries on the left hand certainly look similar to the injuries . . . on the back of the head. Attributing these wounds to a fall doesn't make sense," he said.

Thompson added that the vaginal injuries could have occurred with either consensual or nonconsensual sex. He said ordinarily an aroused woman would have a self-lubricating process which would prevent such injuries but some women's lubrication system doesn't work well. And there were no tests to determine whether that system was working properly. He said he sent his swabs to the crime lab for testing.

Bonnie also had 11 blunt trauma injuries to her head. She had a fracture at the base of her skull that damaged the brain stem and was the probable cause of death. After that blow she would have survived only for 10 to 20 minutes until the swelling of her brain shut down her vital functions. Thompson said he went out to McHugh Creek and looked at the area and the cliff where Bonnie's body tumbled down. He said of the various injuries that it was unlikely they all occurred in a fall. "It's possible," he said, "but I don't feel that that's a likely explanation."

Miovas asked: "Is it possible, in your medical opinion, that all 11, or if you count the hand injuries, 13, were sustained during that fall?"

"No," Thompson answered flatly. He said some of the wounds were more likely caused when Bonnie tried to defend herself and ward off blows. "Attributing these wounds to a fall doesn't make sense." He said, "these injuries are far more likely to be a consequence of multiple blows to the head as opposed to a fall."

"Based on the pattern of injuries and the scene investigation . . . it seemed like a very comfortable conclusion for me to call this a homicide. I could think of no other explanation for this pattern of injuries than to assume that they had been inflicted by another person." Thompson said the lacerations were likely caused by blows from a blunt object as opposed to being cuts from a knife. "My conclusion is that this has to be a homicide."

Thompson said the injuries appeared to have been caused by an instrument of some sort, perhaps a jack handle, a metal bar or a martial arts weapon like nunchucks, a weapon that Dion had once told investigators he owned.

Under cross examination Thompson said that if a beating had taken place at McHugh Creek, before she went over the cliff into the water, he would expect to find blood spatters on the ground and vegetation. Investigators found none other than the drop of blood. His testimony indicated Bonnie could have been beaten elsewhere and still been alive at the time she went over the cliff.

Thompson said if Bonnie fell from the cliff she would likely have hit the rocks below at least once before landing in the water. He said her injuries could not have been caused by a fall from that cliff. "It is not possible," he said.

IN HIS CLOSING ARGUMENTS Miovas said: "Dr. von Hippel, saying it mildly, is mistaken. I'm not saying that he saw Kenneth Dion out there on September 28th . . . with anybody. But he also didn't see Bonnie Craig. And that's clear from the evidence." And, Miovas added, "there is no way Bonnie Craig had sex with this man consensually based on her love for Cameron and what's going on in her life that morning on September 28th, absolutely impossible."

Miovas speculated that only a single drop of blood was found at the top of the cliff because Dion presumably threw Bonnie off the cliff, then went down and finished her off in the water, beating her to death with his nunchucks.

ON JUNE 16, 2011, nearly 17 years after Bonnie Craig's body was found floating in McHugh Creek, Kenneth Dion was found guilty of raping and murdering her. Judge Smith sentenced Dion to a total of 124 years in prison. Then age 42, Dion could be eligible for parole after 39 years, when he would be 81.

In her victim impact statement, the statement allowed her by Janice Lienhart's Victims for Justice campaign, Karen Foster said to Dion: "As a mother, the pain of losing a child is unbearable, and that is magnified when it is a violent act of rape and murder. It is also magnified as you watch and feel the pain your surviving children are going through. And it was magnified even more when I realized that, as a parent, I wasn't there for my kids. I was trying to find a killer. I was focused and intent on catching you. My children did not just lose their sister, they lost me."

"How can you call yourself a man? How can you call yourself a fifth degree black belt? You are neither. You are a disgrace and a coward. You did one thing right when you got that tattoo to say 'Lost Soul'. You truly are a lost soul."

Dion's ex-wife Tammy was present at the closing of his trial and testified to his disappearances around the time of their child's birth. After Tammy's testimony Karen saw her outside the courthouse, gave her a hug and said: "I'm sorry . . . What he's putting you through. I'm sorry."

Tammy said: "Thank you" as she turned and walked away.

Karen Foster later wrote a book about Bonnie's murder and the emotional journey she and her family endured as a result. Assisted by a professional writer, I. J. Schecter, she produced a remarkable account of the event and its aftermath. *Justice for Bonnie - An Alaskan Teenager's Murder and Her Mother's Tireless Crusade for the Truth* was published by Berkley Books in 2014.

In the closing chapter of her book, Karen mentioned that if Kenneth Dion's DNA had been taken and entered into the national register when he was next arrested after Bonnie's murder, her family would have been spared a dozen years of hell.

CHAPTER 12

Man With a Hobby - 2001

ISRAEL KEYES HAD a hobby; he enjoyed killing people he didn't know. He was a cold-blooded murderer who went about his hobby in a ritualistic, methodical way that often involved years of pre-planning and preparation.

His field of play was the entire nation, from coast to coast, and he was expanding his reach when police finally ended his years of bloody recreation. Experts on serial murders said Keyes' intricate planning and years-long preparation for some murders increased his gratification by prolonging the anticipation.

Israel was born on January 7, 1978, one of nine siblings in a strict Mormon family living in Richmond, Utah, near Salt Lake City. Several of the children had Biblical-sounding names like his own, including his sisters Sunshine, Charity, Hosanna and Autumnrose. The family moved to Colville, Washington when Israel was still preschool age; like the others he was home-schooled. As a child, Israel developed a brutal hobby of torturing and killing cats and other small animals. When he was 14, his grandfather gave him a .38-caliber revolver, which Israel secretly outfitted with a homemade silencer. He had an upside-down cross tattooed on his chest and a pentagram on the back of his neck, satanic imagery. When he was 16 he was arrested for shoplifting and sentenced to community service as punishment. He loved hunting and killing any animals he found in the woods and fields.

In Colville the family attended a white-supremacist, anti-Semitic church. As a teen, two of his closest friends were Chevie and Cheyne Kehoe, who later became notorious domestic terrorists and are now serving life sentences for murder. Chevie was involved in the Oklahoma City bombing. Among other crimes, he and his father Kirby once robbed the home of a gun dealer in Tilly, Arkansas, making off with guns, ammunition and cash.

In the late 1990s Keyes' father moved the family to an Amish community in Smyrna, Maine. His sister Autumnrose had become a rebellious teenager so his father decided the family needed greater discipline. Autumnrose later wrote on her church's website: "Around the age of 11 and 12, my heart turned in rebellion toward my parents. My two older sisters and I were in a kind of revolt against them. We had friends they did not like, we secretly listened to music they forbade, and we got away with as much as we could. At 13 I fell into grievous sin that my parents did not know about. I began to doubt God's existence and planned to leave my family as soon as possible and dive head-first into sin. I've thanked God many times for my earthly father, who was a strict man. When my sins came to light by God's mercy, he pulled me away from my circumstances and moved the family to an Amish community . . . My father passed away when I was 18. I regretted so much my rebellion and the cold distance I'd had toward my father."

Keyes father had been a maintenance man, but in Maine the family entered the maple syrup business. Israel became skilled with his hands and built a log cabin when he was 16. While in Smyrna, Israel rejected his family's religion, declared himself an atheist and was kicked out of the house. He then purchased a small, isolated home in Constable, New York, and eventually joined the Army. He trained at Fort Hood in Killeen, Texas, and was stationed at Fort Lewis, Washington. Israel did a brief tour in Egypt and served honorably as an infantryman skilled in mortar fire, handling automatic weapons and neutralizing land mines. During his service he was awarded an Army Achievement medal for meritorious service.

Sean McGuire, a fellow soldier who shared a barracks with Keyes while they were training in Egypt, told an interviewer he was troubled by a dark side that sometimes surfaced in Israel. When Keyes was offended by something that came up in conversation, He would drop his head, knit his brow, lower his voice and say, "I want to kill you, McGuire." Keyes drank heavily on weekends, consuming entire bottles of his favorite drink, Wild Turkey bourbon. His sheer size made him a threat to those around him. Keyes was tall, about six-foot two or six-four, he weighed about 230 pounds and was very muscular.

Israel was a skilled carpenter and well-regarded handyman who did work for neighbors. Those he helped would have been utterly shocked to learn of his sideline preoccupation with murder. His first known attack on a human was the rape of a teenager he encountered on the Deschutes River in Oregon in the late 1990s. He abducted the girl when he encountered her tubing with friends on the river and managed to separate her from her friends without arousing their suspicions. When interviewed after his arrest years later, he said he intended to kill her but decided to let her go and put her back on her tube, then sent it floating down the river. The attack was apparently never reported.

Keyes told his interviewers that before he was discharged from the Army at Fort Lewis in 2001 he was anxious for his military service to end so he could start murdering people. Shortly after his discharge, Israel killed an unidentified couple somewhere in Washington state. He moved to Neah Bay, Washington, established a village market for the Makah Indian tribe and began dating a woman with whom he had a daughter. Later, Keyes told investigators, he killed a person while living in Neah Bay because he felt he needed something to do. "Neah Bay's a boring town," he said. He sank the victim's body in Lake Crescent, Washington, weighting it down in 100-foot-deep water with four or five milk jugs.

———————

IN 2002 THE COUPLE SEPARATED and the woman took her daughter with her to Anchorage. Israel sought to win partial custody of the daughter. "He seemed totally normal," said David Kanter, who worked with one of Keyes' girlfriends. Kanter told a newspaper reporter: "He was quiet; he was more reserved, I guess, but you never would have picked him out for doing something like this . . . In no sense of the word was he in any way weird."

Jim Thompson, a volunteer who helped Keyes on community clean-up projects around Neah Bay, told the reporter: "He would tell me about his days in the armed services and the parties they had. He would lovingly talk about his daughter, or tell me when he'd been up late because she was sick."

Between 2002 and 2006 Keyes initiated an extensive series of travels and killed at least two more people, also unidentified. He opened a contracting business, Keyes Construction, and around 2007 followed his old girlfriend and their daughter to Anchorage. He found a new girlfriend in Alaska and his daughter lived with the couple part-time. His home was in the city's Turnagain neighborhood near many of Anchorage's most prominent citizens. State Senator Hollis French, who lived around the corner from Keyes told a reporter: "he was well-known in Anchorage as a really good handyman."

Paul Adelman, an Anchorage man who hired Israel for several projects, said Keyes was "reliable, unfailingly polite and responsive. You called, he called you back. I completely trusted him with his work. If he gave me a bill, I always paid, no questions asked."

In 2009, after making expensive trips to California, New England and remote parts of Washington State, Keyes decided to fund his murder forays by robbing banks. On April 10, after abducting and killing a woman in New Jersey, he buried her somewhere in upstate New York, then entered a bank in Tupper Lake, New York wearing sunglasses, gloves, a fake mustache and goatee and carrying a .40-caliber Smith and Wesson semiautomatic pistol (plus a .22 Ruger in his pocket). He robbed the bank, fled and buried a toolbox containing the two pistols in a natural area in Essex, Vermont. He then spent the next two years making various trips around the country. The reasons for his travels were never determined but they almost certainly involved scouting for new areas to pursue his hobby, and perhaps committing a few murders. On one trip to Texas he burglarized a home and set it on fire.

In the spring of 2011 he built another homemade silencer, this one for the Ruger, and decided to test it on his next adventure. He flew to Indiana and drove to New York to test the silencer in a remote area, then went on to Vermont to recover his toolbox. Israel planned to go on a bank-robbing and arson spree but decided he would first pick a random target and murder somebody. He initially watched from the safety of nearby woods, targeting a man driving a yellow Volkswagen Beetle. He also picked out an abandoned farmhouse in Essex where he would take the victim. When he decided his first target was not going to work out he switched his focus to a couple living nearby. Bill and Lorraine Currier, both in their fifties, lived just a half-mile from the Handy Suites hotel where he was staying. Their house was a single-family home with no children or dogs and an attached garage, from his standpoint an ideal situation.

From watching outside he determined where their bedroom might be, then cut the telephone line to block any security system signals. He then donned a headlamp to conduct what he called a "blitz attack" on the sleeping couple in their darkened home. He entered the garage through a window propped open by a ventilation fan and found a crowbar hanging on a wall. He used the crowbar to smash the glass in a door between the garage and the house, then reached in to unlock the door, and charged through the house into the Curriers bedroom. He abducted the couple, handcuffed them with zip ties, and took Elaine's purse, wallet and a .38 caliber Ruger she carried with her when alone at a vacation home. Keyes then drove them to the abandoned farmhouse he had scouted earlier. He tied Bill to a stool in the farmhouse basement and went back upstairs for Elaine, but she had broken free from the zip ties and was running for nearby Route 15. He tackled her and was tying her up again when Bill broke loose and tried to escape, shouting "Where's my wife?" The furious Keyes hit Bill in the head with a shovel twice, knocking him down only with the second impact. Keyes then ran upstairs to grab his silencer-equipped pistol, returned to the basement and found Bill back on his feet and shouting. Keyes shot him four times before the elderly man fell to the floor and died. Keyes then returned to the bedroom and raped Elaine twice. Afterward he took her down to the basement to show her Bill's body. As she stood there horrified, he slipped behind her, wrapped a rope around her neck and strangled her to death.

Keyes buried their bodies in a pile of debris in a corner of the basement and drove away in their vehicle, intending to return later and burn down the farmhouse. He also planned to rob a few banks but changed his plans when the Curriers' car had mechanical problems. Israel abandoned the vehicle in a Vermont parking lot, then rented a car and drove to New York. There he ditched his tools, his own silencer-equipped pistol and the .38 he took from Elaine Currier, and flew home to Anchorage. Though he didn't know it then, the farmhouse was demolished soon after he left and the debris, including the bags containing the undiscovered Curriers' remains, was dumped in a local landfill.

While in Vermont killing time after the Curriers' murder, Keyes bought a three-day fishing license and went angling for three days on Lake Champlain.

Bill and Lorraine Currier were reported missing by Bill's sister Diana when they failed to show up at their jobs the following day. Both were reliable employees who would always either come to work or call to notify their co-workers they would be late or unable to make it that day. Bill was an animal care technician at the University of Vermont and Lorraine worked at a health care clinic. They were considered typical laid-back Vermonters, Lorraine with long red hair, parted down the middle, and no makeup. Bill played guitar and loved Simon and Garfunkel.

Essex Police Lieutenant Robin Hollwedell told media representatives that the two "were very good about being at work, didn't take a lot of time off. The fact that they've completely disappeared, none of it seems to make any sense. When two good people disappear from town with seemingly no explanation, that's a concern for us."

Both Curriers had health issues requiring daily medication and their medicines were left in the home, suggesting that they did not leave voluntarily. Their pet birds, which they generally allowed to fly free during the day, were still in their covered cages.

———

JUST A FEW MONTHS AFTER HE LEFT VERMONT, Keyes decided to find his next victim closer to home. On February 1, 2012, he drove the streets of Anchorage looking for someone to kill. He later told investigators he was losing control and starting to break some of his own rules, one that directed he travel outside Alaska in search of victims and another that called for the victim to have a vehicle so Israel would not have to put the person in his own car where they might leave their DNA.

His self-discipline failed him altogether when he saw an 18-year-old coffee-stand barista named Samantha Koenig. She was working in a kiosk in the parking lot of the Alaska Club fitness center at 630 East Tudor Road. When he finally confessed, Keyes told police that his rules went by the boards when he saw her. Homicide Detective Monique Doll reported "He was losing the massive amount of self-control that he had. In prior cases he had enough self-control to walk away" if victim situations didn't meet his criteria. "But with Samantha, he didn't."

Keyes told officers that when he walked up to Samantha's kiosk just before its 8 p.m. closing time he was still deciding whether to kill her or just rob the place and walk away. He didn't want to transport her in his vehicle and was ready to change plans if she didn't have a vehicle. But when he saw her, he felt an overpowering desire to murder her. Public view of the kiosk was partially blocked by high snowbanks and Israel was listening to police calls on a portable scanner with an earpiece. He knew most officers were busy responding to an emergency on the other side of Anchorage.

A surveillance video of the incident at the kiosk showed Keyes approaching the coffee stand and ordering an Americano. He was wearing a ski mask but Samantha served him until he pulled a gun. Then she stepped back and raised her hands while Keyes shinnied through the open window into the kiosk. Keyes ordered her to turn out the light and get on the floor, which she did. A panic button was located next to the light switch but she was too terrified to reach for it. He bound her hands behind her with zip ties, cleaned out the cash drawer and led her out of the darkened kiosk to his car.

The kiosk's surveillance video shows Samantha's cell phone blinking on a shelf as her boyfriend, Duane Tortolani, tried to call her while he was en route to pick her up. Another camera at the nearby Home Depot showed Israel and Samantha climbing into Keyes' white pickup.

Israel told Samantha it was a kidnapping and said he would let her go unharmed if her family paid ransom. She said her family had no money but he told her they could raise it through a public appeal. And when word got out about her disappearance and kidnapping, the public donated $70,000 over the course of several weeks.

When Keyes realized that Samantha did not have her cell phone, he drove back to the coffee stand and retrieved it. While there he was careful to pick up the end pieces of the zip ties he had left earlier. It occurred to him they might contain partial fingerprints. Tortolani arrived four minutes after Keyes left with the phone, peered through the window with his own phone pressed to his ear, then drove away. Samantha's phone was to play an important role in the scheme. Israel needed it to send text messages to Duane and to the owner of the coffee stand. When he drove to another part of town and sent them, the first messages made it appear that Samantha was using the phone, just had a bad day and was leaving town for the weekend.

"He knew all along he was going to kill her," Detective Doll said. Keyes removed the battery from her cell phone to prevent anyone from tracking them. He drove around town for a time before taking her to a shed near his home. There he placed her still alive in the shed and turned on loud music so no one could hear if she was able to scream. He left Samantha bound in his shed, then drove to her house to get her debit card from the truck she shared with her boyfriend. While there Keyes was confronted by Tortolani, the boyfriend, who went into Samantha's house to call for help. Israel then took the debit card from the truck and left before Duane returned. Keyes went back to his own house, got Samantha's pin number from her, then the next day he raped and strangled her. He returned to the house, packed his clothes and headed for the airport to catch a flight to New Orleans and embarked on a cruise in the Gulf of Mexico. When he returned to Anchorage two weeks later, he had sex with her dead body, then took a photo of her body beside a copy of the February 13 Anchorage Daily News, staging the corpse to look like she was still alive 11 days after he killed her. Keyes carefully applied make-up to her face to enhance the impression that she was alive. He made a photocopy of the photograph, then used a manual typewriter to type a ransom note on the back of the photocopy. In it he demanded $30,000. He left the note in a dog park and texted its location to Tortolani. The text said the note could be found "under Albert," referring to a memorial flier for a dog named Albert.

In March of 2012, Keyes took his daughter to visit his mother and four sisters in Texas, where they had moved after the death of his father. There they had become members of the Church of Wells, which believes in strict spiritual separation from mainstream churches. One of his sisters was marrying another member of the church. Keyes' atheism got him into tangles with church elders who urged him to join their faith. Pastor Jake Gardner told a Texas television station that their efforts were a failure. "Even at the wedding the Lord pled with him and pled with him and in the midst of it all he wept and broke down weeping, bawling, even wailing, but he would not repent."

Gardner said Keyes responded to one of the church pastors: "Not everyone has your morals." One of his sisters told Keyes with tears in her eyes, "It doesn't matter what you've done, God will forgive you.

Israel, himself fighting tears, replied "You don't know what I've done. I have to drink every day to forget about it."

———

VIDEO OF THE KOENIG KIDNAPPING showed Keyes' white pickup truck in the background but Israel had removed its license plates as well as a rack and toolboxes from the truck's bed. When police later saw the truck, the plates and two structural items had been replaced and they didn't recognize it. His was just one of 750 similar trucks they were looking at but replacement of the rack and toolboxes, which appeared to be welded on, made it look unlike the vehicle in the video. Keyes name was scratched from the list of possible suspects.

Shortly after returning, he cut up Samantha's body, stuffed the pieces into plastic sacks and dropped them through a hole he cut in the ice of Matanuska Lake. Samantha's father drew $30,000 from the reward fund and deposited it into her account, as instructed. Keyes then began traveling and stopped to make ATM withdrawals in Anchorage, Arizona,

New Mexico and Texas, usually wearing a scream mask, his bizarre attempt at humor. His first withdrawal in Anchorage was $500 just before midnight. Early the next morning, less than an hour later, he went to another ATM nearby and withdrew another $500. Then on March 7 Israel withdrew $400 from an ATM in Willcox, Arizona, the first indication to those tracking him that he was traveling outside Alaska. When that ATM machine pinged on its network, a local FBI agent was alerted and drove rapidly to the bank, but by then Keyes was an hour away in Lordsburg, New Mexico, where he took out $80, then traveled on to Humble, Texas, where he withdrew $480. On March 11 he withdrew another $480 from a machine in Shepherd, Texas.

Surveillance cameras at the ATM machines showed little of value. The suspect appeared to be a man but was wearing multiple layers of clothing, obviously to change his appearance, as well as a full-face mask and glasses. The investigators tracking his withdrawals were using the information to chart his travels. They had a blurry ATM photo and a pattern their suspect was driving along route I-10 in a rented white Ford Focus. The multi-agency team in Anchorage did some calculating and predicted that if Keyes kept moving in the same direction he would soon be in Texas, probably enroute to El Paso. FBI Agent Steve Rayburn sent a BOLO (be on the lookout) to the Texas Rangers, alerting them to his movements and including a photo of Samantha, another of Keyes' vehicle and the third of their still unidentified suspect in his hooded sweatshirt, blue jeans and sneakers with his face obscured.

———————

ON MARCH 13, CORPORAL BRYAN HENRY of the Texas Highway Patrol spotted the Ford parked outside Room 115 of a Quality Inn in Lufkin, Texas. Corporal Henry looked into the window of the Focus, making mental notes about its contents. He checked the motel register but found no guests the manager could tie to the vehicle. Then Henry spotted a man peering down from one of the motel's upper rooms, Room 215 above the spot where the Ford was parked. He moved his own vehicle to a spot where he could watch the hotel exit and the Ford Focus. Shortly afterward a man walked out, loaded some luggage into the Ford and began driving away. Henry called his supervisor in the investigation and was told to find a reason to pull the vehicle over, any reason.

Henry stayed two cars behind the suspect vehicle until his radar determined the Ford Focus was driving two miles over the speed limit, so

Henry passed the other two vehicles and pulled behind the Ford. He turned on his flashing lights and followed as the Ford turned slowly into the parking lot of a local cafe. Henry called for backup, then approached the driver and asked where he was from. The man said: "Alaska" so the Ranger ordered him to step out of the vehicle and asked for identification. Keyes showed his Alaska driver's license. Henry looked at it and suspected strongly that this man named Israel Keyes might be the person they were looking for. When his backup arrived, one man interviewed the driver while the other peered into the Ford Focus and spotted a pair of white sneakers and a roll of rubber-banded paper currency with what looked like red dye on it, the kind some banks use in an automated system to mark stolen currency.

The FBI got a judge to issue a finding of probable cause and the arresting Texans were authorized to search the vehicle. Inside they found a banded roll of dye-spotted cash from the National Bank of Texas, a piece of a gray T-shirt cut to make a face mask, a map with highlighted routes through California, Arizona and New Mexico, as well as the stolen debit card and Samantha Koenig's cell phone. They arrested Keyes and impounded his rental car.

After Lufkin police notified them of Keyes' capture, Anchorage Detective Monique Doll and her partner, Jeff Bell, flew to Texas. When they were able to interview him, Doll showed Keyes the ransom note he had written. "I told him that the first couple of times that I read the ransom I thought that whoever wrote the note was a monster," she reported on her return to Anchorage. "And the more I read it—it must have been 100 times—the more I came to understand that monsters aren't born but are created and that this person had a story to tell."

Keyes was unmoved and replied firmly: "I can't help you." Two weeks later, while in custody back in Anchorage, he changed his mind and asked another investigator to convey a message to Detective Doll. "Tell her she's got her monster," he said.

Doll, her partner Jeff Bell and a team of FBI investigators and government prosecutors began interviewing Keyes at the federal courthouse. He sat at a table, his hands folded in the lap of his jumpsuit.

The interviewers quickly got the impression he had a Dr. Jekyll-Mr. Hyde personality. They knew him to be a murderer, but he came across as a caring father, a hard-working business owner. "There is no one who knows me or who has ever known me, who knows anything about me, really," he said. "They are going to tell you something that does not line up with anything I tell you because I'm two different people basically."

"How long have you been two different people?" Asked one of the prosecutors. Keyes laughed. "Long time. Fourteen years."

———————

"ISRAEL KEYES DIDN'T KIDNAP AND KILL PEOPLE because he was crazy," reported Detective Monique Doll at a press conference after his arrest. "He didn't kidnap and kill people because his deity told him to or because he had a bad childhood. Israel Keyes did this because he got an immense amount of enjoyment out of it, much like an addict gets an immense amount of enjoyment out of drugs."

Keyes told police he almost killed a young Anchorage couple at a beach overlook about a month before he went to Vermont to kill the Curriers. He had his silencer-equipped pistol trained on them and also considered shooting an Anchorage police officer who happened along but dropped the idea when a second officer arrived on the scene. "It could have got ugly," he said, chuckling, "but fortunately for the cop guy, his backup showed up. That's about the time I decided to get a scanner because I almost got myself into a lot of trouble on that one."

At the time he was arrested, Keyes was planning to leave Alaska and become an itinerant contractor working on repair jobs in areas of the United States struck by hurricanes. The scheme would have enabled him to travel a lot and kill people in widespread places.

A Seattle reporter wrote of Keyes that he "saw America as one big killing field." He traveled tens of thousands of miles over 15 years, much of it in search of victims. Between October 2002 and March 2012, he took at least 35 trips throughout the continental United States and Hawaii, as well as Canada and Mexico, raising speculation that he might have committed murders both in the U.S. and abroad. He sometimes visited family members living in the East, Midwest and South, often mixing family trips with murderous ventures in the area. He wore the same striped and padded gloves and carried the same silver and black semiautomatic pistol wherever he went.

During his wide-ranging travels he occasionally stashed murder kits for use when he returned to that area. His stashes included items like shovels, zip ties and large bottles of Drano to spread on bodies and accelerate decomposition. One such cache was recovered intact in Eagle River, Alaska, north of Anchorage, and another in Blakes Falls, New York. He also claimed to have buried murder supplies in Washington State, Wyoming, Texas and Arizona, though those were never found.

When his interviewers showed Keyes the surveillance footage of Samantha Koenig's kidnapping, as well as records and footage of the ATM withdrawals made with her bank card, plus a ski mask found in his vehicle, he confessed.

The interrogators were feeling good about the progress they were making until Israel began going into the details of the murder. Their emotions turned to alarm when their prisoner's adrenaline began to flow and he told them how powerful he felt when pointing his pistol at Samantha's ribs. Prosecutor Kevin Feldis reported amazement at Keyes performance, " . . . his demeanor, the level of detail, the lack of remorse, the enjoyment he was getting out of telling certain details." Feldis said he soon concluded that "This was not the first time he killed someone."

When police found indications on Keyes computer that he was tracking details as they emerged in news media about both the Samantha Koenig investigation and the Currier murders in Vermont, they asked him about the Currier case. Keyes eventually admitted the Vermont killings had been his handiwork and gave them details.

Vermont Police Lieutenant George Murtie was at home in Essex, Vermont when he got a call from a local FBI agent telling him about what had come up in far-off Alaska. A prisoner in Anchorage had just confessed to murdering the Curriers, who had by then been missing for a year.

Murtie had been an officer in Essex for 28 years and knew his community thoroughly, including the location of the abandoned farmhouse. He and another detective drove to the farmhouse and found it demolished and the debris hauled away to a landfill. They mobilized search crews and equipment needed to comb through the landfill. The searchers found evidence of putrefied flesh but nothing more. The remains of Bill and Lorraine Currier were never found though the pistol Keyes used in their murder was recovered by an FBI dive team at the base of a waterfall in New York.

Several weeks after the FBI agent's call, Murtie interviewed Keyes by phone. He found the confessed murderer surprisingly matter-of-fact about the Currier killings. "I would describe it as if I was talking to a contractor about the work I was going to have done and he was describing the work he had done in the past," Murtie told a reporter. "There was no emotion or anything. Just flat."

In one interview with the Anchorage team, Keyes discussed his methods for finding and dealing with victims. "Back when I was smart," he said, (once he reached a hunting ground far from home) "I would let them come to me. There's not much to choose from . . . but there's also no witnesses."

He told of training for his hobby like an assassin. "I had a moving target system," he said. "I could trip the target and it would start rolling downhill on a pulley. It was just a piece of printer paper, but then I would spray paint a black mark about that big for aiming at and that's what I was shooting at with it, at about 50 yards. And that was a plan . . . That's one of the ways I—one of the ideas I had, for carjackings. Shoot out their tire while they were pulling up to a stop sign or something . . . Didn't find any good roads or places to do it, so . . . you can set up in the right spot . . . and sit there with binoculars and kind of stake out who is in the car. Like shopping. If it's in the evening and there's not a lot of people around . . . you shoot out someone's tires, she's by herself and she doesn't have much choice but to stop."

Keyes told his interviewers that he once thought about becoming a police officer. When asked why, he said it would be a great way to find potential victims and pull them over on the highway.

During one interview Keyes asked about media publicity on his confession and any details to be revealed. He said he knew that was probably inevitable but added: "I'm not in this for the glory. I'm not trying to be on TV." The thought that he might consider there to be "glory" in his crimes stunned several of the interviewers. Keyes also boasted about going undetected in his murder spree for so many years. Detective Bell said that when asked for a motive, Keyes replied, "A lot of people ask why and I would be like: Why not?"

FBI Special Agent Jolene Goeden said Keyes "liked what he was doing. He talked about getting a rush out of it, the adrenaline, the excitement." Anchorage Detective Doll noted that Israel "never expressed in any way, shape or form that he was ashamed or regretted any of his actions and he was very self-aware. He was also okay with the fact that he did this because he got enjoyment out of it. He didn't try to rationalize it."

Keyes gave detailed confessions in eight murders and admitted he killed 11 in all, but police believe there may have been more. Though each of his murders was undoubtedly a memorable experience, he didn't know the names of most of his victims. When interviewed, the only names he could recall besides Samantha Koenig were Bill and Elaine Currier in Vermont. He claimed that one of the bodies he left in his wake was recovered but the death was ruled accidental because of the way he staged it. He declined to provide more information about the case.

Keyes told the investigators there were victims in 10 states. Police say there were probably at least 11 both in the United States and places like Mexico, Canada and perhaps other countries. Prosecutor Feldis said: "The most we could get out of him was (that he killed) less than 12 people." The interviewers wondered if he meant 11 so they started referring to "your 11 victims." He didn't correct them as he did whenever he thought they said something wrong.

———————

KEYES USED GOOGLE EARTH TO SHOW POLICE where on Matanuska Lake he had deposited Samantha Koenig's body, allowing them to find her remains relatively quickly. Her body was the only one of Keyes' victims ever found. Keyes also showed them a lake in Parishville, N,Y., where he dumped Elaine Currier's .38 and parts of the gun he used to kill Bill Currier. An FBI dive team recovered the weapons.

The FBI posted Keyes' DNA in a national database and initiated a nationwide search for his victims, asking police agencies and members of the public to suggest possibilities for unsolved cases. One person (by some accounts Samantha's father) started a Facebook page asking readers if they had ever seen Israel Keyes. The page included his picture and personal information. It started as an attempt to find additional victims but was maintained for years as a record of his crimes.

Police looked at several killings that appeared to be Keyes handiwork but were ultimately ruled out as unlikely to be his murders. One was a 12-year-old Special Olympics champion with artificial feet, but a Stevens County sheriff said that murder was unlikely because Keyes was just a kid when the child was killed. Israel was actually about 17 at that time, which didn't necessarily eliminate him as a suspect, but the mother's boyfriend was considered a person of interest in the case. Keyes was also considered a possibility in the murder of two educators in Eugene, Oregon, where a man and woman were shot to death on July 1, 2005 while on a camping and fishing trip. But there were no signs of struggle or sexual assault, Keyes' trademarks.

The interviews went on for several months. At first Keyes was very cooperative and carried on long conversations with his captors, who feigned a friendly manner to encourage him to talk. The prisoner seemed anxious to brag about his exploits and was virtually loquacious though always unapologetic and remorseless. The questioners sometimes shared jokes, bagels and coffee with him. Though Keyes was often talkative he was consistently cagey even though he promised to tell them everything about his crimes. His responses were carefully worded.

The interviewers tried not to seem overeager, one of them occasionally jotting down notes on a legal pad. They nodded at his comments and asked short, encouraging questions. Their sparse note-taking was backed up by an overhead camera that recorded all of their comments and questions, and Keyes responses.

And if he was going to continue to talk, he insisted that there be no publicity on his case. He got a thrill from following news coverage of the murder cases and, before his arrest, had searched the Web for stories about the Currier murders. Police used his interest in the murders to keep him talking, giving him copies of articles about the case and letting him know if a new development was imminent.

Prosecutor Feldis said it was obvious that Keyes enjoyed talking about his crimes not to help victims' families but to control the narrative about his case. He told them it would be useless to attempt to pursue leads without his help. Occasionally he would chuckle and tell the interviewers how weird it felt telling them about such things.

Keyes admitted his research for murder projects included watching movies and reading up on other serial killers like Ted Bundy, the Vermont-born murderer who wandered the country in the 1970s, raping, kidnapping and killing young women. Keyes stressed, however, that he did not copy any of the others; he said his ideas were entirely his own.

FBI Special Agent Jolene Goeden said Keyes seemed to offer clues to his murders to avoid multiple trials in widespread jurisdictions and provide the fastest possible route to his execution. "He wanted the death penalty and he wanted it quickly," she said. "He didn't want to sit in jail for a long time."

Keyes agreed to continue talking as long as his name was not mentioned to the news media. He wanted to keep reporters away from his girlfriend and, especially, his daughter. When a Vermont television station broke the story and Alaska media tried to follow up, Keyes became furious and refused to talk to the interviewers for several months. From that time on he was a difficult prisoner. During one court hearing in the spring of 2012 he lurched from his restraints and broke free, seemingly trying to attack spectators and run from the courtroom, an apparent suicide attempt. He was tackled and Tasered by U.S. marshals as some audience members shouted, "Kill him." He was also disciplined after guards found a paper clip and floss device he had fashioned to serve as a pick to open his handcuffs.

For much of his time in custody after that, Keyes was classified as a "max-max" prisoner subject to the highest-security precautions. Whenever he left his cell he wore full restraints and was escorted by two officers. For a time he was considered a suicide risk. In July of 2012 he was found with a makeshift noose in his cell, suggesting that he was considering killing himself. He was placed in a jail unit reserved for prisoners whose mental health is in question. His cell contained no bed sheets or other implements he might use to commit suicide.

Eventually he was returned to the Bravo module, a maximum-security unit for long-term prisoners. Department of Corrections had decided he was no longer a suicide threat, a judgment based in part on his anxiousness to tell about his exploits. Because the FBI thought he might be a link to other murders in distant communities he was considered a high-value federal prisoner, but since he was arrested on local charges resulting from the murder of Samantha Koenig he was housed in the Anchorage Correctional Complex, a city jail. He was then 34 years old and scheduled for trial four months later.

———

GUARD LOREN JACOBSEN WAS SURPRISED to see Keyes back in the Bravo facility. Jacobsen was a five-year veteran of the corrections system, much of that time working with and guarding prisoners. Keyes was the highest-profile and highest-value prisoner in any DOC lockup. "In the past when we'd have high-profile people," Jacobsen told an interviewer, "they'd been in camera cells on the other side of the building." He said the rumor among the lockup's guards was that Keyes had "made a deal with the feds that he'd tell them more of his story if he could move out of the suicide watch back to Bravo mod."

Keyes' cell had bunk beds, though he had no cellmate, and faced a metal guard table. It had a scuffed, floor-to-ceiling Plexiglas window but the view was partly obscured by a desk. On the night of December 1, 2012 Jacobsen was assigned to work the overnight shift in the Bravo mod. He was the only guard for 15 prisoners and was required to do a visual check of each cell at least every half-hour and a more extensive "formal count" every four hours.

Jacobsen last saw Keyes arranging items in his cell and preparing to climb into bed at 10:12 p.m. Shortly afterward another guard relieved him and Jacobsen left for his scheduled meal break. Sometime after climbing into bed Keyes ducked under his blankets, slashed his wrists with a disposable razor embedded in a pencil and used a makeshift noose to strangle himself. The razor had mistakenly been given to him by another correctional officer and went un-retrieved.

A surveillance video of the entire Bravo mod was recorded by a camera mounted high above the guards' desk. It showed sporadic movement in Keyes' cell until a jerk at 10:24 p.m. Then the prisoner's bed went still.

When Jacobsen returned from his meal break he relieved the other guard and resumed his duties. Records indicated he made a total of 16 checks before his shift ended, walking close to each darkened cell and peering into each but never going inside. He did not see the blood that began pooling on the floor of Keyes' darkened cell sometime after midnight. He later told supervisors that Israel appeared to be sleeping while completely covered by his blanket, which he often did.

Between checks Jacobsen read a novel, conversed with other guards on the internal phone system and researched the purchase of an airplane using an online system. After the day-shift guard relieved Jacobsen and began his schedule of checks the lights came on. The relief officer found Keyes dead in his cell just before 6 a.m. He reported that the body was "pale and in rigor," suggesting that death had come hours earlier.

Jacobsen was fired a week later. His letter of dismissal said his actions on the night of Keyes' suicide were "simply inexcusable." The correctional officers union strongly defended him and said the actions cited in his dismissal letter were standard behavior for the guards, widely known and tolerated by supervisors. In his dismissal hearing, a union representative argued that the actions by Jacobsen were "very common on both day and night shift, but especially on night shift when officers are attempting to remain attentive and awake."

Video surveillance tapes later showed that Keyes was still preparing for bed when the second officer relieved Jacobsen and he died before the fired officer returned to work. The Alaska Police Standards Board moved to revoke Jacobsen's police certificate but later dropped the case. Jacobsen elected not to resume his career in corrections and took a job in the maintenance field.

———

KEYES FAMILY HELD A FUNERAL for him in Deer Park, Washington, near his old home in Colville. They hoped some of his old friends might come but none did. Only his mother, four of his sisters and three brothers-in-law gathered at the funeral home. The family pastor, Jake Gardner, accompanied the Keyes to Deer Park and spoke on their behalf. He titled his sermon "The Funeral of a Serial Killer." Gardner said Israel had earned no one's forgiveness. "He's not in a better place. We believe that he's in a place of eternal torment. All of his crimes . . . all the time the Lord plead with this man are running through his head and he can't get it out for eternity. This man was not only a murderer of others but a murderer of himself last of all."

A Seattle reporter noted that the family declined to say where Israel would be buried. "It seemed poetic justice," he wrote. "Much like Keyes hid the bodies of his victims, his family would hide his."

After his suicide, investigators found four pages of handwritten, weirdly poetic notes scribbled on a yellow legal pad lying under his body. They were soaked in his blood and largely illegible but an FBI forensic lab was able to reproduce them in part. They contained stylized descriptions of death, rape and murder, descriptions that chilled the readers.

"My pretty captive butterfly colorful wings my hand smears . . . punishment and tears," he wrote. "Violent metamorphosis, emerge my dark moth princess . . . come often and worship on the altar of your flesh . . . You shudder . . . and try to shrink far from me. I'll have you tied down and begging to become my (illegible) sweetie . . . "

"Now that I have you held tight I will tell you a story, speak soft in your ear so you know that it's true. You're my love at first sight and though you're scared to be near me, my words penetrate your thoughts now in an intimate prelude. I looked in your eyes, they were so dark, warm and trusting, as though you had not a worry or care. The more guileless the game the better potential to fill up those pools with your fear."

"Your face framed in dark curls like a portrait, the sun shone through highlights of red. What color I wonder, and how straight will it turn plastered back with the sweat of your blood. Your wet lips were a promise of a secret unspoken, nervous laugh as it burst like a pulse of blood from your throat. There will be no more laughter here."

About the Author

Tom Brennan is a newspaper editor and columnist who began his career on the police beat and has covered many true crime cases over the years. He has found that recent advances in investigative techniques and internet availability offer new perspectives on many of the most intriguing cases. The stories are more complex, more nuanced and more riveting than ever shown before.

CPSIA information can be obtained
at www.ICGtesting.com
Printed in the USA
FSHW010750110421
80349FS